HOW SWEET THE SOUND

HOW SWEET

DOUBLEDAY

New York   London   Toronto   Sydney   Auckland

THE SOUND

My Life with God and Gospel

CISSY HOUSTON

with Jonathan Singer

PUBLISHED BY DOUBLEDAY
a division of Bantam Doubleday Dell Publishing Group, Inc.
1540 Broadway, New York, New York 10036

DOUBLEDAY and the portrayal of an anchor with a dolphin are trademarks of
Doubleday, a division of Bantam Doubleday Dell Publishing Group, Inc.

Book Design by Leah S. Carlson

Library of Congress Cataloging-in-Publication Data
Houston, Cissy.
How sweet the sound : my life with God and
Gospel / Cissy Houston with Jonathan Singer. — 1st ed.
p.   cm.
1. Houston, Cissy.   2. Christian biography—
United States.   3. Afro-American singers—
Biography.   I. Singer, Jonathan.   II. Title.
ML420.H674A3   1998
782.42164′092—dc21   97-39137
                                          CIP
                                          MN

ISBN 0-385-49010-0

FOR MY GRANDCHILDREN WHO BRING ME JOY

FOR MY FAMILY, NANCY, DEBBY AND BEN SINGER
—FOR THEIR PRAYERS AND THEIR PATIENCE

ACKNOWLEDGMENTS

The authors wish to thank the following individuals for their kindness and cooperation during the writing of this book. Our respective families: Anne Moss, Marie Epps, Lee Warrick, John Houston, Bae (Ellen White), Laurie Badami, Judy Clay Gatewood, Diane Whitt, Gary Houston, Michael Houston, Donna Houston, Whitney Houston, Honey Davis, Louis Drinkard, Mrs. J. B. Drinkard, Aaron Drinkard, Stance Drinkard, Yvonne and Aaron Norman; Nancy Singer, Debby Singer, Ben Singer, Michael Singer, Esq. (for legal and brotherly counsel), Fay Zinger (for sisterly wisdom), Michael and June Prilutsky, and especially, Esther Glass (for the Golden Books). Friends and colleagues: Jim Cinque, Esq. (counsel), Jolly Dean, Evelyn Nelson, Jean Brown, Barbara Benedict (for faithful transcription of interviews), Anita and Robert Friedman (for encouragement and advice all along the way), Roy Schwarcz, Lee and Cindy Hill, Scott Brown, James Kunstler, Tim Cooper, Jeffrey Sussman, Patrick Milligan, Holly McCracken, Helen Urriola, Bruce Howell, R. Brian Ferguson, Chris Makepeace, Eddie Schwartz (CYD support), Neil Baruch (for early introductions to Buddy, Chuck, Don and Phil), Alan Steinhauer (special thanks for giving us access to the Dave Steinhauer Memorial Wing during the manuscript's preparation) and the staff of Whitney Houston Enterprises, who helped gather materials for this book. The musicians, songwriters, producers and executives who freely gave their time during interviews:

Brooks Arthur, Ilene Berns, Joe Bostic, Jr., Rocky Bridges, Charles Cummings, Dave Davidson, Joel Dorn, Tom Dowd, John Dunning, Paul Griffin, Peter Guralnick, Donny Harper (for his inspirational work on *He Leadeth Me*), Mayor Bill Hart, Tony Heilbut, Joey Helguerra, Gerry Hirshey, Arif Mardin, Hugh McCracken, Joel Moss, Henrietta Parker, Jerry Ragavoy, Michael Rothschild, Gary Sherman, Mike Stoller, Bette Sussman, Billy Vera and Jerry Wexler. Our friends at the Scott Waxman Agency, Giles Anderson and Scott Waxman, for their keen eye, understanding and compassion. At Doubleday, we are grateful for Arlene Friedman, the kind offices of Eric Major, Andrew Corbin and especially the vision, enthusiasm and patience of our editor, Mark Fretz, Ph.D.

Finally, we wish to acknowledge the debt we owe our parents, Delia and Nitcholas Drinkard and Fay and Abraham Singer—though gone, they yet speaketh, in the life they poured into us. And to our heavenly Father . . . from whom all blessings flow.

CONTENTS

Let me tell you about my mother, Cissy Houston. She is a very suspicious lady.

The day I was born, she thought my father was playing a very cruel joke on her, telling her that she'd just had a beautiful baby girl.

"Stop your lyin', John," she snapped from her hospital bed. "I know it's a boy."

My mother had waited almost seven years for a girl. She'd delivered two boys, my brothers, four years apart, and now, the odds of having another boy had overwhelmed her. When the nurses brought me into her room for the first time, she finally stopped fussing with my father.

My mother made up for the seven years she waited for me with a vengeance. By the time I was in fourth grade, she was dressing me right out of *Town and Country* magazine. The other girls were dressing down with their jeans and stuff and there I was with my plaid skirt, bucks and pigtails: my mother's version of Buffy from *Family Affair.* As you can imagine, in the mostly black East Orange neighborhood where I lived, my Buffy getup didn't play real well with the homegirls. At the age of ten, I was already a marked woman.

They waited for me after school. They ran me home, and once they even broke my glasses. I tried to avoid telling my mother what was going on. When it came to anyone bothering her children, she could become a madwoman, regardless of the perpetrator's age or gender. Eventually, she dragged it out of me. My mother visited the principal and told him if he didn't fix the problem, she would. My older brother Michael waited outside my classroom to glare at my enemies.

The persecution would die down for a week, then pick right back up the next. My mother didn't understand why these girls didn't want to be my friends. All she saw was her daughter, a friendly, talkative little girl with nice clothes.

"These girls don't want to be with you because . . . why? Because Mommy dresses you nice?" she said. "Because Mommy combs your hair? I don't understand."

She had dressed me in the nicest, most fashionable clothes she could find. She combed and braided my hair in long pretty pigtails. But the world, or at least the world of East Orange, didn't agree with her vision of what a little girl should look like.

My mother's heart was broken. I wasn't exactly thrilled with the walk home from school or the lack of friends either. Her frustration led her to a solution that was, if nothing else, a bit radical: "Whitney, sometimes you just have to be your own best friend," she said. "Sometimes, you're better off just being by yourself."

My mother was right: it was better to be by myself. She didn't leave me alone for long, though. She insisted on filling up my free time with a double portion of church. At first, I didn't like spending all my time there. But as I saw I could relax there, as I saw that nobody was really looking at you there, that everybody had the same purpose—singing and praising God—I began to enjoy it. I didn't have to try to get everybody to like me, I just cut that out. Soon New Hope Baptist Church in Newark became my second family.

So much of my first family was there already. My mother's sisters, Aunt Reebie, Aunt Lee and Aunt Anne. My Uncle Nicky played organ and piano for my mother's choirs. I joined my mother's choir, which was no small undertaking. At one time or another, Mommy's choirs included some of Newark's finest singers: three of the original members of the Monotones ("The Book of Love"), Judy Clay, Sylvia Shemwell and Myrna Smith from the Sweet Inspirations, and, of course, my cousins, Dionne Warwicke and her sister, Dee Dee. While serving my apprenticeship in that choir, I learned everything I ever needed to know about singing: how to sing when the tempo changes in the middle of a song, how to sing four-part harmony without even thinking about it twice and how to sing a cappella, which is the greatest school of all—your voice is the instrument, your feet are the drum and your hands are the tambourine.

Of course, my mother also put a great deal of emphasis on singing from the heart: applying the words of the song to your life, caring about what you were singing. If she didn't think you were giving one hundred percent in choir practice, she took it personally. There were times we fought the whole way home in the car because of this.

Mommy was right again. She knew exactly where to take a girl who needed a friend. Church. I found a spiritual home at New Hope. I loved it so much that I found another small church with the same spirit right near our house. When I couldn't get a ride to New Hope, I attended this little church. It was here during a revival service a few years later that I made a friend—a friend "that sticketh closer than a brother."

By taking me to church, my mother gave me two wonderful gifts: my foundation in gospel music and a godly heritage. That is what this book is all about—gospel and God. I will tell you why I'm thankful for this book. My mother worked hard her whole life to provide for us. We had a great home life but there wasn't always a lot of time for "rhetoric" (one of Mom's favorite words) about her early years. This is the first time she has ever sat down and committed to paper the story of her life and our family, whose roots go deep in the history of gospel. In these pages, you will read about my great-great-grandmother and great-great-grandfather, John and Victoria Drinkard. In the 1800s, they were among the first blacks to own their own land in Georgia. You will meet my grandfather who left Georgia for Newark in 1923 and dreamed that his children would one day sing gospel. Had his dream never come true, I would not be a singer today. But it did. The Drinkards, the family quartet where my mother started singing as a child, were pioneers of the gospel sound in the New York metropolitan area. My mom was just out of her teens when they played Carnegie Hall, the Apollo Theater and the historic Newport Jazz Festival in 1957. You will read my mother's behind-the-scenes take on the many artists and producers she recorded for as the leader of the mid-1960s first-call background vocal group, the Sweet Inspirations. It is one thing to read the long, glorious list of the artists she recorded with: Solomon Burke, Wilson Pickett, Aretha Franklin, Van Morrison, the Drifters, Chuck Jackson, Ben E. King and, of course, Dionne Warwicke—quite another to sense the vibe of the actual recording sessions. Her first solo record, "Presenting Cissy Houston," which she recorded when I was seven, is one of my all-time favorites. Over the years, I have permanently "borrowed" every copy of it I could find at her house, so I am never without one. You will also read exactly why my mother turned down a recording contract for me when I was fourteen. Hint: she was right. Between the covers of this book, you will also encounter my mother's irresistible wisdom and advice, most of which I took: pray and act ("faith without works is dead") . . . don't change your standards for anybody . . . and her constant theme song: "to thine own self be true."

There is one last piece of advice my mother gave me that may not have made it into this book. But I will share it with you anyway. One summer, when I was a teenager, still living in East Orange, some neighborhood girls visited me, who reminded me of my elementary school enemies. The ringleader had been picking on me most of the summer, though I hadn't done anything to bother her. When she and seven big girls showed up at my door one night, I wasn't really surprised. "I wanna fight you," she said. I conferred briefly with my two friends in the backyard and, though outnumbered, we accepted the challenge. On the way out of the house, my mother, unaware of my tormentor's superior troop strength, sent me into battle: "Whitney, get the one with the most mouth first," she said.

I took her advice. I extended the right hand of fellowship to the ringleader and most vocal of the eight. It worked. I spent the rest of that summer, in fact the next three years until I moved from East Orange, in relative peace.

Thank you, Mommy, for your great advice on and off the battle-

field. I finally have it collected in book form. It will be your written
legacy to me, my children and anyone who wants to consider the life of
the one I call the singer's singer. The one I have been blessed to have in
my life; who taught me so much about being not only a great singer but
also a godly woman. If I can be just half of what you are, I'll be all right
. . . I'll be all right.

HOW SWEET THE SOUND

ONE

Through many dangers, toils and snares,
I have already come.
—*"Amazing Grace"*

They say my father had to leave the South. As a child, I never heard the whole story. Every time I got close, I got shooed out of the room for listening to grown-up talk. But over the years, I picked up some more pieces of the story—from a cousin or when one of my older sisters got in the mood to talk. I knew this much, right from square one, or as we say, Jump Street, Nitch Drinkard had a temper.

My older sisters saw him take Red Smith's gun away from him on the streets of Newark. Red Smith was a bad cop who hated blacks and used to bother my brother. My father took things to heart, felt things deeply, but didn't always show his feelings. It was impossible to read him behind those steely gray eyes and high Indian cheekbones—till he blew! He didn't take any nonsense. He was a Christian. But he was also a straight-up kind of a guy. If you did right by him, he told you so. And if you did wrong, he told you so too. I understand how he was, completely. I'm just like him.

Now, in 1922, Hilton, Georgia, did not exactly welcome men who were straight-up, especially if they were black. Daddy's family went back at least three generations in Hilton, a two-bit town just outside of Blakely, the Early County seat. The Drinkards were tied to the land, farmers in Georgia's own little fertile crescent between the Chattahoochie and Flint rivers, down in the corner of the state where Georgia meets up with Alabama and Florida. I guess I come from a line of folk who knew the land, because some said the Drinkards were the best farmers in Early County. They raised cotton, peanuts, corn, sugarcane, sweet potatoes—you name it, they grew it.

But Nitch didn't win any prizes from the Future Farmers of America, not as a twenty-year-old black kid. Georgia wasn't giving out any awards to third-generation black farmers who owned their land. As a matter of fact, they were lynching them. The social and economic gains black folk had made since Reconstruction following the Civil War generated an angry backlash. By 1890, states' constitutions had conveniently been changed to deprive blacks of the vote. Not only was intermarriage between the races a social taboo, it was outlawed in every southern state. Blacks couldn't even associate publicly with whites, since schools, hotels and most restaurants and theaters were either black or white, never mixed. The KKK was there to see that the laws were observed and social customs upheld.

In the North and in the Midwest, newly arriving blacks competed with whites for jobs, housing and recreation. When black soldiers returned from World War I, they further swelled these ranks. Honoring soldiers for defending our country in Europe meant parades for white heroes, not black. If you were black, you were still a second-class citizen. The Klan rose to defend this principle. In just the first year after the war, seventy blacks were lynched. Mobs in Georgia and Mississippi each murdered three black war veterans—some in uniform. Murders in Arkansas, Alabama and Florida brought the total up to ten. During this same period, eleven blacks were burned alive.

In 1896, the year Daddy was born, the Supreme Court made segregation official. With the three famous words they would use to describe public facilities, "separate but equal," the Justices sanctioned a black-and-white world, hailed by whites and hated by their black neighbors. A generation later the outcome of national segregation was plain to see. The headlines were impossible to ignore. I can imagine my father's surprise as he opened the November 23, 1922, edition of the *Atlanta Constitution*. There appeared the full-page ad placed by the National Association for the Advancement of Colored People (NAACP), which read:

THE SHAME OF AMERICA

Do you know that the United States is the Only Land on Earth where human beings are BURNED AT THE STAKE? In Four Years, 1918–1921, Twenty-eight People Were Publicly BURNED BY AMERICAN MOBS

3436 People Lynched 1889 to 1922

FOR WHAT CRIMES HAVE MOBS NULLIFIED GOVERNMENT AND INFLICTED THE DEATH PENALTY?

THE ALLEGED CRIME	THE VICTIMS
Murder	1288
Rape	571
Crimes Against Person	615
Crimes Against Property	333
Miscellaneous Crime	453
Absence of Crime	176
	3436

WHY SOME MOB VICTIMS DIED:

1. Not turning out of road for white boy in auto
2. Being a relative of a person who was lynched
3. Jumping a labor contract
4. Being a member of the non-Partisan League
5. "Talking back" to a white man
6. "Insulting" a white man

I can just imagine how mad this made my father. But the worst was yet to come. From June until December 1919, there were twenty-five race riots. The Klan and other Klan-like operations whipped the discontented elements of society into a frenzy of hate. It started in July, in Longview, Texas, when several white men went into the black section of town to teach a black schoolteacher a lesson. It was said that the schoolteacher had sent a letter to a Chicago newspaper detailing the recent lynching of a black in Longview. But the white men never found their prey; they were shot. Shocked by the black section's refusal to be intimidated, whites poured into the neighborhood, burned homes, ran black citizens out of town and whipped a black principal in the street. In Washington, D.C., the next week, bogus reports of white women being attacked by blacks touched off three days of riots. Several blacks were killed as mobs made up mostly of white servicemen ran through the streets. In Chicago, where black homes were often bombed to discourage black families from moving into white neighborhoods, a full-scale race war erupted. It began when a young black swimmer drifted into waters normally frequented by whites at a popular Lake Michigan beach. The youth was stoned and subsequently drowned. Mobs of blacks and whites clashed all over the city. Blacks were pulled off streetcars and flogged. Even with the militia on alert early, Chicago was without law and order for nearly two weeks. In the end twenty-three blacks and fifteen whites were dead, 537 were injured and more than 1,000 families, chiefly black, were left homeless.

Just weeks later in Knoxville, Tennessee, troops went into the black section of town and shot it up. "The indignities which colored women suffered at the hands of these soldiers," declared a black newspaper, "would make the devil blush for shame." In Omaha, Nebraska, an angry mob dragged a black accused of attacking a white girl from his jail cell. They shot him more than a thousand times before mutilating his body beyond recognition. Then they hung him above one of Omaha's busiest intersections.

Things were not much better in Hilton, Georgia. Like black folk all around Early County, Nitch could not forget the terror of the Grandison Goolsby Scrape in 1916. In fact, Goolsby was a cousin by marriage. A prosperous black farmer, Grandison Goolsby had, by some white folks' estimation, gotten too big. One Sunday afternoon, Goolsby's son was in a buggy, returning from a wedding, his girlfriend at his side. Down the same muddy road, in the opposite direction, came a white man, Henry Villipigue. For well over a hundred years, the custom had been that when a black encountered a white man on the same road, he was to go into the ditch to allow the white man to pass.

Perhaps if Villipigue hadn't been drinking, he would have left enough room for both drivers to pass easily. But he didn't.

Goolsby's son refused to go into the ditch. Their wheels locked, and Villipigue, outraged, lashed the boy's face with a horsewhip. When the boy returned home that evening, his mother begged him not to tell his father what had happened. The boy did anyway. Goolsby left his dinner and, armed with rifles, he and his sons went to Villipigue's home. Goolsby called for the man from the front door, rather than the back. "Mr. Henry, I hear you done hit my boy and I done come to get some satisfaction about it." From inside the house, Villipigue asked him if it was the same boy he had whipped in the road. When Goolsby answered that it was, Villipigue came out shooting. In returning fire, Goolsby killed him.

That same Sunday evening, Goolsby fled to a black church in the nearby New Hope area. In the church steeple, he barricaded himself in with pistols, rifles and a load of ammunition. Villipigue's relatives, several wagonloads of men seeking revenge, refused to wait until Monday morning for a sheriff's posse. They encircled the church and began firing. But from high above them in the church steeple, Goolsby was able to pick off dozens of the shooters. During the night, a lynch mob rushed the building and set it afire. Goolsby was burned to death. But before he died, he killed or severely injured the lion's share of his attackers.

Grandison Goolsby may have killed as many as fifty white men in Early County that night. Those that didn't die suffered disfiguring wounds. Dozens of men were forced to amputate arms and legs. For years afterward, when one of these amputees was seen in public, black folk would whisper under their breath, "There goes one of old Grandison Goolsby's."

In an act of revenge against the entire black community, every black Masonic hall in Early County, including my father's, was burned to the ground. Some black churches also were torched. The entire Goolsby clan was marked for death. It may well have been some of the Masonic brothers and sisters from my father's lodge who, though in fear for their lives, safely harbored Goolsby's kin. Daddy, who was twenty at the time, may well have been one of those young Masonic brothers. Like his father, he had joined the Masons, as many blacks did, after Reconstruction—just because they could. My father wasn't gung-ho about their doctrine and it didn't strike him that being a Mason and being a churchgoer were at odds. My father wasn't gung-ho about much except his family, his church and his God. But if it was within his power to help a brother, he would. He wasn't a very political person. Later on in his life, he became a union man. But as far as race issues are concerned, I believe he simply dreamed, as he did for years, that one day he would be regarded as just a man, not a "black" man.

For a year after the incident, blacks could not set foot on the Columbia highway, one of the county's major roads. Men still seeking revenge announced their intention to kill any black found walking there. Blacks were not sold high-powered rifles or ammunition for many years afterward. Even decades later, blacks were afraid to claim kinship with any Goolsby.

At the same time, the Grandison Goolsby Scrape shouldn't have surprised anyone. As states go, Georgia always had a violent streak. Lynching was a time-honored tradition. As a matter of fact, along with just a few other states, Georgia led the South in lynchings. And for a very good reason—there were more blacks. In 1920, blacks made up almost half of Georgia's population. Whites in power had to keep their Negroes in line and that's what lynching was about. It sent a message and a warning: you do this and you will come to the same end. That's the message they wanted to leave with poor Jake Davis. Jake lived in Colquitt, Georgia, a mere twenty miles down the road from Nitch's home town of Hilton. In July 1922, somebody found him hanging in a tree. Jake had fathered the child of a white woman.

But there was something else in Early County, that whites hated just about as bad as a black man being with a white woman. That "something" added fuel to the fire that smoldered beneath the surface of the Grandison Goolsby Scrape. Something that could almost place you on equal footing with a white man. Something that had the potential of one day taking over the role of the white man in the South.

It was a black man owning land.

That's what Nitch figured the whole Grandison Goolsby Scrape was about anyway. Henry Villipigue knew old Grandison Goolsby and, like most white folks in Early County, hated him more than other blacks, because he didn't work for no white man. He worked and saved and now he owned his land free and clear. And what's more, he was rich to boot!

At the turn of the century, no other achievement put the fear into whites, and was so cherished by black folk at the same time, more than a black man owning land. It stank of Freedmen's Bureaus, and black folks getting the vote; of Yankee abolitionists and liberal troublemakers. But most of all, it carried the stench of defeat. Of the Union winning and the Confederacy losing. Of once beautifully landscaped plantations, fertile and proud, now scarred by bombs; smoldering and barren. Of a way of life gone and the reliable order, in which blacks knew their place, turned to chaos. Devastated and beyond repair, many of the once grand old homesteads were abandoned by their original owners.

For black folk, owning land was nothing less than redemption! It was Moses and the children of Israel overcoming an evil Pharaoh; a cruelly enslaved people and the cries of their travail finally reaching the ears of God. It was deliverance; to walk on one's own earth, and plant one's own crops after being owned by another for so long. It was something worth living for. Something worth working for. Something worth dying for. The Land.

People knew the name Drinkard in Early County. Not just because they said Nitch's grandfather was the best farmer in the county. But because the Drinkards owned their land. No sharecroppin' for them! When white planters kept blacks from owning land, refused to sell it to blacks, and black landowners were scarce in the South, Nitch Drinkard's daddy *owned* his little piece of Georgia. Nitch's daddy, John Drinkard, Jr., owned it not just because he worked it and earned it by the sweat of his brow. Not just because John's wife, Susan, sick most of her life, chopped that land's cotton. And not just because their nine children also worked that land. John Drinkard, Jr., *inherited* that land. Inherited the farm from his parents, Nitch Drinkard's grandparents, John and Victoria Drinkard. Born in slavery, John and Victoria had sharecropped that soil until they could buy some themselves. An inheritance for their children and their children's children—Nitch's children!

And this wasn't just any old parcel of land. Listen to one of those good old boy overseers writing home about Early County, the "garden spot" of Georgia, in 1859:

> From October 1859 until January first 1861 I was on the plantation of Major Henry Dunwoody (peace to his ashes, his brave spirit flashed out with the guns of Gettysburg in 1863) twelve miles East of Blakely, near Spring Creek. Lying East of Blakely there was a tract of land 12 miles wide and 18 miles long, the finest farming land in the State, every foot of which was owned by people of wealth and inhabited by negroes and overseers. The owners of those plantations were wealthy, educated and refined. Among them were General Taylor, the widow Taylor, the widow Nesbitt, Dr. Hill, Joe Hill, Mr. Jones . . . Their idea of hospitality was, you wine and dine me today and I will return the compliment tomorrow and poor white trash and negroes were considered to be on the same level, if anything the negro was in their estimation on top . . .

These southern Gatsbys would leave their plantations in the hands of an overseer while they spent the hot season in North Georgia. (The "widow Nesbitt" was a personal friend of Teddy Roosevelt's mother.)

> . . . most of those planters were like migratory birds, up north in the summer and down south in the winter, arriving in November or December in time for hog killing and fresh meats, backbone, spareribs, sausage, chitlins and souse. After selling their cotton and seeing the crops planted, they would return to their summer homes in North Georgia about April or the first of May . . .

These rich man's farms were the Spring Creek Plantations, ten miles east of Blakely. Ten miles west of Blakely were Hilton and the River Plantations. From one of these once grand plantations between the Chattahoochie River and the Sowhatchee Creek, John and Victoria Drinkard purchased a parcel of land. Another visitor describes this land, writing from Blakely, Early County, in 1857, ten years before John and Victoria's first son is born:

> . . . there are many acres of uncultivated land—some of it excellent for grazing—some (lime pine land) which would furnish a large yield the planter—untouched and untrodden save by a chance cattle grower or the red deer . . . thousands of acres of rich land on the waters of Colomookee, Sowhatchee . . . and the Chattahoochie River may be redeemed by a judicious system of draining, which has already been inaugurated by our most skillful farmers.

One Blakely newspaper editor referred to Early County simply as "Eden." On either side of Blakely and probably running south as far as Florida, it was a fertile swath of earth that bloomed with vegetables and fruit and oats and cotton and cane for syrup. Between the Sowhatchee and the Chattahoochie there was also a great pine forest where deer, wild turkey, wildcat, coon and possum roamed. Where still ponds hid alligators and great fish. Food and crop enough. That's where Nitch Drinkard grew up. On Drinkard land. That's where he belonged. And that's where he would stay, no matter how many letters Uncle Jim sent him from up North.

Black folk couldn't move out of the South fast enough. Uncle Jim wrote about New Jersey like it was the Promised Land. But Nitch Drinkard wasn't going anywhere. This was his home. He didn't blame anyone for leaving, times were bad—race riots, murders, lynching. He swore if he heard about one more lynching, he might fly off the handle and hurt somebody before he even gave it a thought. It was almost impossible to walk around acting as if everything was all right, when you had some of those horrible scenes still in your head. Lynchin' those boys in uniform was the sorriest, saddest thing he'd ever heard of. He'd spoken to one boy about what life was like over in Europe during the war. He said they'd had them doing all dirty work: pulling up tree stumps, putting in roads. Got gassed a lot. And had a lot of southern boys bossing them around. If you complained, you were branded a troublemaker and they sent you to the front. Boys they sent there hardly ever came back in one piece. When you came home, there was no fanfare. A man told him to take off that uniform, get a pair of overalls and go back to work. Didn't want him marching around in no army suit. Guess he was lucky compared to the ones still wearing their uniforms and swingin' from a tree. It made your blood boil.

There was no answer for such atrocities. No explanation for such cruelty and no place to take the rage inside you. You could take it out on the street and end up like Grandison Goolsby—riddled with bullets and burned beyond recognition in the steeple of a church. Or you could pour liquor on that rage like crazy Hiram, who'd get a bellyful of moonshine and stand around the town square in Blakely cussing out white folk. Eventually, they got sick of Hiram and they shot him dead too. If neither drink nor revenge was the answer, if leaving was out of the question, and if your pride would not allow you to shuffle around the rest of your days, ignoring it all, playing the harmless Negro, then there was only one place to go for answers.

Ebenezer African Methodist Episcopal (AME) was a little country church that stood out in the middle of nowhere on the Columbia highway in Hilton. Nitch's family had been members there for three generations, all the way back to his grandmother, Victoria Hansom Drinkard, an evangelist, who still sat up in the Amen corner, a few short rows of pews in front of the altar. She preached sometimes, as did her son, John Drinkard, Jr., Nitch's father. Nitch was raised at Ebenezer.

Church didn't always give you answers. But there never was a time Nitch didn't leave that place relieved and refreshed. Sometimes it was enough just to hear the words of that old spiritual

> *Through many dangers, toils and snares,*
> *I have already come.*

and know that his parents, his grandparents born in slavery had also sung those words and shared his pain and his rage. But there was more. You could be yourself in church. It was one place the white world did not intrude. You could be yourself there, without feeling like any less of a man or woman. Without any standard of white beauty to try and, of course, fail to live up to. The white world did not come near, because they did not understand what happened there. The worship was different, the music was different and the message was different—it had to be. Black folk came there with burdens, unlike any white Christians. Just a simple homily would not do. The minister had to inspire, encourage, call down heaven, so that his flock could stand up at the end of the service, ready to face whatever adversity or trial came their way that week. Church had to be an experience.

> *Some get happy, they run,*
> *Others speak in an unknown tongue,*
> *Some cry out in a spiritual trance,*
> *Have you ever seen the saints do the holy dance?*
> *—From a song by Dorothy Love*

The holy dance. It was something from long ago; something from Mother Africa that survived the horrors of the Middle Passage, the slave markets and the life of forced servitude. A white overseer, in charge of a large Early County plantation called Gum Bottom or Sugar Tit, observed it and wrote home:

None but Negroes live on the place—the old time, salt-water darkies. They are queer people, are very religious and have meeting six nights a week. They never start to church until nine o'clock and do not break up until two or three in the morning, for after the preacher has charged them with spirituality and wrought them up to a state of religious frenzy, they engage in what they call the "holy dance." They form a ring and, as many as can, get into it; then they dance around and around, singing a mournful and weird song, while others keep time by patting with hands and feet.

   I attended one of their meetings recently, and watched with much interest the intensity and fervor of the worship of these ignorant people. When the preacher got under full headway, they began to shout, and a sister who was more deeply moved than the others went up one aisle and came down the other, moaning and wildly clapping her hands. When nearly opposite where I was sitting, she gave a sudden plunge three or four feet forward and fell upon the floor. Then two others started around the aisle and went through the same performance.

—From a pre-Civil War letter published by the *Blakely Observer,*
December 3, 1896

The unbeliever and the skeptic always misunderstood the movement of God. King David's wife laughed at him when he danced and sang in the spirit. Eli the priest mistook for drunkeness the prayer of a godly Hannah. At Pentecost, doubters accused those full of the Holy Spirit, speaking in other tongues, of being filled with new wine. In 1787, didn't white members of Philadelphia's Old St. George's Methodist Episcopal Church get fed up with the "noisy" worship of black Christians in their midst? Didn't they even go so far as to pull up from his knees while praying, the dynamic black minister, Richard Allen? Several years later, Allen founded one of the largest black denominations in America, the African Methodist Episcopal Church (AME), where blacks could worship as "noisily" as they pleased.

Ebenezer AME left Mother Africa's ring shout back in the 1800s. But they still sang and shouted and "got happy" lining out the old hymns, some from Richard Allen's hymnal, like "Amazing Grace" and "When I Can Read My Title Clear." Ebenezer was a poor church; just a simple wood-frame country church, with a center aisle, a dozen rows of pews, a pulpit, a steeple and a bell. Poor in material wealth, but rich in spirit. They didn't even have a piano, but they could raise the Spirit just clapping their hands and patting their feet, worshipping with songs like "Blessed Assurance," "What a Friend We Have in Jesus" and "That Old-Time Religion."

Some nights, they just sang and prayed—all night. These were people who believed in tarrying, waiting on the Lord. They had revival services, baptisms, evenings where people in the church just stood up and gave their testimonies, healing services and funerals. But always there was music. In fact, Ebenezer was one of those "singing churches."

Make a joyful noise unto the Lord, the Old Testament writer exhorted the people of Israel. There was something about music and song that brought heaven down to earth. Once the Spirit entered their midst, the burdens of the week, their hard trials slipped away. And when the folk at Ebenezer weren't singing, they were listening to others sing. There were jubilee singers; chorales that were inspired by the world famous Fisk Singers, who itinerated around the South, singing the old spirituals from slave times. But it was the male quartets who visited Ebenezer that captured Nitch Drinkard's imagination.

Well-dressed, of exemplary Christian behavior, these men would often stay with one of the church's families while in town. On Sunday, the quartet would stand in front of the church and perform the old spirituals like no one had ever heard them before; in perfect four-man harmony, infectious rhythm and exciting call-and-response-style singing. These quartets would influence singing groups for many decades to come. Nitch couldn't get enough of their sound. When a quartet came to town, he would follow them to other AME churches nearby: Allen Chapel, Shiloh and Zion Watch.

But more than music drew Nitch Drinkard to church. The AME ministers, though itinerant, were well-educated, having attended one of the denomination's several colleges or seminaries. Nitch heard preaching that changed his life; meaty sermons rich with Bible characters that became heroes to him. Like David, a man unafraid of battle, human, with a temper and failings like his own; yet still a seeker of God, one who the Lord said was "a man after my own heart." And Elijah, who called down fire from heaven on the prophets of Baal, then later felt hungry, destitute and abandoned by God. But neither of these mighty men of God spoke to Nitch's heart more directly than Daniel's three friends Shadrach, Meshach and Abednego. Their persecution and their willingness to enter a fiery furnace of affliction with the faith that they would emerge unharmed, spoke loud and clear to Nitch, others at Ebenezer and black folk everywhere. The black experience had been a furnace of affliction, from the hard life of slavery to the angry white backlash of Reconstruction. Sermons about the three young men in the furnace, full of faith and unscathed, gave them hope that better times were coming. Six decades had passed since the end of slavery, the worst of Reconstruction was over and the government was making some gestures to protect blacks from the lawless elements of society—relief seemed to be in sight.

Still, the race riots in various cities, the numerous lynchings of returning black war veterans and the Klan's midnight raids made the story of the fiery furnace a popular subject of sermons in black churches all over the land. Few expressed it more eloquently than Dr. Charles Tindley, a dynamic black preacher from Philadelphia. The son of a slave, Tindley was optimistic but believed that there would always be trials and a furnace of affliction to endure. He believed that real change could only be achieved through struggle. That trials, like the refiner's fire, purified the human spirit.

I welcome this morning, all the persecutions, unkindnesses, hard sayings, and whatever God allows to come upon me. I welcome the hottest fire of trials if it is needed for my purification.

Oh, the things that we have in our lives that can never go in heaven are more numerous than we are apt to think. They must all be taken out before we leave this world. God's way to get them out may be the way of the furnace.

—*"The Furnace of Affliction"*

"You know," Tindley said, "the only way you can really become defeated on your way to heaven is to allow life's difficulties to get inside of you and to turn you sour. One of the things that we have to do—we must do—is to make sure that we do not try to take vengeance. That if we belong to Him, He in His own time will take care of the situation."

Tindley's knowledge of the refiner's fire came through personal experience and at great cost. As a boy, he and his father were so destitute that when Tindley's mother died, his father was forced to hire him out in order to support them both. Tindley poured the trials and hard experiences of his life into songs that ministered almost exclusively to blacks. He wrote the classic hymns "We'll Understand It Better By and By," "Stand By Me" and "I'll Overcome Someday" ("We Shall Overcome"). These songs spoke powerfully to turn-of-the-century black Christians, with simple but memorable lyrics and music that employed the beloved pentatonic scale of Africa and the blues. Unlike white hymn writers of the day, his songs concentrated less on the ABC's of the Christian walk—sin, salvation and heaven—and more on the practical and immediate concerns of blacks: overcoming tribulations in this life, like persecution, poverty and hunger.

"Tindley said one morning he and his family sat down getting ready for breakfast," relates Rev. Henry Nichols, a friend of Tindley. "And his wife said, 'There is no food here.' He said, 'That's all right. Fix the table. Put the dishes on—we'll have breakfast.' And she looked at him and said, 'But, Dr. Tindley, didn't you hear me? There's no food here.' He said, 'That's all right. Fix the table. Let's sit down and have prayer.' And so she did. The children sat and I'm sure the children thought he was gone. And he said, 'Let's bow our heads.' No food; empty plates. And then he began to pray, 'Dear Lord, we thank you for what we are about to receive.' And just then, he said somebody knocked on the door. He stopped and went to the door, and one of the officers said, 'Brother Pastor, didn't know whether y'all had anything to eat this morning. Brought you some food over.' "

That was faith, the kind of faith and the kind of hardship Nitch Drinkard knew about.

He'd grown up poor, at least seven of them living in that shack with the tin roof. A house on stilts, two feet off the ground, with plenty of cold air blowing through the cracks in the floor, especially during the cooler months. Modern comforts such as electricity, gas stoves and indoor plumbing were only a dream. Keeping the family warm required a busy regimen of hauling, storing and chopping wood for the open-hearth fire. The men—Arthur, Nitch, Joseph, Benjamin and W.T., along with their father John—did the plowing. The women and the children—Sally, Leona, Tina and Ruby—chopped cotton. Flossie, the baby, born in 1914, came along too late to help with any work.

In the fall, everybody pitched in to pick the cotton. Every day there were chores to do—even for the youngest children. But there were also special days when their mother, Susan, put up jars of fruit preserves and jellies—a delicacy weighed against the high cost of sugar. Nitch particularly looked forward to the times when his daddy would gather their crop of sugar cane and take it to the mill. After a full day of extracting the syrup from the cane, they would arrive home to find a special treat from Mama—a stack of fresh pancakes waiting to "test" their latest batch of syrup.

Cycles of planting and harvesting set the rhythm of life, from what time you got up in the morning till when you laid your head down at night and how much time you spent in school. Nitch grew up farming nine months and only attending school for three months a year. When he went to school, he didn't go in a horse-drawn wagon like white kids, and he didn't go to their public school in Blakely. Like most blacks in rural areas, Nitch got his education at a local church—Ebenezer AME in Hilton. What was for the Drinkards the house of the Lord on Sundays became a one-room school house the rest of the week.

There were thirteen Drinkards including my grandmother and grandfather and times were hard. Especially during years of panic, when cotton plummeted to ten cents a pound. Or when the rains left you with water in the fields up to your ankles, infested with boll weevils. But they learned to pray through adversity, pray for the things they needed, rely on God for everything. My grandfather John was a lay preacher with Ebenezer AME Church and he took his calling with great seriousness. His entire life he wore a large black hat and dressed completely in black. He was tall and had so much Indian in him he was red, with long straight hair and piercing black eyes that looked right through you. As a child, I was scared to death of him!

He raised Nitch and the rest strict. No fishing, hunting or playing ball on the Sabbath. And there certainly was no playing or singing any secular music, only spirituals. The family went to church two or three times a week and almost all day Sunday. By firelight Grandpa John read to Nitch from the Gospels, Proverbs and Psalms. This nightly ritual paid an unexpected dividend—Nitch became adept at handling the scriptures. Throughout his whole life he was an effective one-on-one counselor, giving advice not just from the mind of man, but from the heart of God.

From childhood on, Nitch came face-to-face with life's mysteries. When he was just eight years old, he witnessed a catastrophic train accident. On February 20, 1905, the westbound Georgia Central left the Hilton station, descended the steep three-mile downgrade to the Chattahoochie and plunged through an open drawbridge into the river. Three men died. The engine, the train's engineer and two men working in the next car all sank to the bottom of the river, while three coaches and a mail car teetered precariously above the precipice over the river, its passengers terrified at the windows of the train. This dramatic, frightening scene, the timely rescue of the passengers and the coaches consumed by fire, would forever be etched in Nitch's memory.

As a boy, his young mind was haunted by scary stories of the Creek Indians who'd only recently been chased from the county. On the outskirts of Blakely there was a mysterious Indian Mound, seventy-five feet high and nearly five hundred around, a silent earthen mound harkening back to a civilization that built it thousands of years ago: at its center was a strange vault of human bones.

But the mysteries that most intrigued him were those of God. He witnessed family members, brothers and sisters raised up from a death-bed only by the power of prayer. He saw the church elders anoint his sick mother with oil and have her resume her cooking and washing as if she had not been sick at all. When they were bereft of food and money, God miraculously provided for their needs. His father taught him to take God at His word, claim His promises: for physical well-being, for financial stability, for guidance in every area of his life—pray for everything! Even for love, that he would find and marry the right woman, a godly soulmate and helpmate as good as his mother. God knew what he needed! John Drinkard taught Nitch that his relationship with God was the most important thing in his life. To pray always for forgiveness if he transgressed, to keep short accounts with the Lord.

John Drinkard taught his son to serve God so that his days on the earth would be long and good. That when he married, he would have many children; that his quiver would be full and God would put a hedge of protection around them. "I have never seen the righteous forsaken or the seed of God begging bread." Go with God and He will go with you. His father prayed often for Nitch, his big hands callused from the plow handles, resting on his son's shoulders. Nitch had to kneel for this ritual now, he was the tallest in the family, over six feet, handsome and tan, high cheekbones and gray eyes, his complexion rich with the red of his father's Indian blood. John Drinkard prayed for his son, that he would be a mighty man of God, a leader, that he would watch and protect his brothers and sisters. And that he would be a blessing to all those whose lives he touched.

Nitch listened on his knees as his father prayed over him and sang in the spirit and shouted. He loved that old man. He worried about both of them: his mother and father. They were so trusting and innocent. He hoped no one would ever take advantage of them because of that. He worried what would happen to them if he wasn't there to watch out for them. He was no mathematical wizard himself, but Dad just handed whatever money he got over to Mama. Didn't even want to think about it. He hoped they met all their commitments, made whatever payments they had to make.

He wanted to please the old man; he would, by God's grace. And yet the times were changing, days were evil. Black men—black soldiers—were hanging dead in trees! You couldn't just shake your head and moan and cry, "God." You had to do something sometimes, too.

But Nitch Drinkard wasn't leaving. This is where he was born, where his parents were born. Where he hunted and fished and sang with his uncles. Folk knew him, respected him. He had three babies, even had a son, William, whom he'd soon show all his boyhood haunts, his favorite ponds to fish. And in those deep piney woods, there were deer and opossum and coon enough to hunt. Oh, they'd have a time!

This was his family's land and not just their land. His grandparents, John and Victoria Drinkard, were the first to ransom that land from white men with their sweat and blood. This farm was an inheritance for their descendants. As the family's first freed slaves, John and Victoria were able to develop the pride of self-ownership and self-determination for the Drinkard family.

Both John and Victoria knew two things well: a life of slavery and the hard work of farming. The elder John Drinkard came from the rich Mississippi delta. Black folk from Mississippi knew how to farm. Down in the delta, they had to figure out ways of draining the land, through ditches and canals, or they wouldn't have been able to do a thing with it. Land sitting on top of the Chattahoochie could get wet, but not as wet as when the Mississippi overflowed the levee! He was an experienced farmer. He knew how to nurture the earth, protect it, revive it when it had been savaged by the elements. He could make it bloom with crops. His ancestors in Mother Africa had taught him the importance of letting the land rest. The Seminoles down in the bayou who had intermarried with his clan had also shown him a thing or two about raising crops in the wetlands. It was no wonder they said John Drinkard was the best farmer in Early County.

After Emancipation, Victoria and John came to some kind of sharecropping or tenancy arrangement with their former master. From the outset, they set their mind to making this property their own farm. The first thing they had to do was save up for a mule. That was the hardest hurdle to cross; it might take two or three years. Then they worked toward buying a plow. In the meantime, they borrowed tools, seed and the various supplies they needed from the landowner at inflated prices. Once the crop was harvested, the landowner sold it and gave John and Victoria their cut, minus the rent on that sad little shack they occupied. As tenants, they were never permitted to look at the books; they could never challenge what they were charged or credited. Those who asked were branded troublemakers. What was clear was that at the end of the landowner's cockeyed balance sheet, John and Victoria were in debt to the landowner up to their ears. In debt, with a brood that eventually included eleven. Nitch's Uncle Jim was born first in 1867. Nitch's father, John Jr., was born four years later. Anna, Wiley, Joe, Evelina, Hattie, Lucius, Dollis, Alabliss and Hansom followed thereafter.

Like many former slaves, John and Victoria were now enslaved to their "debt." Had they chosen to move on before the onerous balance sheet had been wiped clean, the law provided for their capture and return at the hands of the local sheriff. Some tenants were eventually given contracts that dictated exactly how much they were to be paid for their labor. This was supposed to be an improvement. But even with the contract, the landowner still paid you what he wanted. If you tried to escape the vicious cycle of work and endless debt, you were hunted for "breaking" your contract. When they caught you and returned you to the farm, you were usually beaten or whipped. When the authorities finally started to investigate the abuses of Georgia landowners, some killed their workers, rather than let them reveal the inhumane conditions under which they were forced to work and live.

Somehow by the grace of God, John and Victoria Drinkard endured as sharecroppers until they finally obtained rights to their own land. Twenty, thirty years of backbreaking toil, hard labor that made you old before your time. Up in the morning, hoeing and plowing and geeing and hawing with that stubborn mule until you had just about memorized every crease in his behind.

The authorities dictated the daily comings and goings of blacks, modeled on the old Slave Codes. Tenaciously, the Drinkards clung to their land through the terror of the KKK's midnight rides and cross burnings, when they might set your whole crop on fire or lynch somebody you knew because they didn't like the way you voted. They kept the farm through droughts and floods and panics. When cotton was worth next to nothing. When the boll weevil ruined your entire crop. When it was all you could do to scrape together a few dollars to buy pork and flour and salt to put something on the table. They held on to the land as an inheritance for their eleven children.

To be black and own land at the turn of the century—the harshest, most perilous years to be black in Georgia—that was one thing. But to be black and have *inherited* the land, that was something else again—something quite extraordinary, even miraculous. How many other black families in Early County could claim such providence? Is it any wonder that Nitch became taken with the idea that the Drinkards were different, even blessed? And why them?

Why not? That was something his grandmother, Victoria Drinkard, taught him. How many people didn't get their blessings because they never asked! It seemed so simple, but it was true! She taught him to ask. Another wonderful gift she had given him. One more laurel of thanks he would one day lay at the feet of his grandmother when he got to the other side.

As a small boy, he remembered her: this little brown woman, not much taller than he, taking him by the hand to that country church. He remembered her with that long Indian braid of shiny black hair. Getting happy in church. The deacons at Ebenezer didn't let too many women sit up there near the pulpit. But Victoria Hansom Drinkard was different; she was a bona fide evangelist. They even allowed her to "lecture" from time to time. Nitch remembered his grandmother preaching; watching her from the mourner's bench, where those who still had not been converted had to stay. It was during one of her "lectures" that he felt compelled to leave that bench and fall on his knees at the altar, anxious to accept the Lord.

She was an evangelist from Pennsylvania, who'd caught the holiness fire at a camp meeting during the tail end of the "Second Awakening." The first "Great Awakening" swept the colonies in the 1730s. One of its hallmarks was a change in worship music—from the dry rise and fall of singing psalms line by line, to the fervor of new hymns written by Englishmen like John Wesley, Isaac Watts and John Newton. "Amazing Grace," "When I Can Read My Title Clear" and "On Jordan's Stormy Banks," though poetic and lofty in lyric, authentically expressed the heart of the Christian faith. Newly converted slaves adopted the hymns and made them their own. So much so, that after nearly one hundred years, the hymns little resembled their original form. They had become a synthesis of English hymn and African chant. Even some of the verses and refrains had been modified to reflect the hard trials of slavery.

The "Second Awakening," which began about 1780, was a revival that spread through much of the South, and lasted over fifty years. This revival was characterized by "camp meetings." Given the movement of the Spirit, a camp meeting could take place wherever a clearing or field could accommodate a large main tent for meetings. Smaller tents or cabins were set up around the main tent, vaguely reminiscent of Israel's ancient tabernacle in the wilderness. Worshippers could live in the smaller tents for several days while attending the revival meetings. As the Spirit moved through a typical service, like at Pentecost, worshippers both black and white were dramatically converted, spoke in tongues and were miraculously healed. The music was likewise heavenly; choirs of rich black voices further invited the listener to give the Spirit full sway in his or her life. The freedom of the pentecostal camp meetings was a powerful draw to the slaves laboring daily and monotonously on the plantations. At one of these camp meetings in Early County, Victoria Drinkard found the Lord.

After the Civil War, Victoria, John and a handful of other freedmen purchased an old Methodist church from white people in Hilton. They affiliated with the new black African Methodist Episcopal denomination. This small group of former slaves named the church Ebenezer—literally, the "stone of help" that Samuel erected as a memorial to the Lord for helping Israel rout the Philistines.

To Ebenezer AME, Victoria brought the stirring spirituals that she had heard and sung at the camp meetings. And she taught them to her children and later to her grandson, Nitch: "Deep River," "My Lord, What a Mourning" and "Lord, I Want to Be a Christian." As Nitch grew, he, his father and his uncles would carry those songs into the field, singing while they worked. In the evening, however, anxious to entertain themselves and imitate the male quartets that were so popular in the South, they enjoyed souping up those old spirituals quartet-style. Close harmony. They could sing for hours into the night, it sounded so good to them! The natural, pure harmony of fathers and uncles and sons, blending and floating in midair: bass, baritone, second tenor and first tenor. Before too long, they got up to sing at Ebenezer. Then, they began to spend a Sunday a month visiting other churches in nearby Bainbridge, Columbia, across the river and even as far as Waycross. But not for the money. They didn't sing for the money. They sang for the pure joy of singing. Like the song says:

I sing because I'm happy,
I sing because I'm free,

His eye is on the sparrow,
And I know He watches over me.

When he thought of that song now, sitting in church, he thought of his wife, Delia—it was her favorite.

She was sitting next to him, holding the baby. William, four, and Lee, two, fussing on either side of her. He was amazed at how good his life was compared to what it could have been. This was the blessing of God. Nitch thanked the Lord for His goodness; for His watchcare and protection of his grandparents, his parents and the land that linked all three generations. As he began to think about his parents and his grand-parents, how God had protected them all these years, his heart welled up with praise. They had given him an inheritance of more than land; they had given him faith and family and song.

He thanked Him for Ebenezer Church. He'd had so many good times there; so many sweet hours of prayer. So many times he'd sought the Lord and He had answered in such marvelous ways. Though Nitch was still a young man, not yet thirty, he was grown up in the Lord. His faith had been tried and tested. He knew his Bible. He liked to counsel the younger men in the church. He could sense when they were drift-ing away from their wives, and he quoted them the appropriate scrip-tures. "Stolen water is sweet . . . But little do they know that the dead are there, that her guests are in the depths of the grave . . . Can a man walk on hot coals without his feet being scorched? So is he who sleeps with another man's wife." And finally, and most direct: "Young man, cherish the wife of your youth, and let her breasts satisfy you." There was wisdom enough in Proverbs for every occasion, every character under the sun. For those engaged in argument with wives or employers, he liked to counsel: "a soft answer turneth away wrath." And if that didn't work, he winked at them and said, "Brother, it's not the size of the dog in the fight, it's the size of the fight in the dog."

He counseled his own brothers and sisters over matters great and small. With his older brother Arthur gone, the mantle of oldest child rested comfortably on Nitch's shoulders. They loved him and gave him all the respect due the eldest brother. They looked up to him and called on him often. He was their leader and the backbone of the family. Even some of the older folk liked to sit with him and talk. He had a respect for them that made them feel appreciated. He was well liked at Ebenezer. The young women liked him. They knew he didn't live loose, never shirked a job and was good to his parents. They'd seen and heard him sing with his uncles; his face radiant, his high, sharp Indian features gleaming. His clear, pure voice cutting through the air. He would have made a good catch, that is, if Delia hadn't gotten to him first! But that was out of their control. One day he just came back from visiting kin in Florida and brought her back with him. Quiet, shy Delia. She was young when he got her, still in her teens, and he was already twenty-six. They teased him in church, the older men did, about robbing the cradle. And he would blush and sputter and laugh. But she was dark, petite and fully developed. She wore those cute little hats to church and liked to sing that song "His Eye Is on the Sparrow." She was so small; maybe she felt like a sparrow. She would get up in church, in season and out, sick or well, and wail out that hymn, tears streaming down her face. It was her testimony: God cares. He has brought me to this point. He woke me up this morning and put the breath of life in my nostrils. I will trust Him.

Now Nitch looked over at her and smiled. He was filled with gratitude that his wife felt the same way about the Lord that he did. He felt blessed to have a Christian wife; one who could encourage him in his faith, someone who understood the Christian walk. It would have been a nightmare, he thought, for someone like him, who loved the Lord like he did, to be unequally yoked, married to an unbeliever. They had been married only a short time and already his quiver was full: three children. First William, born in 1918, a few months before the end of the war. Then, two years later, a girl, Lee. And finally, in October 1922, Marie. In his heart, he thanked the Lord for his precious family. He prayed that from an early age, they would come to know Him. He prayed that they would always stay together no matter how old they got.

After the service, he shook hands with some of the older deacons, the ones who still remembered his grandmother, and greeted the pastor. He told Delia he would meet her at his parents' home, he would just be a little while. He liked to stay and pray in the empty church on Sundays, late in the afternoon, before the evening service, when the sun was low in the sky. When gleaming shafts of sun would fill the little church with a warm glow. He felt like he was on the mountaintop; just he and God; his special time. Kneeling in the aisle, beside the last pew, he began to thank Him for his family, his children, his wonderful wife. And as he thanked Him and praised Him, an indescribable joy began to bubble up inside him; and he thought that if he didn't give it utterance, he would burst. So he let this living stream have its way with him and he gave himself over to it and praised him in a language he knew not.

So caught up in this rapture was he that when he suddenly felt a shadow cross his face, he was certain it was the wing of an angel, fluttering just above his head. But when he looked up, he saw it was a man, with his hand outstretched, offering him something.

It was an older man from the church; maybe a deacon, he didn't remember. In the man's outstretched hand was a newspaper, folded long, like a stone tablet, revealing that part of the paper with the public notices. He took the paper from the man and began to read. The man slipped out of the church. The paper was a few days old but one particular notice had been circled with a dull pencil.

. . . and that plot known as lot number . . . in County of Early, bounded by Sowhatchee Creek on the North and on the South by . . . belonging to one John Drinkard . . . will be sold for the recovery of delinquent taxes.

The paper fell from his hands. He began to perspire; he felt light-headed.

It was their land.

The words were a jumble in his head. There must be some mistake. The newspaper had made a mistake. Somehow they had gotten hold of inaccurate information; these kinds of people were so unreliable, gossipers who ran that newspaper.

He ran to his parents' home. The looks on their faces told him they had heard and that there was probably no mistake. His mother, a world of sadness on her face, held the limp notice she must have received months ago, but somehow overlooked, when the county first demanded payment. He heard himself tell her not to worry; he would go into town in the morning and fix it.

There was no one to talk to about this. To talk about this with anyone was to invite embarrassment . . . shame. He'd heard of folk losing their land because of things like this! Even if a settlement could be worked out, they would want thousands of dollars. The kind of money no one in the family had. *Man alive, how could you let this happen to yourself . . . your parents? You're a man with a family now; you've gotta start thinkin' for them too.*

He cannot wait. It is Sunday night, the courthouse is locked up tighter than a drum, but he still wants to face their accuser. He hitches up a buggy and rides the ten miles into Blakely. In the deserted public square, the town's strange new electric arc lights burn and sputter, casting an otherworldly glow on the courthouse. He doesn't dare get out of the buggy. He had planned to walk around the building seven times, like the children of Israel walked around Jericho before it fell. But the courthouse's forbidding granite columns and pediment, the arc lights blazing and sputtering have shaken his nerve. He only sits in the buggy, frozen. Blakely is another world, putting on airs and brand-new electric lights. Paving its public square and getting ready for the carefree 1920s. Blakely is a world that's passed him by. A world that cares little for how long his family held the land, nor how hard it was for his grandparents, born in slavery, to first buy that land or how they passed that land to his daddy.

It was up to him to defend his parents; to win back what was theirs. He would go back in there tomorrow and either by words or by fists—it was their choice—get back what was theirs. Drinkards owned that land.

He turns the buggy around and rides home in the night, with only the moon to light his way. The house is dark; the soft glow of the fire is gone. Only a wisp of smoke still rises from the chimney. His parents, Delia, the children are sleeping.

He doesn't unhitch the mule just yet. Instead, he rides a few miles to the river. High above the Chattahoochie, he moves the buggy too close to the edge of the bank above the river. The animal brays and backs up, frightened of the cliff and the river below. He speaks softly to the mule, comforting the animal, realizing, for the first time, it has been hours since he has thought about something other than the courthouse, his parents and the farm. He climbs out of the buggy and ties it to a tree.

He walks back to the edge of ground overlooking the river and falls to his knees; to show reverence for God—as he believes all men should pray—as he prayed in church . . . at home next to his little bed as a boy . . . and on this patch of praying ground, where he has come hundreds of times before. Where the mighty rushing of the Chattahoochie below will drown out his own wailings.

He pours out his whole heart to God; his only witnesses, the moon and the stars swimming in his tears.

Why, God? Why have You allowed this to happen? Heavenly Father, what have we done, what have we done to deserve this? Have we not served You all of our lives? Have the three generations of us not loved You enough? How have we not honored You?

Have You brought me all this way to leave me now? Have I been dreaming? Have You really been with me at all? Can You hear me? Are You there?

He cried for hours. Begging . . . pleading with Him to restore the land to them. The land that his grandparents had hoed and plowed and nourished with their sweat and tears. The earth that his grandparents had clung to for the sake of their children and their children's children. Through storm and flood and drought and evil men. Restore it not for him, but for their sake. For his parents' sake. What would he do with his father? In the middle of his life, he couldn't just become a tenant farmer; it would kill him.

He cried for hours; bitter tears, for the shame he felt, as a son, for whatever he could have done and didn't. The shame he felt as a man, made powerless by another, faceless man. He cried out even the hate he had inside him for that faceless white man in the courthouse. He confessed the murder he had in his heart to visit upon that man. How he wanted to strap on a pistol, ride into town in the morning.

Nobody knows what my father did that next morning—at least, if they do they haven't told me yet. My sisters don't want to talk about it. It's "ancient history," it's buried and it's gone and what's the good in knowin' anyway? Nobody wants to talk about Daddy's parents, John and Susie Bell Drinkard, who lost the family's land. Except my cousin Louis Drinkard: "Lost their land? Back taxes? Shoot. Those crackers just *took* John and Susie's land!"

Whatever my father did, he had no blood on his hands when he left Georgia. He probably went down to that courthouse, told them they were a bunch of lying, cheating SOBs . . . scared 'em and then slipped out like Jesus slipped away from the Pharisees. My father wrestled with his own nature, but I rarely saw that temper get the better of him. Above all, he was a praying man. To have gone in and shot up Blakely, what would that have proved? He knew what it had gotten Grandison Goolsby—killed. I'll tell you what it would have proved. That those Drinkards were nothin' but no-account sharecroppers. That John Drinkard, Sr., wasn't the best farmer in Early County. That he was just some old-time slavery Negro from Mississippi whose grandson shot up Blakely. That's not the kind of man Nitch was.

From the court's foreclosure on the family farm until February 1923, Nitch worked for the railroad. He got his father a job there too. Together they hauled those big fifty-foot timbers out of the pine forest in Hilton, eventually to be treated and used for railroad ties. It was hard, backbreaking work. The other men were roustabouts who cursed and blasphemed all day long, singing the kind of low-down blues that would make a sailor blush. Nitch felt badly for his father and wrote to his Uncle Jim in New Jersey.

Before he left Early County for the North that winter of 1923, Nitch went back to the river many times, as much to pray as he went there to gaze out on the river and remember his boyhood in Early County. He would never get to share his boyhood haunts with his son, William. The long, lazy afternoons spent fishing in Hilton's ponds or along the Sowhatchee Creek. He would never get to sit with his daughters in Ebenezer AME on a Sunday, where he once sat as a child, holding the hand of his grandmother, Victoria Hansom Drinkard. He was saying goodbye to many things. And when it would overwhelm him, he went to his knees, to cry and pray. He stayed there—he didn't know how long—hours perhaps; singing . . . praying . . . tarrying, waiting on Him, until he had his answer. And when he did; when that calm, that peace that passes all understanding had settled over him, he rose.

"When I was a child, I spake as a child, I understood as a child, I thought as a child: but when I became a man, I put away childish things. For now we see through a glass, darkly; but then face to face: now I know in part; but then shall I know even as also I am known."

Perhaps, he was only saying goodbye to the things of his youth. It really was not the setback that he first thought it was. When the Lord closed one door, he remembered his father telling him, He opens another. It was his job to have the faith to believe that God would open a door. That's what he was doing now in February 1923. Walking through that door. He didn't know what the future held. Or even what the North was all about. Black folk talked about it like it was the Promised Land. Well . . . that remained to be seen. For now, he was only to trust and be obedient.

From where he stood, he could see the eastbound train crossing the river, from Alabama, building up a good head of steam, in order to climb the steep three-mile grade into Hilton. He would meet that train in the morning. But first, he would sleep one last night in Hilton. After twenty-seven years, a lifetime in Georgia, he would lie in bed one last time listening to the sounds of the rushing river and the wind singing in the trees of the deep piney woods.

In the morning, my daddy put his parents, the two older children, William and Lee, up in the train. Once he'd helped my mother up the steps, he handed her the baby, my sister Reebie. He put one foot up in the eastbound Georgia Central and turned around to take one last look at Hilton. In his lifetime Nitch would return only once to the land of his birth, to bury his father in the cemetery at Ebenezer AME Church. But that wouldn't be for twenty years and another lifetime's worth of experience.

That wouldn't have surprised Daddy. At the present moment in 1923, Early County was that kind of place: easier to die in than to live in. What would have surprised my father were what and who were waiting for him, up in Newark, New Jersey.

TWO

Is there anybody here who loves my Jesus?
Anybody here who loves my Lord?
—_"Is There Anybody Here?"_

God must have walked close alongside my father during that trying year of 1923. Tragic as it was, losing the land, the family farm worked by two generations of Drinkards after slavery, propelled Nitch into action. He packed up the family and left Georgia with its painful memories in the past. One thing he didn't forget on his journey was God's abiding love.

In my father's travels and trials, he found strength in those old spirituals and favorite gospel hymns such as "Is There Anybody Here?" It is like that for me today; I find encouragement and the Lord's direction in the music that bubbles up from within me. In the winter of 1923, though, nobody was thinking of a little girl to be born ten years down the road. Moving North took every ounce of the family's time, energy, money and attention.

Nitch Drinkard wasn't the first person to land in Newark thinking it might be the Promised Land. In 1666, thirty Puritan families, unhappy with Connecticut authorities' intrusion in their religious life, sailed through the Long Island Sound, down the East River and north, up Newark Bay. When they landed on the banks of the Passaic River they quickly realized that they weren't alone—the Lenni Lenape Indians were there already. This tribe, whose name means "original people," were native to the Delaware River valley, but came to the Passaic River every spring for the abundant clams and oysters.

Fortunately for the Puritans, the ancient Lenni Lenape tribe—rugged and formidable in stature—was so peace-loving, other tribes branded them "the old women." Like their neighbors on the island across the Hudson, the Lenni Lenape sold their rights to the land for little more than britches and guns.

In their new home, the devout Puritans thrived for a while under their spiritual leader, the Reverend Abraham Pierson. At last, they thought they had found a place to raise their families, free of worldliness and the interference of government. They built a church, brought the Gospel to the Lenni Lenape and laid out the first streets of Newark like a typical New England town—an orderly grid, the main thoroughfares running north to south, a pleasant green at either end. But eventually, faraway kings, local authorities and apathy destroyed their vision of pure religion and heaven on earth. Newark was not the Promised Land the Puritans had hoped it would be.

Though Nitch Drinkard landed in Newark some 257 years later, he came with similar hopes. He, too, sought a place he could raise his children, a place where worldliness would not interfere. Stepping off the train in New Jersey, he felt the stiff, bitter wind of February blowing through their flimsy cotton clothing. It was only the beginning of the things he and his wife weren't prepared for.

His first glimpse of Newark was the noisy, dirty and freezing Pennsylvania Railroad station. What Newarkers noticed, if they bothered sizing up new arrivals, was a tall black man, with a red Cherokee complexion—looking more like the "original people" than the Pilgrim he was. My father soon settled the family in a three-story wood-frame tenement just 2,000 feet from where Newark's Puritan forebears built their simple little homes. Like them, he nurtured a godly vision within, listening carefully for guidance from that still, small voice. But from without, forces beyond his control would nearly destroy Nitch's dream. In the process, he too would find that Newark was no Promised Land.

In early 1923, Nitch Drinkard wasn't the only guy in Newark looking for a job. Like a lot of industrialized northern cities, Newark was nearly bursting from the constant influx of immigrants, particularly from Europe. Blacks represented only 10 percent of Newark's people.

As the latest arrivals, blacks stood dead last in the long lines for jobs, well behind the preferred Italians, Jews, Germans, Russians, Irish and Slavs. Even if blacks did land a job, they were the "last hired and the first fired." Many unions still excluded blacks from membership, which meant they had no job security at all.

But in Newark it should have been easier to find work. After all, the town founded by the Puritans on the banks of the Passaic was now one of the most industrialized cities in the country. From early starts in tanning, Newark had been making shoes for over a hundred years— shoes worn in the 1800s by southern aristocracy and slaves alike, by Parisians and New Yorkers. There were breweries, distilleries, foundries, chemical plants, garment makers, thread makers, gold and silver refining. Edison had produced his stock ticker here in Newark and later assembled the team that produced the electric light not far west in Menlo Park. There were specialty shops, department stores, beer gardens, theaters—Newark was bustling with the same pride and entrepreneurial spirit that seemed to be contagious across America.

In post–World War I Newark, people wanted to have a good time, have a drink, make some whoopee! For the few who had money, prosperity degenerated into materialism. Centuries-old family values were falling fast—upstaged by the worldly lifestyles that Hollywood projected in the movie theaters of Main Street and radio paraded through America's living rooms. A spirit of recklessness took many guises: the flapper, the flagpole sitter, the Wall Street speculator and the gangster. Nitch would have none of this. "When God closes one door, he usually opens another," his father's words rang in his head. Nitch had closed the door on Georgia and obediently ventured forth into the unknown. But compared to Hilton or even Blakely, Newark might just as well have been another planet!

He reeled at the stark contrasts: He had exchanged the still beauty of Hilton's fifty-foot pines for hulking concrete skyscrapers. For the clear-running Chattahoochie, he got the dirty Passaic. And for the lazy buzz of cicadas on Columbia highway, he now recoiled at the ungodly din of hundreds of Model T's, cabs and streetcars clanging down the iron tracks of Market and Broad Streets. At these renowned Four Corners, he gaped at a cobweb of electrical wires above the street. The army of trolleys that ran on that line shook him as they rattled past. Within a few years, 2,644 trolleys, 4,098 buses, 2,657 taxis and 23,581 autos would pass through the Four Corners intersection in one day, making it the busiest corner in the world.

Besides the deafening cacophony of vehicular clanging, blaring and bleating, there were throngs of pedestrians jabbering to each other in languages he had never heard before! Dark, swarthy Italians, who had recently picked up the most strenuous and menial street jobs from the Irish, who were moving up in the building trades. Slavic street cleaners in white uniforms and helmets, pushing brooms, cleaning debris from the trolley tracks and singing songs from the old country. Beefy Irish traffic cops, red in the face, pouring bitter rebuke and an angry brogue on an erring motorist.

Along with the strange sounds came other dazzling sights. Men in boaters and derbies, all hail-fellow-well-met. Blue bloods with impossibly straight noses, descendants of Newark's Puritan settlers. Flappers in fancy hats pulled low and sultry over their eyes. Older women wearing winter coats, fur trim pampering their cheeks. Newsboys in knickers, hawking their papers. Jews in long black frock coats, with beards and sidelocks, scurrying up Broad on a sunny Friday afternoon, to reach home before the sun went down and the Sabbath began.

And as throngs of people jostled on the wide sidewalks, a variety of stores catered to every want and desire. Jewelers, optometrists, drugstores, soda fountains, clothing stores, automotive supply and shoe stores all called out to them with flashing electric signs. Not to mention theaters! In 1922, Newark had sixty-three halls to satisfy the populace with more never-never land. Downtown alone boasted eight movie palaces, two burlesque houses and five vaudeville houses. The darlings of the silver screen, Mary Pickford and Marion Davies, could be seen in the movie houses. Manhattan was only ten minutes away through the Hudson tubes, but the Great White Way came calling personally at the Proctor and the Shubert in the persons of Fanny Brice, Ed Wynn and Eddie Cantor. The legendary Houdini slithered miraculously out of chains right downtown. Just off Market and Broad, Nitch saw his first department store—Bamberger's. From the sixth-floor radio and sporting goods department, radio station WOR was already broadcasting their thousand-watt signal as far as Staten Island and the Jersey shore.

It was an almost intoxicating time for this heady town, a feast for the eyes. For Nitch, looking had to suffice—Newark was a closed white society. Blacks weren't welcome downtown. Nitch could not enter a hotel. Nor could he take a meal at a restaurant on Market Street: both these places were off-limits. If one of his kind cared to go to a movie or show, he had to sit in the balcony. "Don't tell me how bad the South was," he later told a young black co-worker. "It's the same up here; you don't have to be a Ku Klux Klanner in a white robe; you could just as well be wearing a business suit and work at City Hall."

Finding housing was just as bad. White landlords didn't like renting to black tenants, especially houses with twentieth-century conveniences. The result was a housing shortage, overcrowding, poor sanitation and horrendous living conditions for blacks. The accommodations these landlords reserved for blacks were miserable shacks, cellars and basements, some of those renting for $15 and $16 a month. Newark's civic authorities solved the very pressing problem of black housing by building wooden tenement houses.

Wooden houses. Cheaper, easier and quicker to slap together than brick, but they were also firetraps. Under the right conditions, they would go up like a pile of kindling.

So that's what some Newark capitalist built up on the Hill, as they referred to the Third Ward: wooden tenements. Less than a mile behind the bustling Market and Broad, two miles north of where Newark Airport would eventually stand, was a ghetto in the middle of the city. Here is where Newark consigned each new wave of immigrants. First the Germans, then the Jews, who were still scattered there, and finally the blacks.

If Newark turned out not to be the Promised Land, then Court Street, where Nitch settled the family, was hardly paved with gold. A narrow thoroughfare about a mile and a half from the river, one of Newark's first streets, Court ran several blocks off Broad. By 1923 this street that the Drinkards would call home was in the middle of Newark's most tawdry neighborhood. The Great Depression hit the black community in Newark years before the stock market crash of 1929. As the racism of "last hired, first fired" drove up black unemployment, evictions were common even in the substandard housing on the Hill. Homelessness became such a problem that eventually Newark became fertile ground for Communist agitation. There were demonstrations and fiery speeches right downtown in Military Park. The police granted, then at the last minute revoked demonstration permits, causing further riots. City Hall ignored these social problems. With this atmosphere of unemployment and hopelessness and unrest, organized crime flourished in the Third Ward. Bootleggers were only too happy to provide the balm with which the Third Ward's black community would ease their pain. Nitch's neighborhood was also close by the red-light district, called the Barbary Coast. Of eleven burlesque houses in this country, two were located a few short blocks from Nitch's front door. Gin mills, speakeasies and clubs, many controlled by the underworld, were showcases for black talent. The Newark writer Amiri Baraka proudly points to this area, not Newark's Symphony Hall, as the true cultural center of black Newark. He might be right. But my father couldn't move us out of Court Street fast enough! He saw its worldliness and despair as a threat to his children; its hustling lifestyle, a challenge to everything he was about. He sternly forbade his children to venture away from the block. And for the next twenty years, he raised us strict and kept us close. Amazingly, for the little that we knew of the streets, we could have been growing up in a remote New England hamlet!

This is where I was born: 199 Court Street, on the corner of Court and Broome Street. Crammed together in a top-floor apartment of a three-story tenement, we shared a pull-chain toilet located on the back porch with my father's sister, Tiny, who lived in the other third-floor apartment. That building was full of Drinkards! Aside from my Aunt Tiny across the landing, down on the second floor was my father's brother Benjamin, whom we all called Shorty. And on the ground floor was my mother's mother and older sister, both named Emma. Across the backyard in another tenement lived my grandparents, John and Susie Bell Drinkard.

By the time I came along, the last day of September 1933, my mother and father had eight children. Joining William, Lee and Marie was Hansom, or Hank as we later called him, the first one to be born in Newark in 1924. My sister Anne followed in 1927, and three more followed her: Nicky (1929), Larry (1931) and finally me. They named me Emily—a name I never liked. Most of our early years, especially on Court Street, we were dirt poor, like most people in the Third Ward— lots of immigrants, Italians, Jews, Germans, and mostly blacks trying to make ends meet. But not everyone there was poor. There were some people in that neighborhood who were filthy rich, buying Duesenbergs with cash. It was from those people that my father desperately wanted to protect me and my brothers and sisters.

I am speaking of the sportin' life. People who didn't work for a living but ran numbers, sold women and hooch. These men and women of the high life hung out and plied their trade in the more than one hundred saloons, speakeasies, clubs and after-hours joints in Newark. Most of them were right in our neighborhood; some of them were just down the block and around the corner. Places like Miner's, which had burlesque. Villa Maurice, on Washington Street, with its promise of "a galaxy of girls and music." The Golden Inn Bar and Grill, the Cotton Club, the Alcazar and the Kinney Club, from the late 1920s the sportin' life's headquarters. The Kinney Club was open until sunrise entertaining New Yorkers, high-class pimps, call girls, hustlers and even whites, curious for a peek at exotic black life.

Three blocks from us, between High Street and Washington, was the most notorious section of all, called "the Coast," short for the Barbary Coast, once the Mediterranean haunt of wild-living wayward pirates. If you couldn't find a wild ride from the goings-on in these clubs, then it didn't exist.

Newark winked at the Third Ward. The city knew it existed, but conveniently looked the other way. Like the cops and the crooked politicians who were paid off by gangsters like Longie Zwillman, friend of Meyer Lansky and Lucky Luciano, who greased the right palms so that illegal hooch continued to flow in the Ward.

Music was the main ingredient fueling the sportin' life. Not only did Newark produce lots of homegrown talent, but once the clubs, after-hours joints, speakeasies and theaters were in full swing, Newark became a magnet for top musicians: the great barrelhouse pianist Fats Waller, Billy Eckstine, Count Basie, Duke Ellington, Jimmy Lunceford, Lucky Millinder, Louis Jordan and His Tympany Five. Entertainers like Bill "Bojangles" Robinson and Josephine Baker played and partied in Newark. Some talented locals like pianist Donald Lambert and the growly, incomparable Willie "the Lion" Smith were born in the Third Ward and went on to great acclaim. Right on Court Street, the Coleman brothers owned and operated a black hotel that bore their name; that's where Ruth Brown, Big Maybelle and Billie Holiday stayed when they were in town. There were locals who had their own following like Broome Street Slim, the same Broome Street that crossed Court in front of our apartment, Harry Payton, a musician named Sparrow and a harmonica player named Sheffield. Some of them could read music and some of them couldn't. Some of them, like the Shaw Brothers, "played in crazy keys," which drove the horn players nuts. They played the day's standards like "Dinah," "Stardust" and "Prisoner of Love."

In places like the Orpheum there were elaborate revues, scenery and pit orchestras. Just four blocks from Court Street, this grand theater had a marvelous history. Built in 1871 to show off products of Newark's industry, it was later converted to an opera house, which by 1923 showed that it had seen better days. The Orpheum catered exclusively to black folk. In its heyday, some of the biggest names in black entertainment performed here, including Bill "Bojangles" Robinson, Ethel Waters and even the "Empress of the Blues," Bessie Smith.

During Smith's weeklong engagement, the Orpheum's managers doubled the price of admission, to fifty cents for a matinee and one dollar for an evening performance. Despite the steep cost, the shows were sold out. On Thanksgiving night 1925, a New York photographer from *Vanity Fair* magazine came to see the legendary singer perform, accompanied by the Marx Brothers intimate and Hollywood actor

Robert Benchley. Benchley's companion described Smith as a sorcerer who elicited "hysterical shrieks of sorrow and lamentations" from the crowd with her "crude and primitive" music. While the average worker in 1925 earned twenty dollars a week, Bessie Smith was paid a cool thousand for her stint at the Orpheum.

Smith was a sorcerer so powerful, she even cast a spell on gospel singers, among them Mahalia Jackson. Miles away in the Deep South, a fourteen-year-old Mahalia Jackson was also listening to Bessie Smith. "Bessie was my favorite, but I never let people know I listened to her . . . I'd turn on a Bessie Smith record . . . and play it over and over . . . Mamie Smith has a prettier voice, but Bessie's had more soul in it. She dug right down and kept it in you. Her music haunted you even when she stopped singing." Smith's music haunted many of the greatest singers and songwriters of gospel music, especially Thomas Dorsey, often called the father of gospel music. He was just a few years older than Nitch, born two hundred miles up the same Chattahoochie River that ran through Early County. So impressed was Dorsey with Bessie Smith that he found himself a substitute Bessie to accompany early in his career, Ma Rainey. Through Bessie, Ma Rainey and others the blues crept into the gospel music of Thomas Dorsey.

Thomas Dorsey has always been my favorite gospel composer. Perhaps because he never denied how strongly he was influenced by the blues. At the same time, he readily admitted that Charles Tindley, who preached the "Furnace of Affliction" sermon and wrote the gospel classic "We'll Understand It Better By and By," was his inspiration as a songwriter. Gospel and blues coexisted for Thomas Dorsey through much of his early career—it was all just music to him. Unfortunately for Georgia Tom, the church did not share his laissez-faire attitude on such matters. Throughout the 1920s, the church would not touch his gospel compositions.

My father felt similarly. He and the church knew very well what the blues were about—despair. Li'l Son Jackson, a blues singer who turned his back on secular music for a career in the ministry, could have been speaking for many church folk, including my father:

You see, it's two different things—the blues and church songs is two different things. If a man feel hurt within side and he sing a church song then he's askin' God for help . . . but I think if a man sings the blues it's more or less out of himself, if you know what I mean, see. He's not askin' no one for help. And he's not really clinging to no one. But he's expressin' how he feel. He's expressin' it to someone and that fact makes it a sin, you know, because it make another man sin. Make another woman sin.

"When you're through with the blues," said Mahalia Jackson, "you've got nothing to rest on. Gospel songs are songs of hope. When you sing gospel you have a feeling there's a cure for what's wrong . . . Blues are the songs of despair."

The songs of despair were right outside our windows on Court Street and even in our tenement where folks staved off eviction by throwing a rent party. The rollicking barrelhouse piano and the blues shouters were the sportin' life's sound track. Just around the corner from the building our family occupied were the after-hours joints. These featured the same diversions as the Coast but conveniently ran all night. The sun rarely rose without a brawl and the foulest curses filling the street under our windows. My father kept a close watch on the neighborhood's lawless element. These local characters were poor role models for my older brothers. Nitch was afraid for my mother, my brothers and sisters and my grandparents. Not just for our physical safety—God forbid one of us got caught in the middle of a fight between two of these drunken rowdies. But also because we were so young and impressionable. The things we might see in a neighborhood like this would stay with us for a long time. He wanted to keep us from seeing these things at so early an age—or even at all. They went against everything he believed and taught us.

Unlike some of the men living the sportin' life in the Ward, my father never shirked a job. He took whatever work he could get. The Public Works Administration (PWA) offered jobs fixing the streets, the sewers and the trolley tracks. It was a public assistance-type check that you earned with backbreaking work. He made eighteen dollars a week and the city gave us clothes to wear. Later on, a job opened up for him at the Singer sewing machine factory in nearby Elizabeth. This was one of those northern industries that sent trains down South to bring in black workers by the thousand. My father could read and write. But come payday he helped a lot of men who still signed their name with an "X."

These were the dirtiest, hottest jobs on earth. My father worked in the foundry, pouring hot steel into ingots, banging and shaping these things into cast-iron sewing machines. Behind the foundry in Newark Bay, ships would pull right up to the dock and take those sewing machines halfway around the world.

Nitch quickly earned the respect of his co-workers at Singer, especially much younger men. One such young man, Bill Hart, later went on to be mayor of East Orange. He remembered my father counseling some younger men in the foundry.

"Management had threatened to fire some guys who were being sued for nonsupport by the courts. Mr. Drinkard would sit down with them and talk to them—he put more than one couple back together again.

" 'Be a father to your children,' " he told them. " 'Don't be a father to the beer joints and the taverns . . . Stay married to the same woman.'

"All the old-timers had respect for him; some older, some younger. Because he was a real leader without ever assuming a leadership job—a union head or something like that. He'd maybe be a shop steward for his area. He didn't want the top job; he wanted to be the guy who held other folk up.

"He was a realist. He never talked about the South. If you knew him for any length of time, though, you knew he was very upset about things that happened down there. He thought that things were no better here. Like a lot of people, he'd heard of things happening at night in Newark that never got reported.

"He wasn't afraid to speak up. He wouldn't hesitate to tell you if he thought you were wrong—even if you were the boss! He took this white foreman aside once—this was the head boss—took him over in the corner. In those days, everyone brought a dinner bucket. These men were working so hard, they didn't have no little bologna sandwich. They had their pots of greens and neck bones, mashed potatoes. Twenty minutes before lunchtime, these guys would heat up their food with a piece of red-hot iron. They'd just throw that red-hot ingot right into their lunch pail! Well, this white foreman says, 'Hey! That stuff stinks, get that garbage off this iron. It stinks in here.'

"So Mr. Drinkard says, 'Mike, I know you're Polish. And if your Polish folks were heating up some kielbasa or sausage, which I don't like the smell of, I'd have sense enough to know that's their food. Don't call our food something that stinks again. Unless there is a union rule about heating our food on iron, we're gonna do it.'

"His main message to everyone was to trust in God and go to church. He wasn't afraid to get down on his knees and pray in public for someone. I remember once, some young fellow's mother was real sick in the hospital, and Mr. Drinkard got down and prayed for her right there in the plant."

And he sang. Bill Hart heard my father sing during lunch hours in that foundry. He sang gospel—the old quartet spirituals. The ones he sang down in Georgia with his uncles.

"Every lunch period, I'd go down to those locker rooms just to hear him sing. It was like church in between those lockers some lunch periods. This man was really a great singer. They would beg him to sing at that foundry.

"He was very good at lifting people up when they were in the dumps. He used to say, 'If you think you're in bad shape, take a look at your fellow man.' He was so good at lifting people up; I sometimes thought that maybe he was in the dumps."

If my father was down in the dumps, we never knew it. He was not a complaining man. He did everything through prayer. He prayed all the time. I mean literally. Openly and inwardly. I know he did because that's what he taught us. He knew what it was to pray without ceasing. He praised God all the time; for everything—the good and the bad. My father was really a minister without being ordained. In the home he taught us everything we were supposed to know about God and Jesus.

As each of his daughters came of age, he urged—he required—each of us to teach Sunday school, which was just as much of a learning experience as a teaching experience.

My sister Anne remembers him praying at the dinner table: "He prayed very strong and sincere. He always prayed that God would take care of his children, keep them together, that was his heart's desire. I guess it was because some of his family life hadn't been what he had wanted or desired it to be. He wanted us to remain close-knit at all times, so he prayed for that. In church, he prayed for that; he'd openly pray for his children.

"He prayed for times to get better: during the Depression the foundry laid him off and he was forced to work with the PWA in exchange for a public assistance type check from the city for rent and food. The city also gave us clothes. Even though my father worked hard for this check, he considered it to be on the dole and hated it. He prayed for times to open up where he could resume his job at Singer or get a decent job and really support his family; he did not want to be on public assistance. He really prayed hard for that. I can remember him praying and even crying about that."

For a brief time, my father started a small grocery store in the neighborhood. This didn't last long. With his big heart, he let his brothers, sisters and other relatives run up tabs they couldn't possibly pay. Eventually, he had to close up shop.

He was not the complaining sort, but we knew things were not going well.

It was the middle of the Great Depression. Thousands were unemployed, without any source of income. Countless numbers of blacks were on the relief rolls. The city gave us food. One night a week, my Uncle Shorty would go down to the market area and get a sack of surplus vegetables. Then, on another night, he'd go over to Fischer's Bakery on Waverly Avenue and get a large sack of day-old cakes, cookies and breads for a quarter.

My mother had eight children to feed. In those days, in our kind of families, women didn't work. The man would "make the way" and the woman would mind the children and the home. My mother never complained either. But I'm sure my father worried that he wasn't holding up his end.

He needn't have. My mother never would have held my father's responsibility to provide over his head. She loved him. They were not demonstrative, they were very modest; all we ever saw my father do was give her a peck on the cheek when he left the house. They saved the rest for the privacy of their room. But we knew they were very devoted to each other. Besides, she was so quiet and soft-spoken. There were only two things that were important in my mother's life: her kids and her God. Church was my parents' whole life.

She was a steward in our church, St. Luke's African Methodist Episcopal, around the corner from Court Street on Charlton Street. My father was a trustee. She wore those crisp, milky white uniforms that went with her position. She was petite but full-figured and I'll bet she turned a few heads in that uniform. My cousin Honey, Aunt Tiny's daughter, remembers my mother singing "His Eye Is on the Sparrow" in that church. "I remember her standing up and singing that song," recalls Honey.

> *I sing because I'm happy,*
> *I sing because I'm free,*
> *His eye is on the sparrow*
> *And I know He watches over me.*

"She had a beautiful voice that just rang out so clear—it was like bells when you heard it."

Honey's mother was my mother's best friend. They were like two sisters, although Tiny was actually my father's sister. They both had the same temperament, real quiet. Tiny lived across the hall from us on Court Street and my mother and she used to bake together.

"Some of the things they cooked," remembers Honey, "I never learned how to make. Like apple butter roll and apple dumplings. I could never make biscuits like those ladies. They'd take that biscuit dough and just choke it up and those biscuits would be so light and fluffy. Cissy's mother had this churn and she would make buttermilk— my mother used to love it! The two of them used to make jelly too. You would come home and the whole tenement would be smelling sweet, like jellies and jams; and you knew just where to go: straight up to the third floor!"

My mother was a homebody. She never left the house, except to take us all to church. There wasn't a time that she would take a vacation, go away, go anywhere. She was there in the home all the time. We were never without her. Momma was a very kind lady. She nurtured not only her own family but other family members—her sisters-in-law, her brothers-in-law, her sister's children. Even kids in the neighborhood called her Momma; she looked out after them too.

"If she was angry, you didn't know it," remembered my sister Anne. "And I know there were times that she should have been angry. But she didn't show her feelings, at least anger. You never heard her yelling at us. She would punish or spank us—but even that was not in a loud, boisterous way. The disciplining she left to my father.

"She did everything in a quiet way. Many people never even heard her talk, she was such a quiet-mannered person. She went about her daily chores, cleaning, cooking, taking care of the younger children, teaching us and babying Cissy. Cissy was the baby and kind of sickly when she was little. Because she was sickly and was the baby we gave her a lot of attention and spoiled her."

Well, that was always a running argument in my house. I was never sassy or pouted until I got what I wanted. I was respectful to my mother and father. But I did have my own head; and my head could be strong! My father never played favorites. But if he was going to go soft on any of his kids, he had good reason to go soft on me. They say I favor his mother, who died the day I was born. Maybe every time my father looked at me, he saw his own dear mother, Susie Bell Hubbard. I was also his baby. Flossie, his youngest sister, born only four years before my oldest brother, liked to get up under my father and act like *she* was his baby. As soon as I got old enough, I set her straight on who was my father's pride and joy. I can still remember how proud I was to march with my daddy in the Mason's parade. Every year that was our special occasion.

I was a sickly baby, though. I was born in Newark's City Hospital, but there wasn't any money for doctor's visits. My parents probably didn't even have a crib for me at first. As the story goes, when I was a newborn they laid me in a dresser drawer. I do know that my mother doctored me at home. I still have the marks on my wrist from where she tied garlic to try to bring down one of the high fevers I ran as an infant.

During one of those high fevers, my mother left my sister Anne to watch me while she went to get me something at the drugstore. Anne was six years old and a little self-conscious about the new eyeglasses she had to wear. They had wire rims like the glasses that are so popular today. She peered in the carriage at me and I started to go into a convulsion. Poor Anne thought she had scared me with her glasses and brought on the convulsion! When my mother returned from her errand, Anne threw herself on my mother's mercy for scaring the baby. My mother smiled and assured her that neither she nor her glasses were to blame.

We wanted to know more about my mother: where she came from, what her childhood was like. But we never learned much, except for a few basic facts. She was born Delia Mae McCaskill outside of Pensacola, Florida, in a little town called Cottondale. Her mother left her at a young age—as early as eleven years old. She took her other daughter, Emma, the one she preferred over my mother, up North and left my mother with her husband. My father met her several years after that and married his beloved.

That's all I know. I don't even know the exact circumstances of how my mother and father met. There were some subjects my parents considered "grown-up" talk and we as children were kept in the dark.

Their secrecy about some subjects grew out of an instinct to protect us from knowing things before we were ready to deal with them. After I was born, my mother had three sets of twins who all died at birth. My parents kept us so close, raised us so naive, that except for my two oldest sisters, Lee and Marie, none of us knew my mother was even pregnant!

That's how much she kept things to herself. She felt we were too young to know things like that. Even the word "pregnant," because it was so obviously linked to sex, was considered a cuss word.

My mother also felt that the past was not as important as the future. The past was gone. She and my father had suffered things in the South they wanted to forget. Things they didn't want to pass down to us—to scare us or hold us back. What was most important now was the future; raising her children, training her girls.

"She never talked about the past," says my sister Anne. "She was too busy teaching us, the older girls, how to do things, how to run a house, how to clean, how to wash, how to iron. Teaching us from the Bible and practical things, like 'Together you stand, divided you fall.' To always stick together as a family—you can disagree, yet be together. Be together, no matter what. When the deal goes down, you be together."

There was an urgency about her concern that we always stick together, that we master the practical skills of running a home. It was almost as if she was getting us ready for the day when she wouldn't be there for us. She would softly sing a hymn while going about her chores, a hymn we never forgot. It was a strange one to pick for a favorite; it was about the final judgment, when the heavens would be shaken. An old mournful spiritual that went back to slave times. "My Lord! What a Mourning" was sung slow, almost like a dirge:

> *My Lord! what a mourning*
> *My Lord! what a mourning*
> *My Lord! what a mourning*
> *When the stars begin to fall.*
> *You'll hear the trumpet sound*
> *To wake the nations underground*
> *Looking to God's right hand*
> *When the stars begin to fall*

I know why she sang it. It was the kind of hymn that someone who was heavenly-minded would sing. Someone who saw beyond the daily affairs of man. Someone who saw the big picture. Someone who savored the day when she would behold her Lord face to face, no longer through a glass darkly.

Most of what she taught us about being a Christian was not from the Bible. It was by her own example, her quiet, gracious manner. The way she cared for others—her brother's and sister's children, my father's family. Her meekness; although there were times we all wished my mother would have spoken up.

Like with her own mother. She was a big bossy lady that none of us liked. Apparently, leaving her husband in Florida was more important than caring for her little girl. She just left my mother there and took her favorite daughter, the one that was light-skinned like her. My mother was beautiful and brown, but she was made to suffer the sick racism that blacks inflict on each other—"I'm better than you because I'm light-skinned"—from her own mother! Still, my father settled both of them, my mother's mother and my mother's sister, on the first floor of our tenement. I guess every time my grandmother saw my mother, she was reminded of her failure as a wife and a mother. My mother never held it against her, though. She respected her mother and had forgiven her a long time ago. As a matter of fact, she honored my grandmother by naming me Emily, after her. But my grandmother could not forgive herself. So she grew into a bitter person, unable to love herself or anyone else. She had no use for church either. She hid from the light, behind her apartment door, as we all clattered down the stairs for church, every Sunday morning, evening, and midweek service. My mother continued to care for her; respecting her, bringing her food. But my mother's meekness, her turning the other cheek, only poured down coals of fire on my grandmother's head. She became even more embittered and bossy toward my mother, which my father wouldn't stand for and told my grandmother so. My grandmother knew how staunch my father was as a Christian, how involved he was at St. Luke's. She was just waiting and watching for him to slip up, to blow his Christian testimony. She enjoyed drawing him into an argument to see if he'd take the bait and lose his cool. There was tension between them; a powder keg ready to explode. This grieved my mother terribly. She assumed that her meekness would one day win her mother and her sister to the Lord. Instead, it seemed to drive them further from her and God.

My oldest brother, William, also brought my mother a lot of stress. He had an awful temper—if you crossed him he'd just as soon burn your house down. By 1933 when I was born, he was fifteen years old and already arrogant and mouthy. He thought the world owed him a living and was always getting into trouble, gambling and fighting. The sportin' life characters of the Third Ward, the sleek-suited pimps and numbers runners, had gotten to him and twisted up his mind. He should have been working with my father at the foundry; my father could have gotten him a job there as he would later get jobs there for my brothers Hank and Nicky. But William rejected my father's lifestyle. He was looking for easy money and he'd get into trouble, rippin' and runnin', gambling and fighting. Tough guys would come to Court Street looking for him. One day a big redheaded Irish cop who hated blacks roughed up my brother on the street. My father came running down the steps, got Red Smith in a bear hug and took his gun away from him. But when my father tried to talk to my brother later, William just blew up. He had no ear for discipline. He had inherited my father's temper and the two of them would set each other off. Their words erupted into arguments, the kind of arguments that made it impossible for them both to stay under the same roof. So William, my mother's first child, drifted off, leaving seven of us at home.

All my mother could do was pray. And worry, which drove her blood pressure up. She probably inherited this medical condition from her parents. Black folk in the South were never known for healthy diets. I'm sure having all those children so young also contributed; she had four before she was out of her teens. Every week, my mother ran herself ragged keeping the two outfits the city gave each of us children—fourteen outfits—washed and clean, ironed and crisp. And they always were. Even with William gone, we were still nine mouths to feed—on eighteen dollars a week.

Eighteen dollars a week! I know things were cheaper then, but still, I don't know how she did it.

"I could never understand how she did it. But we never missed a meal," says my sister Anne. "She stretched what she had to make a meal: southern foods when they could get them—neck bones, white potatoes and collard greens. There were times when she'd make things for us from the most basic ingredients she had in the house. Like corn bread. Sometimes we'd have just corn bread and milk. She stretched those eighteen dollars so that we managed to have a meal every mealtime. And if there wasn't enough, she would go without a meal. I remember her doing that so the children could eat.

"She never complained. But there were times when I saw her crying. I would ask her why she was crying and she would just say, 'Nothing, it's nothing, honey.' I figured it was because she wanted more for us than she had to give. And it made her feel very sad."

My mother did the best she could. She had a lot of children—small children—to take care of. A few years after I was born, she had a set of twins. She lost them at birth. A few years after that she had another set, which she also lost. This last ordeal, along with the vigil she maintained to feed her seven growing children in the midst of the Great Depression, and the tears she shed for her mother and her wayward son, tipped the delicate balance of her health. When I was almost five years old, my mother had a stroke. At the time she wasn't even thirty-five years old.

My mother's stroke placed a far greater burden of responsibility on my forty-one-year-old father. As the Depression cast its long shadow over Newark, he had already lost his small grocery store and had been laid off from his job at the foundry. He was breaking his back, fixing the streets of Newark for the PWA, barely making ends meet on eighteen dollars a week.

He lived in the worst vice-ridden neighborhood in Newark, right next door to the red-light district. Its cheap allure had already stolen away his son; his first son, William. He would grieve for him the rest of his days, as surely as he still grieved right now for his mother, dead only a few years at fifty-nine. He and his wife had just lost two sets of twins; then after the last set, my mother suffered a massive stroke.

My mother lived. But one autumn night, only months after she returned home to us, another unexpected tragedy befell us. A flash fire that started in a paint store beneath our tenement completely consumed our building and the rest of the block. As my father stood helplessly on the street, holding me in his arms, he must have known for sure that Newark wasn't the Promised Land. In fact, he may have wondered just what more could go wrong, how much hotter the furnace of affliction could get.

Through the long season of prayer my father no doubt had, I hope he felt the assurance of what waited for him, literally, around the corner. For on Mercer Street, there was a storefront that would change his family's life down to the third generation.

THREE

I wonder just what I've done
To make this race so hard to run.
Then I say to my soul, "Don't worry"
The Lord will make a way somehow.
—*"The Lord Will Make a Way Somehow"*

My sisters stood against the fiery night sky and cried. Their clothes, their schoolbooks, Anne's fourth-grade penmanship awards, were all gone. My brother Nicky, just eight, stood on the sidewalk in front of our burning building and wept for the new baseball glove Aunt Flossie's husband had just given him. Six-year-old Larry was confused and scared by the noise and searchlights of the fire truck, and the loud white firemen bellowing commands in "his neighborhood," and the hacked-up front doors and windows of "his house." Larry just hid behind my mother.

Tears rolled down my father's face. He cursed Newark under his breath and rued the day he had come here. At least in Georgia, no matter how bad things were, he could have always fed his family. Even as a tenant farmer, he would have had a piece of land to work and food enough. William, his son, would have helped him; the way he had helped his own father, and his father before him had helped his grandfather. He could have spent time with his son every day, talked to him— been an influence in his life, instead of these Third Ward bums who taught him to drink and gamble and cared nothing for his soul. He would still have his son right now if it weren't for Newark!

His wife—wouldn't she be well now if it weren't for Newark?

Climbing those steep stairs every day, pregnant, wrestling with this awful poverty, living so close to her mother, hadn't all this further aggravated her, driven her blood pressure up till she had this stroke?

He looked into the flames consuming every inch of their three-story building, the cinders floating drunkenly into the night, and lamented the day he ever got on that Georgia Central train. Just then in his deepest despair he felt a hand on his arm.

"We're praying for you, brother," offered a tall, good-looking man. He had seen him before. And the woman by his side, with her strange Moorish hat, Nitch remembered her from somewhere also. Yes, of course, now he placed them. They had come up to the house when they heard about Delia's stroke and offered their assistance in any way they could help. They were two missionaries who had just been sent by the Church of God in Christ to open a small storefront in the Third Ward. They had asked if his children could attend Sunday school with them one Sunday. He told them they already worshipped together as a family at St. Luke's AME on Charlton Street. Oh, yes, yes, the man had exclaimed, he knew the pastor, a good man; thrilled my father was a Christian but anxious not to appear to be stealing any sheep from St. Luke's pastor. He introduced himself as Elder Wyatt, the lady as Mother Gillespie. They were new in the area and only trying to plant a small work for the Lord. My father agreed, the Third Ward could use all the help it could get. "Where sin abounds, grace all the more abounds!" my father quoted the scripture. The man complimented my father for being an AME man for these many years; this was a denomination that had done so much for our people. Likewise, my father said that he had heard good things about this new Church of God movement too: how it had grown out of a well-known revival in California and was now multiplying all over the country by leaps and bounds.

Before Elder Wyatt and Mother Gillespie left our house that day, my father had agreed to send us to his storefront for Sunday school. As they said their goodbyes, my father eased the man's fears about appearing to steal St. Luke's sheep. Who knows, my father gestured grandly with a wink: one day, maybe he and his wife Delia might just skip a Sunday at St. Luke's and join their children at his storefront. My father waited a beat until the man knew that a trustee and his wife from St. Luke's were just kidding.

"Yes, and a little child shall lead them," the man said mockingly, wagging his finger at my father. They all had a good laugh over that one.

It was agreed that we would attend in a few weeks as soon as my father had gotten my mother settled in. The stroke had paralyzed my mother's right side: she would have little use of her left arm and she would have to learn how to walk again with a left leg that wouldn't obey her brain's commands.

"We are praying for you, brother." Elder Wyatt squeezed my father's arm again, jolting his thoughts back to the fire. My father mumbled some thanks and they disappeared into the night.

As 1937 drew to a close, the Depression continued to bear down on Newark and the rest of the country. FDR's New Deal raised people's hopes but didn't bring instant relief. In Europe, a madman named Hitler was gaining power.

My father had to find us a new home. Anxious to get as far away from Court Street as he could, he started walking south, right off the Hill. He walked almost three-quarters of a mile; a long walk in any city, where just one block can put you in a neighborhood so different, it feels like another town. He stopped just one block short of Clinton Avenue, outside the old Jewish section. He didn't want to go too far; he wanted to be within an easy one-block walk to St. Luke's on Charlton Street. He had to think of my mother now and how much she would be able to walk.

My mother would never be the same again. The stroke changed her life and ours. My mother had always been a homebody. Now she would rarely leave the house unless my father was taking her to church. It took a lot out of her to drag that leg. Now, only an emergency would bring her down those two flights of stairs to the street. But we were happy to have her home. She seemed more fragile now and we worried about her. My older sisters would take turns rubbing her bad leg, to keep the circulation going, while she lay in bed.

With William out of the house a lot, the next oldest, my sister Lee, stepped into the elder-sibling role. She was seventeen by the time we moved to Hillside Place, old enough to share in some valuable adult conversations with my parents. But to whom much was given, much was expected. She was now required to run important errands and take care of some of my father's official business—bill paying mainly, such as making sure insurance premiums were paid. What Nitch lost in William going his own way he recouped twofold from Lee, his daughter. She was eager to please, knowing she was filling the oldest child's shoes. She became my father's trusted confidante and would remain so for many years. Marie (or Reebie, as we called her), the next oldest, now began to help my mother around the house, also tending to my needs; at four years old, I was the youngest. Hank (Hansom) was a dreamy twelve-year-old; on the brink of being a teenager but in truth still years younger. Anne, a nosy ten-year-old, positioned herself near Lee and Reebie, ready to "catch any hints," as she called them, morsels of family information and news (was my mother pregnant or not?) that Lee or Reebie might care to drop her way.

Nicky (Junior), eight, Larry, six, and I were considered the children. We were thick as thieves and I loved my brothers dearly, especially Larry, who was only two years older than I. We laughed and played and when my closest brothers weren't home I missed them terribly. I waited at the window for Larry to come home from school so we could continue our antics. When I got old enough, they taught me how to climb trees, fight and ride a bike. They toughened me up, played boy-type games with me, probably played too rough with me, but I thank them for it. My brothers gave me a head start on life, even before I was ten years old.

The city helped us move into 38 Hillside Place. It had more of a neighborhood feel; everyone knew each other and there were even several families from our church—St. Luke's. Right across the landing, there were the Coxes and the Millers and the Forshays were in the next building. On the corner were the Epps; my sister Reebie would marry the oldest boy and stay with him her whole life. Good, solid, working-class, churchgoing black folk. There were people in that neighborhood who wanted to move up to an even better neighborhood. But when he hit Hillside Place, my father breathed a deep sigh of relief: the Court Street bums were behind him now. We moved into the third floor—a sorry day for Miss Georgia underneath us. Three teenagers and four little kids bouncing up and down that long hallway. On the top floor was a Muslim family—we called them "moosh Americans."

The fire had taken all of our most precious possessions: pictures of my parents as children, all of my sisters' grammar school records and awards, family Bibles, letters and books. There were things we lost that were of great value, irreplaceable. The fire made us suffer the shame and embarrassment of being put out in the street. And not just us. In engulfing the whole block, it burned up the tenement next to us, where my father's other brother and sister lived. It scattered the Drinkards all over the Third Ward.

The fire was a devastating event. But in a strange way it brought my father closer to his vision of raising his family the way he chose, in a godly environment. Like the Israelite who addressed his foe, "ye thought evil against me; but God meant it unto good," and Romans 8:28, "And we know that all things work together for good to them that love God, to them who are the called according to his purpose." My father could see the glimmer of opportunity rising out of tragedy.

First, it forced him out of Court Street, one of the worst neighborhoods in Newark, if not the worst. It would have taken years to save enough money to move out and find another apartment. Second, it separated my mother and father from the bitterness and tension of living so close to my mother's mother. My father "did the right thing" and moved my grandmother and my mother's sister across the street from us on Hillside Place.

Third, though he loved his brothers and sisters dearly, my father had already begun taking a different path from them when they were still living in Georgia. They were not as staunch in their Christian faith as he was. Like his own father, he wanted everything God had for him. His brothers and sisters were lax about attending church. He wasn't worried about their influence on him. On the contrary, they were probably sick of him telling them that they were "raised in church" and needed to get back in there. No, he wasn't worried about their influence on him. He was concerned about their influence on us, his children. For the next ten years, until we were all grown, he hardly let us visit any other homes unless he was with us. Relatives, friends, whatever.

Finally, the Court Street fire, and to some extent my mother's stroke, brought us into sharp focus before the eyes of Elder Wyatt and Mother Gillespie from the Overcoming Church of God in Christ. After we were settled on Hillside Place, Mother Gillespie came early one Sunday, collected all seven of us and took us back to Mercer Street.

It was a small storefront, with folding chairs and an aisle down the middle. Forty people would have packed the place, which we often did, what with all my cousins who came and the other kids from the neighborhood. It was small and warm and felt like family. It took us a while to get used to bigger churches after that.

"That's really where we were converted," remembers my sister Reebie.

Even though it was a children's Sunday school, there was a lot of heavy teaching going down in that storefront. The foundation of our Christian faith was imparted to us here by two selfless missionaries, Mother Gillespie and Elder Wyatt. They weren't married; I believe they were both single. They saw the Third Ward in Newark as their mission field, the way another missionary might view the Amazon or China. Elder Wyatt, a tall, good-looking, middle-aged black man, taught the boys. He was the minister of the church; he preached and he taught. Mother Gillespie, who was also black, middle-aged and attractive, schooled the girls and visited the sick. My sister Anne was particularly taken with her.

"She wore a hat like a Moor's hat, a straight robe and a sash, always in pale, neutral colors. Everything always matched. That's what fascinated me so much about her—she matched everything up so perfectly. And everything matched perfectly because it was simple. And so was she; kind and simple, never flashy."

Say what you want about the Holiness people, of which the Overcoming Church of God in Christ was a part. A lot of people criticized them for separating themselves from other Christians because they thought they'd found the only way to God and spiritual perfection: by being pure, denying the world and the pleasures thereof. Never being seen in bars, women wearing modest clothing, way-long dresses that exposed no flesh. Their speech seasoned with "brother" and "sister" and "praise the Lord."

People might have made fun of them, called them holy rollers for getting happy in church, for getting full of the Spirit and marching, even leaping around the sanctuary. Let them talk. My father never thought there was anything wrong with getting too much of God and neither did we. Mother Gillespie had a pure heart. She never taught us we were any better than anyone, nor any less than anyone. She taught us to be as good as we could be, the best we could be, always, that's the lesson she put home to us.

She taught us the scriptures by giving us recitations. There were Easter programs and Christmas programs that your parents came to see you participate in. Knowing the joy you'd bring your parents with a well-performed recitation gave a lot of kids the incentive to learn their part—a particular scripture—well. Mother Gillespie took a special interest in my sister Anne.

"She would take me on outings because I was the middle child, about eleven years old. She would take me places over in Brooklyn like the zoo. That's where I first saw the elephants and fell in love with them. When I went to stay with her, it would always be an intellectual session—one-on-one Bible study. As young as I was, I enjoyed it and looked forward to it."

She took other kids from the church—and even kids from the neighborhood who didn't go to the church—on trips to Coney Island. Free of charge; none of us could have afforded it anyhow.

But the main feature of the Overcoming Church of God in Christ was the music. This is where we first experienced music . . . heard it . . . sang it . . . and experienced it as something spiritual.

"It was basic congregational songs that we sang a cappella," says Anne. "But she made it real to you because she explained the words. She explained what they meant or could mean in your life. If you took those words and let them mean something to you, then it would come out differently when you sang it. Because it would be coming from a different place. Not from the throat, but from the heart."

From the heart. No other word better describes the real birthplace of the Church of God in Christ denomination. It is most closely linked to an incredible revival in California, the Azusa Street Revival in the early 1900s. But the roots of this revival and the Church of God in Christ were really born years before, in the heart of the Holiness Movement—the same movement that changed Victoria Drinkard's life. Followers of this movement from just after the Civil War were white Methodists, men and women who simply wanted more of God. Many of them had been swept up in revivals at camp meetings—multiple days, even weeks, of services usually held in rural areas under a large tent. Here, the power of God was manifest in healings, dramatic conversions and ecstatic praise and worship. But these Methodists were not content with just experiencing God in a dynamic way once or twice a year when a camp meeting was scheduled. They wanted to live the camp meeting experience all year long. The Holiness men and women believed that by separating from worldliness and seeking God with a whole heart, they would reach spiritual perfection. By the turn of the century the movement had attracted black Christians, who established Holiness churches, many in major cities with sizable black communities. Then, for several weeks in 1906, the Pentecostal fire fell at a Holiness church in Los Angeles, the Apostolic Faith Gospel Mission, 312 Azusa Street. Christians who attended the revival believed they shared the same experience that first-century Christians experienced on the Day of Pentecost—an ecstatic heavenly language prompted by the indwelling Holy Spirit. So dynamic were the services that two men from the Holiness movement visiting from Memphis experienced the revival and went on to found two entirely new denominations—the Assembly of God and the Church of God in Christ.

Music has always been a key feature of revivals. Dating back to the Great Awakening of colonial times, the music of the English hymn writers Isaac Watts and John Wesley was used to stir the spirit and bring heaven to earth. When the newly converted slaves worshipped at these revivals, and at the camp meetings that followed later in the wake of the

Second Awakening, they made these hymns their own. They accented and elongated unexpected syllables for rhythmic effect, patting their feet and clapping their hands in tempos remembered from a faraway but still vivid homeland. Under the great tents of the camp meetings, visitors listened to the rich voices of spontaneous black choirs, raising the hymns, calling and responding to each other beneath the vast canvas. As the poetic but deeply felt lyrics and simple melodies of these English hymns met the rhythm and improvisational techniques of Mother Africa, the spiritual was born.

The Azusa Street Revival also produced a new and dynamic black worship music. This time it emerged from the individual in the throes of Pentecostal rapture—singing in the Spirit and testifying to the goodness of God. Born in the city, this new music built on the foundation of the hymns and spirituals but charged them with a power and conviction that had never been heard before. This time the music was more personal, emotional and rhythmically irresistible. It drew the young and those who resisted the traditional church experience to the Spirit's new urban outpost—the storefront church—where the young Church of God in Christ denomination and its unique music spread like wildfire. You could hear the sound for blocks—tambourines beating at fever pitch, a cappella harmonies and joyful hallelujahs.

As slaves once used the unique rhythm and improvisational technique of Mother Africa's music to transform English hymns into spirituals, the Church of God in Christ now ignited these hymns and spirituals with Pentecostal fire to create a dynamic, new music for the black church—gospel.

At the Overcoming Church of God in Christ on Mercer Street, just around the corner from Court Street, the Drinkard children first heard the new music.

My sister Reebie learned to play the tambourine there. She says, "We learned to get a lot of rhythm; to clap our hands in time. We learned syncopation there. We didn't have any music there, just tambourines, foot-patting; we sang a cappella."

My sister Anne's description of the Spirit-led music at the Overcoming Church of God in Christ makes it sound like the "spontaneous choirs" of the camp meetings in the 1800s:

"Someone would start a song over here and the rest of us would pick it up all over the church—in harmony," says Anne. "You could just feel true harmonies going through the whole church!"

We were just children. And only now, as I look back, do I really appreciate Mother Gillespie and Elder Wyatt. They were not just Christians who were totally sold out to God—that would have been enough! But they were also incredibly talented teachers. I am convinced that Mother Gillespie had designed every detail of her person and demeanor to focus our complete attention on her: from the simplicity of her dress to her graceful manner and the attentive gaze she fixed upon you—as if at that moment there was nobody else in the world that mattered more than you. Because she was so single-minded, so pure in her mission of teaching us spiritual truth through music, she created in us something that I don't even think she knew she was doing. Maybe she did. Her teachings sparked in us the desire to try to sing together on our own.

I don't remember when my brothers and sisters first tried it. We were probably all fooling around, playing church one day. Nicky imitating Elder Wyatt, shouting, "Give me a song, give me a song." Anne, Larry and me, his mock congregation, started to raise a hymn, like in church. And something must've just clicked when we heard what was coming out of our mouths.

"It was a miracle . . . or a mystery," says Anne. "We were in perfect harmony. It just fell right in. If Cissy was singing lead, I'd fall back into her harmony part and the rest of them would fall in around me. The same thing would happen if I took the lead; Cissy, Larry and Nicky would fall in around me. It was just something that happened automatically in our heads, our minds, or . . . our souls."

Once my father got a load of us, that was the end of my carefree childhood! He had Reebie teaching us songs, rehearsing us every night of the week. We sang at St. Luke's AME. When relatives came over, all they ever wanted to do was hear us sing. I'd run in my room and hide— boy, that would make my father mad! You have to remember, I was only five years old! I wanted to keep playing like a normal kid—hop-scotch, skully, jump rope. Eventually, when threatened with corporal punishment, I relented and joined my brothers and sisters. "All right now, children," he would say. "Strike me up a tune." My aunts and uncles always wanted to hear me sing "I'm Waiting and Watching." I got sick of that one in no time. I was just being a normal kid; contrary, wanting to do something other than what my parents wanted me to do.

Looking back, the discipline of rehearsing, learning new songs was good for me even if I was on the young side. I might have pouted and stuck my lip out a mile long, but I couldn't deny my daddy anything. Not when I saw how happy our singing made him. He'd listen to us and get this big smile on his face and nod his head in time to the song. "Sing, children," he would say, smiling. "Sing, baby," he would say softly, if I took the lead.

My father's burdens—surviving, feeding us all during the Depression, the recent blaze on Court Street and my mother's stroke—for a moment must have eased as he leaned back in his chair and listened to us sing.

He still had his problems. God didn't wave some magic wand over his life. The fires in the Furnace of Affliction would still burn; he would still have to go through the fire. He knew that. But as he listened to his children sing to him now, he could imagine himself, like Daniel's friends, Shadrach, Meshach and Abednego, walking about in the very midst of the fire, yet unharmed, for the Son of God was walking with him, by his side all the while.

He closed his eyes, and thought back to Hilton, Georgia, when he was a boy, singing with his father and his uncles in the fields and in the house at night. No audience, just singing for themselves, in the glow of a kerosene lamp.

You know, my God did
Just what He said, uh-huh
Oh yes, He did, uh-huh
Oh yes, He did.
You know, He healed the sick

And He raised the dead, uh-huh
Oh yes, He did, uh-huh
Oh yes, He did . . .

It felt so good, singing in my soul; Nitch, his uncles, their faces raised, their breath as one, blowing the tight quartet harmony into the air. They sounded so good. Drinkards! The best farmers in Early County . . . the best quartet singers in Georgia. The best. Just like his children now. Singing in my soul. Thank You, Father; You have given them this song, You have given them the harmony of brothers and sisters in their throats and in their hearts. Keep them together, I pray . . . protect them . . . use them; may many come to know You through their voices.

Inside my father's heart a vision was being born. A vision not for himself, but for his children—the Drinkard Singers.

FOUR

I sing because I'm happy,
I sing because I'm free . . .
— *"His Eye Is on the Sparrow"*

Once my father knew we could sing, he wasted no time. He assigned the task of teaching us songs and rehearsing us to my sister Reebie. Reebie was a strict teacher—she didn't take no stuff. Reebie got a lot of enjoyment out of singing with us, and the special joy of teaching others to sing; something I wouldn't find for myself until I was a teenager. She would forever be my model as a teacher.

"We got our joy from singing," says Reebie. "We just sang for the joy of singing. God had given us that gift. It wasn't a gift to go out and make money with either. We just loved to sing. And we mostly sang in our house. We'd sing in the kitchen after dinner and rehearse in the living room. These were the most joyous times in our lives—singing together."

I was the alto, I was just turning six years old; my brother Larry was the bass, he was eight. Anne would lead and at twelve was the oldest in the group. My brother Nicky had that high tenor and he was ten years old. Anne would start a song in any key and we could fall right in behind her—in perfect harmony.

As Reebie remembers it, "We'd take a song out of the hymnbook, and sing it straight first, to get the melody. Then after the melody we would go into different parts, then we'd ad-lib different things into the song. I was the one who would figure out the backgrounds. As they got older, Anne and Cissy would both have input.

"Cissy was so small, we had to stand her on a box," laughs Reebie. "She always had this extra tone to add to the harmony, and a big voice. She did most of the leading because her voice was so big; it would just reach out.

"God gave us almost a perfect gift. No matter who started off a song, we would each find a note that would blend in together behind them. We all had that ear for harmony; automatically. It was amazing! That's how I knew God was in this plan all along."

Had he not felt God's calling on us my father never would have encouraged us to sing. But he sensed an anointing on us and he was thrilled. Not thrilled in the way a pushy stage parent or a frustrated singer might be. He could have stood up and sung with us anytime he wanted to—he was that good. Other than church, we never knew he sang. It wasn't until years later that we learned of him singing during his lunch break at the foundry.

Nor was he in it for the money. That was not what he was about. To my father, gospel singing was a ministry, there was a message in the music. A message of hope that lifted you up—God loves you, God cares for you. Gospel singing was an honorable profession. In the black church, Christians gave great respect to those who sang gospel. They were considered God's ambassadors—like the quartets of my father's youth, who traveled from church to church.

"How beautiful upon the mountains are the feet of him that bringeth good tidings . . . that publisheth salvation; that saith unto Zion, Thy God reigneth!"

He saw us as junior ambassadors—not just sowing the Gospel but also reaping the blessings of singing God's Word in our own lives. He wanted people to know we were his kids, that we were untrained and look what could be done. He wanted us to be an influence on other kids. He wanted us to be an example to bad kids. He was very proud of us, not just as his children, but as Drinkards, carrying on the name of his grandparents, Victoria and John Drinkard, the best farmers in Early County.

We took one step backward, however, in our choice of repertoire. We'd gotten the singing bug at the little storefront on Mercer Street, where the Spirit blew where it wanted and improvisation reigned. What we learned with Reebie was "quartet." This was the kind of singing my father did with his uncles in Georgia. Four voices perfectly programmed, harmonizing with precision on mostly old spirituals. Little or no opportunity to improvise, which was counter to the testifying-type music that we experienced in the Holiness storefront. It would be a few years before the churches would accept the "new" music—gospel music. But we were bitten with the gospel bug and we still found ways to work that fire into the Drinkard Quartet. That's what our daddy dubbed us—me, Anne, Larry and Nicky. Lee and Reebie sang too, but mostly functioned as coaches, and when we began to sing outside Newark, Lee handled the business end.

My father couldn't have been happier. His children had been blessed with this gift, he had escaped Court Street and in the middle of the Depression, when some men were selling apples on the streets of Newark, he was working. No, it wasn't the greatest job, it was backbreaking work. Sometimes the temperature would reach a hundred and fifty degrees in that foundry, and the pay envelope was a little slim. But it was something. We were still poor, trying to feed nine mouths (ten when my brother William decided to show up) on one salary. We weren't out of the Depression yet. But on Hillside Place people pulled together and became more than just neighbors; they became family. If you needed a cup of sugar, you went across the landing to the Coxes' or next door to the Millers'. The Depression taught us to share; one of my father's favorite theme songs. "Cast your bread upon the water . . ." Help someone in need, and when you're in need, the Lord will help you. We didn't have much in the way of clothes and furnishings, but they were clean. My mother, like women up and down that block, cleaned the house right to the curb. As on Court Street and in hundreds of other old-fashioned and dilapidated buildings where blacks and other immigrants were forced to live in Newark, the toilet was still on the back porch. But it was spotless; there were never any odors. No matter how poor we were, come Christmastime we always had the biggest tree.

Finally, my mother and father were realizing their dream; to raise their children the way they wanted to, in a godly household. These were the best years of our lives.

We were poor but we made our own cheap fun. Larry, Nicky and I would take a magazine and a running start and slide down the hallway on the new linoleum; from the kitchen right through the three bedrooms all the way to the living room! We'd knock pieces of plaster down on Miss Georgia's head underneath us and she'd scream bloody murder. "I'm gonna tell your father." She didn't have to; Annie was a big tattletale. We'd gang up on her and beat her up! But we made up by nighttime; we slept in the same bed. Reebie and Lee, the big girls, had their own beds; the boys slept in the other room. I was always getting into trouble; a little tomboy, tearing my clothes, trying to do everything my brothers were doing; climbing trees in the backyard, down on my hands and knees shooting skully, and proving I could fight just as good as they could. We were like three peas in a pod; me, Larry and Nicky, the young and the restless. Nicky, the oldest of us young ones, was the spitting image of my father, intense around the eyes, red complexion. Larry was good-looking, all the women would go crazy over him. I was a perfect combination of both my parents. I had the fire in my eyes from Nitch Drinkard and Delia McCaskill's sweetness in my smile—when I wanted to smile. I bumped heads with Lee sometimes—the youngest and the oldest. Lee was the junior matriarch; tough, but more of a fighter with her mouth than with her fists, a good negotiator. My brother William and I just didn't get along, probably that oldest and youngest thing again. Hank was a sweetheart. He was good-looking like my other brothers, but gentle, a lot like my mother. Everybody always took advantage of Hank. Anne was in the middle. At twelve, she was getting too old to slide down the hall on her butt with us, yet she wasn't old enough to be invited into my parents' world with Lee and Reebie. Occasionally, Reebie or Lee would "drop a hint," and she would pick up on some inside dope from the grown-up world. As I got a little older, Annie became my idol: she was tall, graceful, had her own friends and she was book-smart. In the lower grades she was always pulling a penmanship award. In high school she was chosen as her school's valedictorian. Always sweet, and a little sensitive, she was always there for us in later years, like Lee, to put a roof over our heads. She palled around with Hank and gave him a room in her house in the last years of his life. Reebie was a lot like my mother, sweet and taking refuge in her religion. No matter what life dealt them, "the Lord would make a way." As I got older, I felt that it didn't hurt to be a little proactive too.

My mother was the first one up in the morning. She'd get a fire going in that coal stove and cook breakfast for my father. Then she'd fill his lunch pail with some of last night's leftovers, kiss him goodbye and get him off to work. That's how I woke up in the morning, smelling some kind of food—biscuits or pancakes. We all ate breakfast together, usually some cooked oatmeal. Mommy said grace. Before I started school I had Mommy all to myself, once the others had gone off to Charlton Street School a few blocks away. I watched her clean up the breakfast dishes and start her cleaning. One of the ways she stretched my father's twenty-five dollars a week was by sending Lee down to Prince Street in our old neighborhood to shop the stalls run by Jewish merchants. Three pounds of chopped meat cost a dollar. Mommy would mix that up with bread and stuff and make a family-sized meat loaf. Twenty-five cents bought us three pounds of neck bones. And collard greens were three pounds for a dime. At the bakery, for twenty-five cents, you could get a big bag of cupcakes, buns, raisin bread and doughnuts. I've never lost my taste for doughnuts because of that place.

My mother would give me lunch and start cooking dinner around the same time. If she was making spaghetti, that sauce would be cooking all day. She'd start baked beans early in the morning; simmering a big pot of beans all day with molasses and bacon strips. Sometimes, we'd lie down and take a nap together. Then we'd get up just in time to turn on the radio and listen to my mother's favorite soap opera, *Portia Faces Life*.

"*Portia Faces Life* . . . [organ swell] . . . The world's most popular bran flake cereals, Post 40% Bran Flakes and Post Raisin Bran present . . . *Portia Faces Life,* a story respecting the courage, spirit and integrity of American women . . ."

According to the show's script, Portia Blake was married to a handsome young attorney, Richard Blake, who fights corruption in Parkerstown, a fictional city. After her husband Richard is killed, Portia, who is also a lawyer, is left to raise their young son alone. She falls in love with Walter Manning, a doctor, but he is stolen away from her by Arlene, an evil hussy, who becomes Portia's rival. Arlene later tricks Walter into marriage. After months of pining for Walter, Portia realizes she must forget him. She continues her late husband's crusade against corruption, battling the crooked politicians of City Hall and trying to help the poor people they have consigned to the town's worst slums.

The story sounded as if it was torn from the pages of the *Newark Evening News,* a story my mother had seen unfold right before her eyes "in the town's worst slums"—Court Street. Where gangster Longie Zwillman hobnobbed with the Third Ward's corrupt politicians and racketeers.

Portia's law school education might have been beyond my mother and most women of the 1940s. But there were plenty of traits my mother could identify with in "tiny, resolute and brave" Portia. Portia was the heroine, something new to radio but not to American women, especially black women. Men were absent as Portia—and my mother— faced down her trials. Like Portia, who always took the high road in dealing with her adversaries, my mother also never gave the devil an opportunity. She never lost her graceful, quiet demeanor, never resorted to anger or revenge when wronged by her mother or her sister, who gossiped about her, or when she was cheated by a merchant on Prince Street. I wished my mother would have stood up more to people. She was always so sweet, but so subservient. I adored my mother, but I knew I would never be like that. "Vengeance is mine saith the Lord," she would quote when one of us urged her to fight back. Another reason she liked that hymn so much, "My Lord! What a Mourning," the story of God's ultimate judgment.

What my mother didn't know, along with millions of other women, glued to their radios at four o'clock every afternoon, was that Portia was not what she seemed. First of all, Portia wasn't real; she was a fictional character played by an actress. Thousands of people thought Portia was real; they would write in to warn her about other characters in the serial, they would remember characters' birthdays and send in birthday cards. *Portia Faces Life* and her cast of thousands was in reality just two or three actors and some sound effects. And the only corruption worth a crusade was against the show's producers, who grew rich while they would deliberately suppress the identities of and underpay the performers who created their product. I would learn all about this kind of injustice much later in life.

My sisters would come in from school, have a glass of milk and talk to my mother. They'd start their chores and I would wait outside on the porch for Larry and Nicky to get home. My father was pretty strict; we weren't allowed to stray off our block. And there was no visiting other people's houses. Our house was similarly off-limits, even to friends. Our house was private, only for family members. The only people outside of family who ever visited were a few deacons from church and Reverend Warrick, who came over every Sunday for dinner.

At five o'clock, someone from the neighborhood who also worked at the Singer factory would pull up with Daddy. My father would get out of the car with a newspaper under his arm and an empty lunch pail and wave good night to the driver. If it was still light and warm enough to sit outside, he'd sit on the porch, talk and laugh with us about whatever happened in the neighborhood that day—light stuff. Heavy problems he discussed with my mother or Lee. He'd let us stay out a little while longer. But don't try to be out past dusk, and don't let him have to call you either. Mommy wanted us all inside, eating together.

Daddy said grace. He had a high-pitched voice; there was nothing muddy about it. If you were a block away, you could hear him call you; his voice was just that clear and strong. He prayed with great sincerity: strong, nothing by rote. He always prayed that God would take care of his children, keep them together, that was his heart's desire. I guess it was because his own family was broken up now; since Georgia, his brothers and sisters were scattered in several northern cities. He wanted us to be close-knit at all times, so he prayed for that. "Keep this family together," he would pray. "Keep me able to take care of this family; let my family know that they are brothers and sisters, from the heart." That's what he would say, "From the heart, you're brothers and sisters.

Blood . . . blood comes first; God, then your blood." That's the order he taught us. He didn't allow us to fight. He didn't believe brothers and sisters should fight. At all. I think my mother may have differed slightly on this point. She believed brothers and sisters could express their differences; argue even. But when the deal goes down, you're together, you're brother and sister, you stick together.

Sometimes Daddy asked one of us to say the grace: "Larry . . . Cissy, say grace, bless the table." And you better have it right. None of this "God is good; God is great" stuff. That was a prayer for infants!

On Sundays, my mother would reinforce what we'd learned in Sunday school by discussing the lesson at the dinner table. That was the main topic of discussion at dinner many nights. For dessert, Mommy might have made a cake. On holidays or special occasions, she would make a cake that had different-colored layers. We looked forward to that. Usually she made some tea cakes, sweet but not too sweet. We never ate a lot of sweets.

We each took a turn helping with the dishes—one week at a time. After they were cleared, my father would say, "All right now, children, strike me up a tune." One of us would start it off, maybe Annie leading one of his favorites, "Jesus, Keep Me Near the Cross," me, Larry and Nicky falling in behind her. If we had any homework to do, now was the time. My father sat down in his chair in the living room and read his paper. He was always on the lookout for a better job, always looking to better himself. He smoked a Camel—the only bad habit he picked up at the foundry—and listened to the radio. Mostly news. He took an interest in the political scene, voted, but never discussed his opinions on politics or world events with us. That was considered an adult conversation. Sometimes a couple from church might come over to see my father. Lots of people depended on my father for his counsel. Marital or otherwise. My cousin Honey Davis says that her brother and his wife counseled with him before they were married. She says they called my father "Uncle"—even Honey's sister-in-law. My father couldn't turn anyone away who was seeking counsel. "Don't send a dog away hungry," my father used to say. "And don't send a man away hungry, especially when he's thirsty for wisdom."

If we were singing in a few days, we would rehearse in the living room. We laid out our clothes for the next day, washed and got into bed. Daddy stayed up in the living room smoking a cigarette. He was usually the last one to bed. Then Nicky would start crying.

"What's the matter?" my father called from his room.

"Gotta go to the bathroom, Daddy," Nicky whined.

My father turned on the light for Nicky and led him to the back porch. When Nicky was through with his business, my father took him back to bed, wrapped the covers around Nicky and went back to his bedroom.

Just after we moved to Hillside Place, my mother had a second stroke. It may have been stress; my grandmother and her daughter, my mother's sister, continued to be a source of aggravation, although they were now living across the street instead of in our building. William was already starting to gamble—where he was getting the money to do that no one wanted to know. The talk of our country being drawn into the war in Europe and the draft that was sure to follow might have concerned her for Hank's sake. She had one son who'd gone off of his own will, she couldn't bear the thought of a war taking another son from her. Or maybe it was just that her body couldn't take the stress of delivering another set of twins—an event which usually coincided with her strokes.

Whatever the reason, my mother's hospital visits almost became part of a routine in our family. She would leave, sometimes in the middle of the night, while we were asleep, and return a few days later. We children would get the word from a neighbor or a relative that Mommy was coming up the street with my father and we would all run to the window and wait for her. We'd all squeeze into that narrow window—I was the smallest, so I automatically got to rest on the sill, Larry, Nicky and Anne fighting for the best spot above me. My older sisters and Hank were usually elsewhere or helping bring my mother home. From the window we could see my father coming up the street, pushing Mommy in a wheelchair. When she saw us she would wave and smile. That smile was worth a million bucks. Everything was okay in our house again.

Unfortunately, this happy routine was usually followed by a distasteful one. It was determined that my mother needed some time to rest in bed without having to care for "the younger children"—me, Larry and Nicky. My brothers were sent to aunts and uncles still living around Court Street. I was sent to the dreariest house on earth: Aunt Juanita's.

Oh, I begged Anne to go with me, so I wouldn't have to go alone. I hated it! It was in the ironbound section, then known as Down Neck, where the river wraps around a piece of Newark like a snake. I thought I was suffocating there. It was the darkest, spookiest place you could imagine. Big, dark drapes, no daylight coming in, big, dark bed, too high to climb up on, even if you wanted to. We didn't like Aunt Juanita. She was attractive but not pretty. She was dark-skinned, had a nice figure and long black hair. But she was mean. Mean to me and mean to Anne. And she dipped snuff! She was nothing like our other aunts, my father's sisters Sally, Tiny or even Flossie. At Tiny's, I could play with my cousin Honey. Aunt Sally had a houseful of kids my age and she made these great melted cheese sandwiches we called "cheese things." At Flossie's you could hear the blues on a phonograph or the next-best thing—the gospel of guitar-playing Sister Rosetta Tharpe. You'd always get something nice to eat at one of these places, some hugs and some fun. But not at Juanita's. She was cheap with her food and always acted like she was doing you a favor. Juanita didn't have any children; maybe that's why she had such an attitude. The way she got in our family was by marrying Uncle Oscar, my mother's brother. Uncle Oscar was a sweetheart, we all loved him. I guess he just saw Juanita's fine shape and long black hair and was gone! Juanita was also tight with my mother's mother and my mother's sister, who already had an ax to grind against my mother and father. So I would end up spending a couple of days here; praying all the while that Mommy would get better quick and send for me.

Mommy continued to do all her chores. She had to drag that left leg, and her left arm wasn't much good either. She still had to cook and was forced to stir a pot with that bad arm. I remember her also spanking me with it once because I was fresh. After the second stroke, she had a hard time coming out to see us in school plays and things, without my father pushing her along in her wheelchair. If she was outside in the street now, she was in that wheelchair. That's how the whole family would go to church now. My father pushing my mother in the wheelchair and we kids in tow.

My mother continued her important work, giving my older sisters their chores, showing them how to run a household. It was during this particular time each day that, according to Anne, Mommy taught them much more than housework.

"When I'd come home from school and while I was ironing or while I was washing or whatever, that was when she would do her talking to her girls. She wouldn't talk to us until we started our menstrual cycle; that's where I was and she was showing me how to take care of myself," says Anne. "She'd take us one at a time and talk to us about life, what to expect. She would talk to each one of us in a very soft, sweet voice. And then she wouldn't go but so far because she didn't want to put anything in our heads to make us fearful or uncomfortable about what we had to face as women."

Rather than the philosophy of sex education today—knowledge is a good thing—my mother and father's generation thought that the more you knew, the more you would do. In their minds, they feared that if we knew the facts of life, we might be tempted to put them into practice at too early an age. The longer they could keep us from this information, the longer we would stay pure, innocent and inexperienced. That's why we never knew when our mother was pregnant. She would hide her pregnancies from us. To have openly revealed her pregnancies might have invited too many embarrassing questions from us. Sooner or later we would have discovered just how Mother got pregnant with those babies! My cousin Honey Davis nearly got the whipping of her life just for saying the word "pregnant." Lucky for Honey, my father was there to stay her father's hand of judgment. But I'm sure he discussed the incident with my mother.

If Anne thought that during these "intimate" talks with my mother, she was going to learn more about my mother's childhood, more about why our grandmother had left her in Florida, she was sadly mistaken.

"She may have told my older sisters things like that but she still considered me too young, at thirteen, to know things like that," says Anne. "She told us she got married early, twelve or thirteen . . . she just never talked that much. She was too busy teaching us, the older girls, how to clean, wash and iron. We had to do all that by hand then. Washing was by hand—we had the tub with the scrubboard.

"Together you stand, divided you fall . . . she would tell us that over and over again. She always taught us togetherness. Family. She connected that with what the Bible said; what God wanted us to be."

Above all we were taught that there was no problem too great for God to bear. We were taught this during a steady diet of church. We were not like other kids. Compared to most kids in the neighborhood, we had a lot less play time. We went to two churches. We continued to go to Sunday school at the storefront on Mercer Street early Sunday morning. At eleven o'clock, we joined our parents at St. Luke's on Prince Street. We spent all day in church on Sunday. But it was enjoyable. There was no fuss; all of us knew that was what was expected of us. We didn't go to the movies on Sunday, no recreational-type things. And if you didn't go to church—you stayed home.

My mother and father were heavily involved there; my father was a trustee, my mother was a steward, dressed in her crisp white uniform. Besides his trustee duties, such as depositing the weekly offering in the bank, many people in the church depended on my father for his godly counsel. He was also the trusted friend of the pastor, Reverend Warrick.

After the eleven o'clock service was over, if we weren't singing at another church we'd go home, then return at six o'clock for African Endeavor Christian League. Here we learned more fundamental Christian teachings like in Sunday school. Sometimes, we attended night service. But generally my mother and father wanted us home Sunday night, to finish our homework and get ready for school. They weren't religious fanatics. They only wanted to teach us what God meant, what life was all about.

I never resented it. In fact, I ate it up. I liked church. I liked what was going on there; I liked singing, and I liked learning about Jesus. When I got old enough, I taught Sunday school—kindergarten, junior, intermediate and senior.

All we knew was church. Sunday morning, Sunday night. Tuesday night, they called it "class," they'd have revival services that night. Later on in the week was choir practice. Other than that, we didn't have a whole lot to entertain ourselves with in those days. We'd sneak and play cards sometimes, which wasn't allowed. If my father came in the room, we'd throw the cards underneath the bed and look dumb.

"Were you playing cards?" my father would ask.

"Nope," we'd stonewall.

"Don't lie to me, now," he'd warn. "I can't trust you if you lie to me; I don't know when you're telling the truth and when you're not."

Still, we stonewalled.

Then he said, if you lied and he caught you in a lie, there was nothing in the drugstore that would kill you any quicker than he would.

That did it. We were undone; a stammering, whimpering confession usually followed.

One thing, above all others, we were warned about doing: playing church.

"We used to play church a lot," Anne laughs. "All we knew was church, so that was our pastime. But if my father caught us, it was on!

"My father caught us one day. He had warned us about it and then he caught us after he had warned us.

"Nicky could preach; and we were his audience; me, Cissy and Larry. Cissy was almost eight, Larry was ten, I was fourteen and Nicky was eleven. Nicky would get up on a little box and he could really preach. Sounded just like a preacher too. He was imitating Reverend Wyatt from the storefront church and other preachers he'd seen. He'd call for song and we'd give him a song just like in church. Cissy would beat a tambourine and sing, then I'd sing a song and then we'd all sing one together. We just had 'service' at our house. That was our pastime.

"One day we had a cousin up from down South who was visiting. She was real religious and sanctified too. Nicky was preaching, we were singing and she thought she was in church.

" 'And you know what God said,' preached Nicky.

" 'Amen . . . amen,' we answered. 'Preach it, brother, oh yeah, oh yeah.'

" 'Then, give me a song, give me a song,' yelled Nicky, 'so that we reach God with our singing!'

"Well, when we started singing," laughs Anne, "our little cousin jumped up and started shouting—I mean literally shouting like she was in church. We got so scared, we ran out of that room. My father heard the commotion, came in the room and figured out what happened.

" 'I told you about playing church,' he said. And then we got it!"

He must have discussed this episode with my mother. Always a moderating influence, she may have convinced him that we needed some constructive diversion to stop playing church. He bought us a Victrola and we started buying the records that were available then—no jazz or blues records. All gospel. The Swan Silvertones, the Nightingales, the Harmonizing Four.

God forbid my parents had caught us playing church when our pastor, Reverend Warrick, came for dinner. Other than one of my relatives, Reverend Warrick was the only other person to ever enter our house. This was one of my mother's favorite times. It was usually Sunday, when she cooked chicken, a full complement of greens and white potatoes. Maybe she even made one of her multicolored cakes to celebrate the occasion. Or brownies, which my mother was baking even before they were available in stores. Reverend Warrick usually brought his wife and Mansel Jr. Reverend Warrick was soft-spoken and handsome, tall with high cheekbones like my father's people. An intelligent man, he prudently complimented my mother's delicious dinner. Such sincere praise made her feel good; made her smile, made her feel that he knew cooking wasn't easy for her since the stroke. She appreciated him; appreciated his teaching and was glad she and my father had trusted him as their spiritual leader. "Behold, how good and how pleasant it is for brethren to dwell together in unity!" was the scripture that came to her. Mommy also liked his wife, and she especially liked that Reverend Warrick was never seen without her. That kept them all from gossiping! He was educated and different. Unlike many pastors in the black community, he didn't go in for a lot of emotionalism and shouting. He was more of a teacher; teaching from the Bible. He had his moments of coming up with the joyous sound of shouting, but for the most part, his forte was teaching.

My mother and father liked that about him. They were mature in the Lord and were ready for the meat of the Word rather than the milk that many pastors still seemed to be feeding their flocks. Besides this, my father was the one man in St. Luke's that Reverend Warrick could trust. There were always mumurings within a congregation. A pastor was always a target for gossip. A friend within the congregation was much to be desired. A friend like my father, gifted in personal counseling, was a friend to be coveted; even loved.

There was another reason my mother felt warmly toward the pastor and his wife. But at this point it was still a secret. Oh, how Annie—or any of us—would have died to know! But only one other person in my family knew. My mother had not even shared this secret yet with my father; my sister Lee had sworn her to secrecy. My oldest sister had fallen in love with the pastor's son; and he with her! Mansel Jr. was as tall and attractive as his father, all high cheekbones and dark, flashing eyes. At nineteen, Lee had inherited my mother's petite build and cute shape. My mother could see them together; they made a handsome couple. When the two of them were in the same room, as even now, there was electricity in the air that even my mother noticed. She longed to talk about the romance with Mrs. Warrick, but Lee had made her promise she would tell no one.

Knowing what she knew, my mother tried not to smile like a fool as Mrs. Warrick helped her with the dishes. My father put his arm around Reverend Warrick and walked him into the living room. He unburdened himself to my father as he'd done many other times when his heart was heavy with church problems. He didn't have to tell my father that offerings were down—my father was the church's trustee and deposited the offerings in the bank each Monday. No doubt Reverend Warrick lamented that it was pretty hard to ask congregants to tithe in the middle of the Depression. He longed for a larger church building. They had been forced out of their first building on Charlton Street—

the ramshackle building down an alley had been condemned. Now, he felt like a gypsy; having to relocate quickly, for the benefit of the congregation, around the corner on Prince Street. It was particularly depressing to him when he looked around Newark and saw every denomination under the sun with glorious brick-and-granite edifices. The Reverend also felt unsettled with the denomination. They had moved him before; and they had the power to move him again. And what about the congregation? He knew the Drinkards appreciated his teaching ministry, but what about the rest of the congregation? Maybe they wanted a more dynamic man; a man who gave them more of a quick fix every Sunday. A man who didn't make them think so much. Someone who didn't make them thumb through their Bible so much.

Someone who did more hand-holding.

It was Reverend Warrick who needed someone to hold his hand now. My father knelt with him in the living room; he invited the pastor to kneel with him as he approached the throne of grace on his behalf. Reverend Warrick had been to college and seminary. His hands never hefted anything heavier than a few wooden folding chairs in church and a stack of hymnbooks. By contrast, my father's education was limited to a few months a year, for a handful of years, in a little country church in a hick town way down in Georgia. His hands were callused from hard labor; first from the plow and now from the foundry, where he poured molten iron all day. But the pastor loved to pray with my father. He removed his suit jacket, folded it over a chair and dropped to his knees with my father. They prayed: first my father taking all his pastor's concerns before the Lord, then Reverend Warrick thanking God for his friend and praying a special blessing over our house. My father rose to his feet, singing, as always, his favorite hymn, his testimony, "I Would Trust in the Lord." Before my father was on his feet, he was calling for us.

Oh, no; we had to sing again. I hid under the bed. The others—Annie, Nicky, Larry—filed into the living room.

You have to understand. I loved to sing. I loved to stand up there with my brothers and sisters and hear our voices blend. The funny way each one of our notes found each other and hung out there as one note in the air in front of us—almost like we had no control over it. The funny shapes our mouths would make to sing a certain note; how we'd look at each other and have to keep ourselves from laughing up there. Oh, I loved to laugh—I was only seven or eight. I wanted to be doing kid things, like any other kid.

"Baby . . . ," my father called from the living room. He didn't know yet that I was hiding.

As I lay there under my bed, I thought of all the singing we were doing. We weren't just singing in St. Luke's now. My father was taking us to sing down in Elizabeth where he worked. We didn't have a car. In the middle of December, we'd walk down to Market and Broad to catch the bus. Only the bus to Elizabeth didn't always show up on time and you'd be standing there freezing. And don't you dare talk about being cold! Perhaps a tear or two, since I was the "baby." Once we got to Elizabeth, when I'd just gotten comfy in that warm bus, we had to step back into the night and find our way to Liberty Baptist Church. We wore Liberty Baptist out! But every time we sang on a gospel program there, they would hold us until last. There weren't too many children's groups then and we were so good that we always brought the house down.

We'd wait out the whole program in a room where I usually fell asleep. By the time my father came to get us, I was in no mood to sing. And I usually let him know by sticking out my lower lip.

"C'mon, now, baby," he would gently coax me out of my slumber. "C'mon, now."

I was so small, they had to stand me on a box so I could be seen.

I would keep remnants of the pouting routine going at least into our first song. Then a sharp look from Daddy would stop all that. Besides, I had discovered a new diversion: watching my skirt. Two ladies from our street who ushered at St. Luke's had sewed us some nice navy pleated skirts. It was my first experience, at seven, with pleats. I was fascinated! Especially the way the skirt snapped every time I swished my butt. Even while I sang, I couldn't take my eyes off my rear end.

Reebie put a stop to that.

"Quit lookin' at your butt!" she'd hiss.

Liberty Baptist and other places where we sang in Elizabeth were always packed because lots of people from my father's job used to show up. We would open with "I Will Guide Thee," move on to "Borrowed Land," "You'd Better Min' " and "I'll Fly Away." I was so tiny to have this big voice coming out of me that I always caused a stir. When people came down front and started throwing money at me, I'd jump off my box and pick up those bills. My brothers and sisters would get so mad at me because I wouldn't share my money with them!

My father would always be there, watching us, just out of sight, but not far enough so that we couldn't see him, encouraging us, rooting us on. Not in an emotional way; my father tended to keep his emotions under wraps. You knew he felt things strongly, though. Sometimes he couldn't help himself. Every so often, while watching us sing, a stray tear would roll down his cheeks.

"Sing, children," he would say.

"Sing, baby," he whispered, if I was singing the lead.

I was his baby. How could I deny him the joy we gave him singing by refusing to sing—hiding under the bed. Besides, one more minute and he'd come looking for me and I'd catch it from him! With that in mind, I crawled out from under the bed, dusted myself off and ran into the living room.

I joined my brothers and sisters—Reebie and Lee also sang with us that night—in front of the window, our little backdrop.

"All right, children," my father said. "Strike me up a tune."

I began one of his favorites, "I Will Guide Thee."

I will guide thee
With thine eyes,
All the way from earth to heaven,
I will guide thee with thine eyes.

My father beamed. Reverend and Mrs. Warrick also radiated a certain amount of pride. After all, the first place we sang was at St. Luke's. Mansel Jr. just gazed dreamily at my sister Lee, helpless under her spell.

My mother also glowed. This was the one source of entertainment she enjoyed the most.

"My mother was especially proud of Cissy," says Anne. "She would just sit back and marvel. She was so small to have such a big voice. Cissy was really her pride and joy."

In January 1940, Mommy's joy was made full. Mansel Jr. asked Lee to marry him. Finally, the cat was out of the bag and my mother could talk with Mrs. Warrick about their two kids spending their lives together. Mrs. Warrick spent a few mornings and evenings with my mother, planning Lee and Mansel Jr.'s big day; a May or June wedding would be nice . . . a trousseau . . . bridesmaids' dresses. But neither Lee nor Mansel Jr. allowed these two ladies to bask in the big event to come. In fact, Lee and Mansel Jr. wouldn't wait. They wanted to get married right away—in a few weeks.

There was no time for elaborate plans. Like most folks did then, Mansel Jr. and Lee had the ceremony in the house. Reverend Warrick came to 38 Hillside Place and officiated. There was a feast prepared by my mother, Reebie and my father's sisters. Relatives, friends, neighbors and well-wishers crowded both the front and back porches. I never saw so much fried chicken, and my mother made a few of her multicolored cakes.

Three months later, in March 1940, Lee announced she was pregnant. Mommy's first girl-child, at nineteen and a half, was now a mother-to-be. Her girls were growing up. With the wedding, Lee's parcel of responsibilities were split between Reebie and Anne. Reebie, at eighteen, was the most eligible young Drinkard woman in the house. Always sweet and a homebody like my mother, she continued to help Mommy with the housework, which had become much more difficult to handle since her second stroke. Though only thirteen, Annie was the girl next in line, and could not be denied. She inherited some of Lee's big, important family jobs outside the house, like paying the family's grocery bill at Dorfman's Grocery across the street.

Mr. Dorfman knew we were a big family. When Lee used to pay our bill, he would always give her a sack of graham crackers for all of us. When Annie inherited Lee's job, paying Mr. Dorfman, he continued to give her the graham crackers. But Annie decided it was her prerogative to distribute them as she saw fit. She would offer Nicky the graham crackers in exchange for Nicky taking her turn washing dishes.

"You're gonna do the dishes, right?" she would make Nicky promise.

"Yup," Nicky promised.

Annie would give Nicky the crackers—but Nicky refused to do the dishes. He always welshed on the deal. Annie would cry and cry. Then she'd turn around in a week and trust him all over again. We used to just laugh at her; she fell for Nicky's hustle every time.

With Lee married and expecting, my mother began to concentrate on grooming Reebie and Anne for adulthood, particularly Annie.

"Mommy was just like a mother hen," says Anne. "She wanted all her baby chicks up under her and didn't want to get up off them until she was ready."

She worried about her two oldest boys as well: William, twenty-two, living the fast life, and fifteen-year-old Hank. Every day the newspapers and radio were full of more and more alarming news of Hitler's advances in Europe and with it, talk of America's involvement in another war intensified. William was of draftable age right now; Hank was safe for a few more years yet. Still, she worried.

If Mommy was a mother hen, reluctant to get up off her baby chicks, she could now envision Annie not only walking but flying on her own very soon. Lee had fallen in love, married and become pregnant at such dizzying speed that my mother worried it could happen again before she realized it. She felt a particular urgency in resuming the ministry of getting her daughters ready for the world.

"She began to teach me how to iron," says Anne. "While I ironed she would talk to me in a soft voice. I took over Lee's job; she was the ironer. Oh boy, there were so many things to iron. My mother's church uniforms, all the school clothes and my father's white shirts—one for each day of the week. And you'd better not scorch them. This was not with an electric iron; this was the iron that came off the stove, the smoothing iron. She started me off on things like sheets that didn't have to be really ironed, just smoothed over. Then I graduated to shirts, all the boys' shirts and my father's shirts. He was a very particular man. You did not leave a wrinkle in his collar and you did not put a lot of starch in the collar—just enough to make it stand.

Lee came by the house every day—big and round, due anytime—to talk with my mother. Sometimes Lee's pal, my sister Reebie, would join them. They'd sit in the kitchen and drink Pepsis, talking quietly and laughing. I looked at Lee, my oldest sister, with wonder: she was the first pregnant woman I'd ever seen up close! And she was related to me! Half of me was curious about her "condition" and the other half was scared to death. I knew from cousin Honey Davis' experience that this was something charged with the secrecy and mystery of the forbidden. Lee respected my mother's sense of modesty and kept herself slightly aloof from us younger children. Wisely, she didn't encourage any question-and-answer sessions from us.

Annie hung out in the kitchen with my mother and Lee. Now that she had inherited a few of Lee's responsibilities, they couldn't ignore her. A new, almost womanly, self-confidence emboldened her around them. Still, when Lee had a question or confession that was for my mother's ears only, she would make Annie feel like the thirteen-year-old she was; by flipping her a dollar and asking her to run across the street and buy them each, Annie included, a fresh Pepsi. The free Pepsi was scant consolation for Anne. She would much rather have been sitting at their table, eyes wide, drinking in a mysterious, exotic account of Lee and Mansel Jr.'s conjugal adventures. Annie would race back to the kitchen, only to find them discussing the price of neck bones on Prince Street.

My mother recognized Annie's feminine aspirations and rewarded her with extra time and attention. As Annie entered womanhood, my mother showed her how to care for herself.

Her time with Annie was not complete, though. She had another visit to the hospital—another stroke. We younger children repeated our ritual of waiting at the window, praying inside for Mommy's safe return. Sure enough, our faith was rewarded! Before long, Mommy was coming up the street in her wheelchair, Daddy behind her. This time the stroke had paralyzed the left side of her face and the smile she managed now was a little lopsided.

She could rarely see us sing in places outside of Newark now, but every time we did she would make sure days in advance that my skirt was clean. Before I left the house, she would put pretty bows in my hair and give me a kiss.

On December 12, 1940, I stopped being the baby. Just two months after we celebrated my seventh birthday, Lee delivered a girl. Which made me an aunt, my mother explained to me. An aunt? You mean like jazzy Aunt Flossie with her fancy hats and that narrow butt she liked to switch as if it wasn't so narrow? That's right, Mommy knowingly nodded. Just thinking of me as an aunt, Flossie or anyone, made me bust out laughing.

Lee named her baby—my niece—Marie Dionne, after Reebie (Marie), her closest sister. Practically every day, Lee would bring her little baby over to our house. We would all take turns watching her in her carriage. She was so cute: a headful of dark curls, her father's high cheekbones and flashing eyes. I could hardly wait for my turn to watch her.

But my mother was beside herself. She was so proud of Lee; my mother had raised her first girl-child well. Lee was not only an obedient, respectful daughter, but a trusted confidante, one who could think and act in the family's best interests. She had kept herself pure, in a world very different from down South, a world where it was easy to fall. She had kept herself pure and found a good man, the Reverend's son. Now this beautiful baby daughter—and granddaughter—was a blessing to both of them.

For the next year and a half, Lee visited almost every day. When the baby was young, she'd come over in the mornings and keep my mother company while we were all at school. When Lee went back to work, she would leave the baby with my mother and come pick her up in the afternoon.

Then, in the summer of 1941, just before I entered the third grade, something wonderful happened. Lee became pregnant with her second child. Little Marie Dionne would have a sister or a brother. Lee purposed in her heart to surprise my mother. If the baby was a girl, she would name it after Mommy—nothing fancy; just what everybody called her in the family—Dee Dee. It would be Lee's surprise. But Mommy was keeping her own secret.

In December, the Japanese bombed Pearl Harbor, drawing the United States into the war. In Charlton Street School, they told us about the four brave boys from Newark who had lost their lives on that base. While the rest of the country may have been slow to waken to the imminence of World War II, Newark had gotten early signs. In 1940, factories were already filling orders for the Army. During the spring, we were the first city to test a complete blackout, on May 25 and 26. My mother may have picked up on these clues and started to worry about war a year or more before we were in it. Or maybe it was just her mother-hen instinct, worried that William or Hank would be drafted— a premonition. She was right to worry. Hank, sweet Hansy with my mother's gentle personality, would be drafted; serve in the Pacific and never be the same again.

Perhaps it was also a premonition that she had about that night.

She didn't want us to go to church that night. It was a Tuesday night and she never stopped us from going to church.

"That's the night she wanted us all to stay home," says Anne. "But I insisted on going. She was still sitting on the edge of her bed, waiting for us, when I came back from church. That's where she would sit; her legs dangling off the bed to draw the blood down to her feet. My sister Reebie and I would take turns rubbing her legs to keep the circulation going in the side that she'd had the stroke. Reebie hadn't rubbed her legs yet. My mother told Reebie she wanted me to do it that night. So I rubbed her leg down. It was about midnight when I finished and she had lain back down."

Annie got into bed. A half hour later she was just beginning to doze off.

Then she heard my father yell.

FIVE

My Lord! what a mourning
When the stars begin to fall.
—"My Lord! What a Mourning"

Annie jumped up and ran into my parents' room. My father had yelled for Reebie, the oldest, but Annie reached their room first. My mother was having a seizure, hemorrhaging, rocking back and forth on the bed. Blood was pouring from her mouth, her nose and her ears.

"I ran to get a spoon to put in her mouth so she wouldn't bite her tongue," says Anne. "Blood was coming from everywhere. I got a pail to hold the blood. By the time the ambulance came, I had almost a full pail; even the plasma, the purple part and the white part were coming out."

The next morning, Anne filled in us younger children on Mommy's condition, sparing us the more graphic details. We had slept through the worst of her attack and the ambulance arriving and Anne saw no reason to alarm us. She thought Mommy would have to stay in the hospital a long time this time. Daddy was with her in the hospital; there was nothing to do but wait. Perhaps a relative would come by and bring us news. We just took up our usual post at the front window. No one felt much like eating breakfast; we just waited.

After a little while, some kid from the neighborhood saw my father rounding the corner.

"Your father's coming," he shouted up at us.

Oh, it was Daddy! Daddy to save the day again. He would come up

Hillside Place, big, strong Daddy pushing my mother's wheelchair. A few neighborhood kids whom she'd fed, who called her "Momma" would approach her shyly, a little afraid of her wheelchair. She would smile at them, inquire softly of one, adjust another's collar, then look up at us. And even her little smile, still crooked from her stroke, would pull us out of our worry. We got our mommy back one more time.

"Get out of that window! Don't you know your momma's dead?"

It was mean Aunt Juanita, yelling up at us from the street.

"Get out of that window!" she yelled again.

Something was wrong, very wrong. My father was pushing no wheelchair. He was a shambles; his normally neat suit looked slept in and he was hanging his head, weeping, leaning on Juanita's husband, my mother's brother Oscar.

My mother's dead? Dead? What does that mean? Is she still in the hospital? Where's Mommy? I heard Annie start to cry above me; Larry and Nicky just wandered off in a daze. Hank bolted for the back of the house. He had busted out on the back porch and had one foot over the wooden railing, about to throw himself over, when Annie put her arms around him and held him back.

My mother had suffered a cerebral hemorrhage. She had died in her own bed at home. The only thing the doctors at the hospital did for her was pronounce her dead on arrival. After she died we learned her secret: In the last six months of her life, while Lee, twenty-one, visited her every day pregnant with her second daughter, Dee Dee, while she cooed and fussed over Lee and baby Dionne, my mother was herself pregnant with twins. Like the other twins, they died at birth. My mother was just thirty-nine years old.

I ran down the stairs to the street. A few houses down, Mr. Underwood had a woodshed where I would sometimes hide. I sat down on a stack of logs and hugged my knees to my chest. I had just been with my mother last night. The tea cakes she'd baked yesterday were still on the stove. I had kissed her good night.

"Died." It had a terrible sound. It was a word I associated with my grandfather, Papa John, my father's daddy, who scared me with his long white hair, his red skin and those eyes that looked right through you.

He'd "died" when I was six, two years ago, and I could still remember my daddy crying in the kitchen, holding on to his sisters, Aunt Sally and Aunt Tiny. I never saw my grandfather again after that day; never saw him walking through the street to our house with his cane and his all-black getup and hat. I saw a dead bird in the yard once, a baby sparrow that had fallen from its nest, so still and frozen. Then, death was far away. Now, it was right in my house. All I knew now was I would never see my mother again. I knew that, and I knew I hated my Aunt Juanita for telling us that way: "Get out of that window . . . your momma's dead."

My mother's funeral was a blur to me. I was there but I've blocked most of it out. Someone got me dressed and fixed my hair. Anne remembers it better; it was on her birthday.

"When they had the funeral," says Anne, "we all had to go up and look at Momma. I stood there and I just looked to see if she was breathing and she would never move. I kept watching to see if she took a breath, but she never did.

"It was like she was sleeping, that's why I looked for her to breathe any minute. I didn't fully understand, even at fifteen. We were brought up so naive that at my age I still didn't know what death was until she had gone. Then we realized what that meant."

My cousin Honey Davis was also there.

"See, Aunt Dee Dee had been in and out of the hospital and she had her little illnesses. But she would always bounce back. Maybe her health wouldn't be so good, but she would always come home to supervise. No one expected . . .

"Cissy couldn't stop crying. She had on a little white dress and she looked so cute, but she and my uncle both—he was carrying on so terrible. And my father had to hold him and hold my mother. She was taking it so hard. She and Aunt Dee Dee were like sisters. She was fainting and I had my eye on her. She got stiff as a board . . . It was so sad, with all those children hollering. The saddest thing was the older brother, William. He was trying to get into his mother's grave."

Thank God, we had my aunts. Aunt Sally and Tiny came over to our house after the funeral. Aunt Sally was my favorite aunt; I loved her.

"You better not bother that gal," she'd say about me. She had daughters but I was always the baby around her. After the funeral, Aunt Sally cooked and with all my relatives and cousins around, I almost forgot the reason they were at my house. But after the last of the relatives had left, there was no longer any pretending.

"After she left, there was a great sadness in the house," Honey Davis remembers. "Sometimes everybody would get together and just cry. It was a long time before . . . well, I guess things never really did get back to normal."

My mother's death changed everything in my house. To this day, my sisters still don't like to talk about it. After more than fifty years, it still brings tears to their eyes. I think about her all the time. She was so young! Was she happy? I can't really see how she was, having babies every two years. Never really getting to see her children grow to adults. She loved my father, of course, and loved us kids. I wish I had the power to go back in time and make her life happy, buy her things and treat her like the queen she really was. Anything good that's ever happened to me in my life, she's always there in my thoughts. Sometimes I feel guilty for the milestones I've reached and the many ways I've been blessed; with every new milestone I feel as though I'm leaving her behind.

In April 1942, however, I was very far from feelings like this. I was eight years old and needed my mother and missed her terribly. I felt so alone. I would spend many hours out in that woodshed, crying to God. Praying somehow He could bring her back, and if He did, how good I'd be. I'd never climb another tree. Or tear my dress fighting. I'd never slide down that hallway and knock plaster down on Miss Georgia's head. I'd sing like a mockingbird and never have to be called twice to rehearse. I cried my heart out in that woodshed. I must have disappeared in there for a good long while.

"Where you been, girl?" my sisters would ask me.

"Just playin'," I'd say.

I guess they were satisfied with that answer. Because I was the baby, they assumed that after Mommy died I just went back to my kid routine. I did. I had school, I had some girlfriends, like Jolly Dean, Evelyn

Nelson and Cookie Jackson, I had my little haunts. They assumed because I was so young that I hardly understood what had happened. They were right—I didn't. But not understanding what had happened to my mother didn't stop me from having strong feelings. My older sisters knew my mother more intimately, knew more things about her, knew her more as a woman. I knew her less. But that didn't mean I loved her less or missed her less. They gave me a lot of attention: saw to it that I was fed, dressed in clean clothes, made sure I wasn't hanging out with the wrong kids or going into the wrong places. They made sure I was safe. For that I can never repay them. They guided me in a path that led to life.

But they were hurting so bad themselves, they could hardly be expected to know what I really needed. Nor could they give it even if they were so inclined. I needed my mother's love. My aunts, my sisters, Reebie, they did the best they could—they went above and beyond the call of duty. But I missed that love I lost, my mother's love. I was so young when I lost her, eight years old. I can hardly remember much about that love. But I have been looking for it my whole life.

No one asked me how I felt. No teacher, no friend, no relative drew me out in that way. I'm not so sure I would have known what to say had they asked. I'm not so sure I would have *wanted* to talk about it. These weren't such warm and fuzzy times. But the message I got was that this was an inappropriate topic of conversation. "You don't need to be talkin' about that now." I don't remember anyone in my family actually saying that to me; maybe they did and I just blocked it out. But that's the message I heard loud and clear. It took me decades to even think about talking about my mother. Someone should have asked me how I felt. If I felt as if information was being withheld from me about how my mother died, can you imagine the way I felt when nobody would talk about her after she was gone? If I am now as an adult overly suspicious, I know just where it started.

Reebie became my new mother. Lee was also a mother figure to me but she was married and out of the house. So my care and discipline fell to Reebie, the oldest (twenty years old) in the house. I must say that Reebie made the supreme sacrifice for me. She gave up her early life to raise me. She'd already had a few offers of marriage, but with her responsibilities at home, she could hardly give them serious thought. In those days, there was considerable pressure on a woman to be married by eighteen. At twenty years old, you were already getting cockeyed looks from some circles. But Reebie paid that no never mind and took care of raising me. And not just me. She had three under her besides me: Larry (eleven), Nicky (thirteen), and yes, even Annie at fifteen. She was not only our caregiver but also our full-time singing teacher, cook and coach. For my father, she was the de facto momma: she cooked for him, made sure his work clothes were cleaned and pressed and made him his lunches. Each Friday, he would come home from work and hand her his whole paycheck.

Daddy became our focus. After Mommy died, all of our love went over to him. He missed my mother terribly. At forty-six, he had spent half his life married to my mother. She was a good woman, almost a child herself when he found her and fell in love. She submitted her will to his, trusted him and followed him North. They'd survived life on one of the worst streets in Newark. Now the two of them were just realizing their dreams: a nice little place in a good neighborhood, near church, where they could raise their kids in a Christian home. He was always one to keep his feelings wrapped tight. I would hear him crying softly in his bedroom. I wanted to run in and hug him but his door was closed.

I "bonded" with no one after Mommy died. At school, I didn't feel ostracized or strange for not having a mother, though I'm sure I was one of the few kids who didn't. Divorce was not as commonplace then; parents didn't leave, they stuck around to raise their kids. I had some friends, Jolly Dean especially, who helped me forget my pain. We never once talked about my mother; we just cut up an awful lot and she made me laugh. There was a woman from church who had been a friend of my mother's. Miss Hall was sort of a godmother to me and Larry. She got us some things beyond the essentials my father provided that we might not have gotten. Miss Hall bought me my doll, my black doll, and later a nice bathing suit. My aunts continued to reach out to me. Unfortunately, this also meant some days were spent at dreary, dark

Juanita's Down Neck. I begged Annie to come with me but she avoided it and, more often than not, I ended up there alone. Besides her apartment's somber, oppressive mood, all I remember now was staring at the picture of my mother that Juanita had up on the wall. She was the only one in the family who had a picture of my mother. For years, we asked her for it and she refused. She waited until she was nearly dead to lend Reebie the picture so we could copy it and have our own. Better times were spent at Aunt Sally's, where she made our favorite "cheese things" and I got to play with my cousins. Aunt Tiny also came over bringing my cousin Honey.

"I felt so sorry for Cissy," says Honey. "My heart used to go out to her. My mother used to go get her sometimes and bring her over. I felt so sorry for her not having a mother. She was the baby and we all called her 'baby girl' and she became real precious to everyone, for she was so young. There was a lot of sympathy that went out . . . Reebie was a good little substitute, she did what she could, she cooked, she cleaned and she made them all do their share . . . My uncle didn't go berserk, he didn't go haywire, he stayed home and he went to church."

Honey was right. My father didn't go to pieces, and Reebie was a good substitute. She was a great substitute; she looked after me, she kept me in line, she was wonderful. But she was a substitute. I missed my mother's touch, the days I used to stay home with Mommy, watching her cook and listening to *Portia Faces Life* with her. I talked to no one about Mommy dying. When the pain got too great, I found myself going back to the woodshed to cry and pray. But for the most part, I stuffed my feelings away somewhere. I guess I was a tough little kid; I know I was a tough little kid! But I was walking around with a Mommy-size hole in my heart.

As the months wore on, as we tried to recover from the shock of losing the most important person in our lives, we began to take some small steps toward putting our lives back together again. I was old enough now for Reebie to give me some chores, as no doubt my mother would have done. We all had something to do to keep the house humming along. This helped cement a routine back in our midst. In time, even my father returned to normal. He continued at the foundry and never stopped going to church, drawing sustenance from the Word, Reverend and Mrs. Warrick and his duties there. He became more important to us than ever. And we became more important than ever to him. After my mother died, he really took it to heart to continue to take us out to sing. He buried his grief in us. With our faces always before him, at a gospel program, at a quartet association or singing at a local church, he had no time to think of her face.

"He'd come over our house to visit my mother," remembers Honey Davis. "He'd miss his wife so bad, he said the only thing that kept him going was those children. Sometimes at night, he said, he'd go home and wake them up in the night and say, 'Get up and sing me a song.' "

We did not disappoint him. We rehearsed several times a week; a full rehearsal, without fail, every Thursday night. He bought Nicky and Larry some spiffy six-button double-breasted gray suits. We practiced microphone technique with a broomstick, and as we started to sing on some of Newark's gospel programs with promoters like Ronnie Williams, Lee was pressed into service as our business manager.

If it wasn't for singing, I don't know what would have happened to us. Singing, rehearsing kept us together. We were never lonely for somebody to play with, that's what saved me. We were still singing quartet at that time. Later on, when Nicky started playing piano, we graduated to gospel. But quartet was without music, we sang a cappella.

Today, gospel leans more toward praise. Gospel got more personal, more emotional when instruments were added. It picked up that gospel beat. But the material we sang in quartet was really a throwback to the old spirituals; stories about hard times, things that had to do with living in that era—all the way back to slavery. Sung without music; just perfect harmony. "You'd Better Min'," that was one of the old spirituals we did as a quartet.

> *You'd better min' how you talk,*
> *You'd better min' what you talk about,*
> *Got to give account in Judgment,*
> *You'd better min'.*

Then we also did "We're Living on Borrowed Time."

> *Oh, we're living down here*
> *On borrowed time, Lord,*
> *We're living down here*
> *On borrowed time, Lord,*
> *We're living down here*
> *On borrowed time*
> *And I don't want my living*
> *To be in vain.*

We knew these gospel tunes by heart. The words, the music, the rhythms, the meaning, it all seemed to be part of us. Week to week we practiced and sang, but even more importantly, we lived those songs. That's why we understood so well both the sorrow and the triumph, the low points and high notes of God's judgments and blessings. Especially now that Mommy was gone, the familiar gospel hymns took on a deeper meaning for me.

We joined a Quartet Association that put us on a circuit of churches and programs where other quartets would appear. One of the bonuses of being part of that organization was the yearly convention in Atlantic City. Not only did we have family down there but we also got to go swimming in the ocean. I loved it! But we had only one bathing suit, which was stretched to fit everybody. It was a blue bathing suit. I must have been eleven years old. It was my bathing suit, but it was stretched to the full extent of my sister Reebie. Me, Annie and Reebie had to use the same suit. I'd be in the water enjoying myself and Reebie would call me out. Annie needed the suit. Then she'd stay in the water forever and Reebie would call her out. Then Reebie would put it on. I would cry and cry and cry, but that's the way it was.

I could never stay mad at Reebie, though. This girl had a lot on her plate. She was not only the chief mover behind the Drinkard Quartet; she was also in charge of the house—making sure groceries were bought, meals were prepared, my father's clothes were clean and his lunches were made. On top of all that, she also had to mind us—me, Annie, Nicky and Larry. It would have been a big job for any woman but Reebie was just twenty years old. It required a special kind of person and some supernatural help!

"My life after my mother had passed . . . I'll tell you this," says Reebie, "I had to take over where she had left off. Because there were five left under me—Hank, Annie, Nicky, Larry and Cissy. Because my dad was a praying man and he prayed for his children, after my mother passed I had to become a praying person too. My conversion had come before my mother died, as a child in the storefront Holiness church on Mercer Street. You accept the Lord at conversion, and as you grow each day, it becomes stronger.

"But as a teenager, you will slide back. That's what happened to me. I used to love to dance; I was a great dancer. But just before my mother died, the Lord got ahold of me one Sunday in church. I just went haywire! It was a feeling that you just can't explain. God was in control of me . . . my mind, my heart, my soul, everything. It was such a beautiful feeling, there's no explanation for it. Everyone needs to experience it for themselves.

"Everything changed; everything became brand new. The way I used to love to dance—now I loved to serve God.

"Singing became different for me too. Like the song says, 'I sing because I'm happy, I sing because I'm free,' it feels like everything just goes and I lose myself into what I'm singing. It's a great joy, a great uplift to me. I have no control over it because it's coming from within and it's true. It's very true.

"You can't explain how you feel. You're giving God praise and the song you're singing, you're applying it to your own life. And self is gone. God has taken over.

"You've got to be truthful with yourself. If you are somebody else out there, the audience will feel you. Many groups perform. But gospel isn't about 'performing.' It's giving God reverence, giving Him praise, and it comes from within. You can't just say, 'I'm gonna do this thing like this group or that singer.' That's performing. First, you've got to be born again. There's no doubt about that. You can't half-step with this thing. A true gospel singer—you've got to have the Spirit of God within you."

I guess I was still "half-steppin'." I know I loved to sing with my brothers and sisters. But I didn't know what I was really singing about. Unlike Reebie, I also loved to dance!

Every Saturday morning, as soon as Reebie and my father left the house, Annie and I would crank up that old Victrola and put on the latest record she'd bought. She loved Billie Holiday. Annie sat on the bed and studied Lady Day's picture on the record jacket. I just studied the sound and swayed around the room to the dreamy beat. Dinah Washington was really my style, though. I didn't know it at the time but Dinah had started as a gospel singer in Chicago with the Roberta Martin Singers, a female quartet we'd soon be sharing the same stage with. Wherever she came from, I loved what she put on "Smile" and I waltzed myself around the room to it all day long.

> *Smile when you're feeling blue,*
> *Smile and it might come true . . .*

Jimmy Witherspoon was also one of our all-time favorites. Annie bought the records every Friday down at Lubinsky's record store on Market Street. She had gotten a really good job at ODB, the Office of Dependent Benefits. This World War II-era government office made sure that the dependents of GIs overseas got their checks. Annie was a real pioneer: at sixteen she was part of the first big government hire of blacks in Newark. She went to work dressed nice, with heels every day at the "Pru"—the twenty-story Prudential building that the government took over.

She never knew it, but I admired her so much. I'd look up at her like she was Alice in Wonderland: tall, slim, light complexion. She had nice things to wear, her own friends and always somewhere exciting to go. It would be a few years before I was old enough to hang out with her. In the meantime, I had my own little gang.

I'd probably known Jolly Dean since kindergarten. But we didn't get real tight until fifth or sixth grade. She caught me still halfway in my tomboy stage, before I discovered Ernest. He comes later. I was a good fighter; my brothers Larry and Nicky had taught me well. That's how Jolly and I palled out so tight. Jolly was real tough—wanted to beat up the boys. But she'd much rather be laughing with me. She was taller than me, a little bit overweight, and like the rest of us she wore an elastic band around her head and some bangs. Jolly lived just down the block from me on Waverly Avenue. Like me, she was the baby of her family— one of eleven children. Jolly was her real name. It seems that after eleven children, her mother just ran out of regular names. Her mother was religious, went to the Baptist church. Jolly's father was a real thrifty man. While we were still on Hillside Place, that man with eleven children and a job at the bakery had saved enough money to buy a house in the neighborhood.

Jolly and I were always laughing. If she wasn't snapping on someone in the crowd in some hilarious manner, then she was snapping under her breath at the teacher. But that didn't happen too often in sixth grade at Charlton Street School. That was the year we both had Miss Preston—the meanest teacher in the school. If you were bad in Miss Preston's class, she would make you put your seat up and sit in the hole between the seat and the desk in those old-fashioned school seats. Even then, we thought this was child abuse.

"Look out," Jolly would whisper. "She's gonna Prestonize you!"

That word produced even more gales of laughter. Miss Preston's class was also the first class Jolly played hooky from. Jolly would leave at lunchtime and never come back. She was so silly, she'd go across the street to Juanita Gurley's house to eat and play records. It's a wonder Miss Preston didn't see Jolly herself from the window. I tried to talk her out of playing hooky. But that was Jolly, a little daring and full of fun. Like me, she never used her fighting prowess to monster anyone. She always took up for the underdog.

Once she took up for a new girl in class named Dolly Bernard. Her first day in class, Dolly had been threatened by Moselle Wells, from

Prince Street. Moselle didn't say a word; she just looked across the room at Dolly, balled her fist up and placed it over her eye—the universal symbol for "you're getting a black eye after school." Jolly diffused the situation by taking up for Dolly—but not without skirting a potentially dangerous rumble. Moselle Wells was from Prince Street, the bad neighborhood I was born in.

"We wouldn't even *attempt* to go around there," recalls Jolly. "Girls over there would beat you up just for looking prettier than them."

After school, Jolly and some other girls in the crowd hung out in the after-school activity room. They'd play ball, do arts and crafts. But I had to go straight home! I had Reebie-designated chores to do and a pretty rigid schedule.

After I finished my chores, I struck out on my own or with Larry and Nicky in tow. We met up with the crowd over on Charlton Street. The crowd consisted of Jolly, Evelyn Nelson, Evelyn Cooper from Broome Street, Cookie (Barbara) Jackson and Betty Boo from Charlton Street. Evelyn Nelson was petite, five foot one, dark and considered fine. As a matter of fact, her nickname was "Black Beauty." Evelyn and I became fast friends because she too could take care of herself in a fight. Her boyfriend was Spivvy O'Neal. The O'Neals had money and lived over in the new projects on Somerset. Spivvy had taken dance lessons from Bill "Bojangles" Robinson. Spivvy and Evelyn would later marry. Cookie Jackson didn't fight but she could sing—not gospel, just popular tunes. She liked my brother Larry, who was generally irresistible to girls. Me, Larry and Nicky would "entertain" the crowd by singing for them by the stoop—mostly popular tunes.

"Go ahead," Evelyn Nelson would snap. "Who do you think you are . . . Sarah Vaughan?"

Of course, "Sassy" was a Newark native, one of our most famous singing stars. She was a good deal older than us, but she was just starting her career then during the war, in the clubs right in our neighborhood. The Piccadilly, Lloyd's Manor, Emmett's were the restaurants and clubs that featured name entertainment like Dinah Washington, Billie Holiday, Arthur Prysock and Ruth Brown. And these performers didn't just do a "fly-in." They lived the Newark high life—eating, drinking, jamming and staying at the Coleman ("For Negroes Only") Hotel on Court Street. They said that Billie Holiday was even going with a guy named Melvin over on Dickson Street. Bebop jazz played by little combos was also the rage in these nightspots.

At the time, of course, these clubs were off-limits to us. But each neighborhood had its own little place that catered to the kids. In Evelyn's neighborhood on Charlton Street there was the Canteen, sometimes known as Graham Auditorium. They held dances here, with live music; admission was a dollar. More often than not, though, you went into places like this after school for a hot dog and a soda and danced to the jukebox. There was Liquor Jim's in Jolly and Evelyn's neighborhood where they jitterbugged and danced the Philly Dog to records by Buddy and Ella Johnson, Ruth Brown and B. B. King. I was never allowed in Liquor Jim's. If Reebie would have caught me in there, I would have paid with my life! Evelyn and Jolly still remember Reebie pulling me out of places like that.

But I did sneak into the Green Lantern. This was one of those neighborhood places across the street from our house on Hillside Place. Ooooh, I could dance and I played all the records I could and ate potato chips in that place until Reebie caught up with me. I got a good beating for being in that place. But I never fought her. First, it was unthinkable to raise a hand to my sister, who had now taken my mother's place. I was also secretly relieved to be reeled back into the family nest. There were things out in that world that I was afraid of. The allure of the music was there, I won't deny that. But there were some other aspects of the scene that scared me, having been raised so sheltered. There were junkies—cool-looking sophisticated junkies who hung out at some of these nightclubs. Even at restaurants like Emmett's, the cool fellows smoked reefer outside. I didn't understand these things; they repulsed me. I couldn't see how anyone would want to be part of something that would steal their money and their looks. Sometimes I'd see women junkies on Spruce Street—emaciated, stopping men on the street, ready to do anything to get money enough for their next fix.

At heart, I was a big daddy's girl, a sheep who'd strayed from her pen at 38 Hillside Place. I was really happy to be back in my father's house, even if it took a beating to get me there.

Make no mistake about it, although Reebie administered the discipline the penal code was established by my father. It was his idea that I not visit places like the Green Lantern, his idea that I not be on the street past dusk and his idea that I rehearse, do my chores and obey Reebie. He was continuing the same plan he had for our lives before my mother had died. But now he was trying to put our family back together again. We knew this instinctively, and rather than dealing with our feelings of loss, we gave him complete and loving sway in our lives. He was a good daddy, a little strict, but he was good. We loved him.

My father measured out our days, weeks and years on a pretty rigid schedule. Sundays was church. All day. Sometimes, evening services. Weekdays, we were to come straight home from school, finish any chores that might have been left undone, then go out to play. The boys washed and waxed the floors. There was washing and ironing for us girls. My father came home around five o'clock and we were to be upstairs before dusk. Daddy relaxed, read his paper and smoked a Camel in the living room until Reebie had dinner on the table. Then we all sat down to eat together. After dinner, each of us had our own week to do the dishes. When that was done, we'd rehearse in the living room while Daddy supervised. Thursday night, in particular, was a rehearsal night. Friday or Saturday night we usually sang in different churches as part of a Quartet Association program.

Daddy continued to stay active at St. Luke's. He performed his trustee duties, counted and deposited the church's weekly offering. He was present at every church service there was and made sure we were there too. African Endeavor Christian League on Sunday nights and revival on Tuesday nights. Reverend Warrick still paid Daddy visits at home. But besides Reverend Warrick, he never brought a man friend home. He had girls and he was protecting them. Every so often, I would still hear him crying in his room. Many a time, I'd get up in the middle of the night and see him sitting alone in the living room, smoking in the dark, his glowing cigarette the only light in the room.

When the war ended, my father was waiting to minister to Hank, in whatever way he could. Hank had served in the Philippines. A shell had exploded so near him, it permanently damaged his hearing. God knows what else he saw there. He never told us, but he was never the same Hanky. My father did what he could for him. He was twenty years old and needed a job. So Daddy took him to work with him at the foundry.

The routine of chores, church and rehearsal bore fruit. We were called to sing in Philadelphia, in Washington and in many other churches in the metropolitan area.

Then Nicky picked up piano. There was a family named Miller in the next building. They had a piano and Nicky learned how to play it without even a lesson. It was something incredible, almost as astonishing as finding out we could all sing. Nicky began to accompany us when we sang. What we lost in Nicky as a singer, we gained threefold in him as an instrumentalist. We were now able to return to our first love—gospel music, the first Christian music we heard as children at the storefront Holiness church. These were our roots.

Even our rehearsals became more exciting. Reebie threw herself into teaching us the music that she most enjoyed. We left behind the rigidly prescribed harmony parts of quartet and the old spirituals. We had graduated to the "new" music and we enjoyed the freedom we had to improvise and solo. Gospel was like a new tool, a way of singing we had fun applying in unexpected settings. We put the gospel beat behind some old hymns and ballads. We "gospelized" "He Can Turn the Tide," "I Believe" and the poem "Trees." We even took an old spiritual, "Listen to the Lambs," and turned it into a gospel selection.

Listen to the lambs, listen to the lambs,
Listen to the lambs, all a-crying,
I want to go to heaven when I die.
Come on, sister, with your ups and downs,
Want to go to heaven when I die.
Angels waiting for to give you a crown,
Want to go to heaven when I die . . .

Gospel was just starting to catch on. Churches were open to it as they weren't before. People began to talk about us. Herman Lubinsky, the man who owned the record store over on Market Street where Annie bought her Billie Holiday records, wanted to record us on his Savoy label. The Coleman Brothers inquired through Aunt Flossie if they could record me solo—gospel, pop, whatever I wanted. My father killed that deal in a heartbeat. I'm glad he did too. I wasn't ready for all that then. Still, looking back years later, I could have stood the encouragement.

"My father didn't aspire for us to be 'stars,' " says Annie. "He just wanted us to stay together and sing. He believed in the message, that gospel music was a message in song. I don't think he particularly cared about the money either. Because we sang for nothing many, many times.

"He was proud of us. Everywhere he went he just wanted everyone to know that these were his children and that they could sing without any formal training."

Even though we were becoming known in the New York metro area, even though we had already started appearing on the gospel shows of Ronnie Williams, one of the Northeast's biggest gospel promoters, and even though we were being asked to record by the foremost gospel label, Daddy still kept us sheltered, kept us close. Even when we visited his sisters' houses in the neighborhood, we rarely went without him. I was twelve years old and I still wasn't allowed to go to parties—even in our neighborhood—especially in our neighborhood. I would beg for permission all week; ninety-nine percent of the time, I wasn't allowed to go. In a strange way, I was glad not to go. These parties were unsupervised and were among the first places where girls would become pregnant.

One day, I was riding one of my brothers' bikes. I had no business on that bike; the seat was way too high for me. But I wanted to prove I could ride anything they could. I fell down on that bike and hurt myself. The seat went up between my legs with such force that my genitals swelled up.

Lee took me to the doctor. I was embarrassed to have the doctor look at me there. But more embarrassed when he asked me whether I had gotten my period yet. I hadn't. Lots of girls I knew had it already. I was beginning to wonder when I would get mine.

My father went nuts. He wanted to kill! He thought some boy had bothered me and he was going down in the street to look for him. He would have killed somebody for me. That was how much he loved me.

We would have killed for him too. We loved him with the love we would have given to two parents. We worried about him. Not just because, as children, we were afraid we'd lose another parent, but because we knew how devastated he had been by my mother's death. She was a wonderful mommy; we would never forget her. But now we had to look after Daddy. We had always loved him, but now we drew even closer through our daily routines.

We waited for him, looked for him to come home from work every day. We sat down and ate dinner together every day—there wasn't a day that we didn't. No basketball team practice, no Girl Scout meeting prevented it. On Tuesday night we went to church with him, on Thursday night we rehearsed in front of him, on Friday night he took us somewhere to sing.

We seemed to be putting the pieces back together again. We had a good little family life. That's why it was all the more shocking when my father sat us down one evening and announced he was getting married. When we heard to whom, I almost fainted.

SIX

How precious did that grace appear,
The hour I first believed.
— *"Amazing Grace"*

From my father's announcement, it was apparent that we had severely misjudged him. I suppose we naively thought we could
meet his needs, fill up his lonely days and nights. Of course, we
couldn't. After Mommy died, my father didn't go off the deep end.
Nonetheless, he was hurting inside. It had been six years, a long time
since he, now a robust fifty-two-year-old, had been with a companion.
We couldn't expect him to wait much longer before he found happiness, some female companionship again. He was a good daddy, he
deserved to marry again, we told ourselves. But I was in shock. I just
couldn't get used to the idea that I would have to share Daddy with
anyone. None of us could come to grips with his choice of a woman.

Her name was Viola Jewel and she was ten years younger than
Daddy. Attractive enough, I guess, Viola was a little bit full of herself.
She called herself "young Viola," practically referred to herself in the
third person. He'd met her in church.

She was so unlike my mother. My mother was quiet, a homebody.
Viola was always running here and there. My mother was a devout
churchgoer, ministering in the church like a woman from Bible times.
Looking after the children of the church, inquiring after the sick and
the elderly. Viola had lots of other interests besides church. Most of all,
Viola saw how much we children dominated my father's life—how
important we were to him. And she aimed to change that.

"My uncle was a good-looking man," says my cousin Honey. "All the women in that church were after him. Viola Jewel took her time, she got close to him first."

We were further frustrated because my sisters and I already had someone picked out for Daddy. A nice woman in the church who was more my father's age and temperament.

I said nothing to Daddy, I was too disappointed and hurt. And besides, I knew that once my father's mind was made up, he didn't change it. That didn't stop Lee, Annie and even Reebie from trying to talk him out of Viola. Of course, the more they protested, the firmer he became in his convictions. The only thing they did was increase the backlash of resentment Viola would bring into our house when she eventually moved in. That was only a matter of time. She had a son by a previous marriage whom her mother was watching. Once she squared that situation away, she was on her way to 38 Hillside Place.

I was probably of a mind to give Viola a chance because I always take up for the underdog. I'll give anybody a chance, at least once. Besides, I reasoned, if Daddy really loved this woman, who were we to interfere in his happiness?

Right away Viola got off on the wrong foot with Annie. I don't know what it was about, but Viola's attitude was something pitiful. Just the way she locked up her food in our house was rude. She locked up sugar with a padlock. My brother Nicky busted the lock one day while she was out of the house. That didn't sit too well with her. She didn't know who did it and nobody would fess up. She assumed it was either Larry or Nicky, so she had it in for both of them. She got sick of both these teenagers hanging around the house, eating the food she bought (with my father's money). So she hatched a plot to drive both of them from our house. She seduced my father into thinking that Larry and Nicky would both be better off, broadened even, by a little travel. She suggested they both go up to Boston, where my father's sister Ruby lived. Ruby's husband would get them both a job on the docks.

I cried the day Nicky and Larry packed their bags and headed for Penn Station. I had given Viola a fair chance. But with this latest stunt, she made me sorry I had ever treated her nice. She had sent away my beloved brothers—my playmates, my protectors.

"Viola was jealous of all his children," says my cousin Honey. "She thought she was doing him so much good, 'cause he didn't look his age at all."

I don't know about all that. My father was smoking more than ever now. If Viola relaxed him so much, why was he smoking so much? He'd even developed a dry, hacking cough.

"Those children . . . I mean, who could take Aunt Dee Dee's place?" says Honey. "They don't even make women like that anymore. They stopped making that breed a long time ago . . . He used to come over to our house and cry. He used to come over and cry about the situation, the tension between the children and the wife and the way things were going. Like he said, he never would have looked at another woman had his Dee Dee been living. But he knew his wife was gone and she'd never come back. Life had to go on. But if she had been living, or if there was anything he could have given to bring her back, even if it meant his right arm or his eye, he would have done it. But he couldn't and he had grieved a long time. He told my mother and father that."

My beloved Larry and Nicky were gone. And just Viola Jewel's presence in my house made me miss my mother all over again. Then, the same month my father announced his plans to marry Viola Jewel, Reebie announced her plans. She would marry Joe Epps at the end of the month!

I had nothing against Joe Epps. He was a neighborhood guy who lived two houses away from us on the corner—a real sweetheart. He had grown up the oldest in a single-parent house, a bunch of brothers and sisters under him. Like Reebie, who was the "momma" in her house, Joe grew up the "father" in his house. Joe and Reebie had waited to marry until Joe had come out of the service and two years beyond that until Reebie thought things, like raising me, were under control. Now they couldn't wait anymore. Reebie was twenty-five years old already, plenty old enough to get married. I had no argument with Reebie's happiness; Joe was a great guy. But he was taking away the only mother I'd known since Mommy died. Sure, she beat my butt and ran me out of the Green Lantern and hounded me until I did my chores. But she loved me and I loved her. She fixed my meals and cared about the way I looked before I left the house. I was always "her baby." Ironically, she and Joe would never have children; so, for the rest of her life, I would remain the closest thing to her own baby.

Now, in the same month my father was withdrawing from my life with Viola, Reebie was also leaving me for Joe. My house, my haven of rest was shaking. Whatever stability I knew there since my mother died—my father's sure return every evening from work, Reebie's fixing dinner, hanging out with my two brothers—was being shaken. Where could I go now for love and security?

Ernest Spears gave me the attention I craved. Lots of guys liked me at school, but I usually wasn't interested.

That changed with Ernie. I guess Ernie was the first guy I really loved. We started going together around sixth grade, but because my family thought I was too young to date, I had to keep him a secret. I went with him almost into high school. In all that time, he wasn't up to my house once; we never went on a date, I had to meet him in secret at the playground or at a party. He only ever met two members of my family: Larry and Nicky. They knew about him and they kept my secret.

He was one of Evelyn Nelson's cousins. I don't remember how we originally met but I'd noticed him at Charlton Street School way before the sixth grade. He was a year older than me and good-looking. He was built beautifully—a dark, black, smooth, wonderful-looking guy. He was a Golden Gloves boxer and he didn't like anybody else talking to me.

Kids today don't know how lucky they are. They can go on dates, they can go to a movie together. I couldn't do any of that. Kids didn't socialize in each other's houses then. Well, if you spent enough private time somewhere with someone, you were liable to get pregnant. And back then that was the worst possible thing in the world that you could do. You were totally ostracized if you let that happen.

Your home was private, just you and your immediate family; maybe a relative or two were your only visitors. The only places kids had to socialize were the after-school activity center, which I wasn't allowed to attend, the playground and the local juke joint like the Green Lantern— also off-limits for me. The place where Ernie and I met up each week was the movie theater. If Larry, Nicky and I finished our chores by one o'clock on Saturday we could go to the National Theater on Belmont Avenue. It was twenty-five cents to get in and a nickel for popcorn. If Reebie left us some extra money, we'd buy a Dixie Cup with the movie star's picture on the inside of the lid. They showed serials then; Roy Rogers, the Green Hornet and newsreels. My favorite actress was Maureen O'Hara; she was pretty, redheaded and tough. The National was a total kid environment, a place to meet your friends and pull stunts you never could have dreamed of getting away with in your house. When Jolly was eleven, the matron busted her down front, smoking a cigarette. She embarrassed Jolly all the way up the aisle as she ejected her from the theater.

I stayed all the way down front too. Ernest and I parked ourselves in the third row and kissed through three showings of the same movie. Today, Evelyn Nelson swears I had to get glasses because I ruined my eyesight sitting so close to the screen at the National with Ernie. Please. Who was watching the movie anyway?

It was all very innocent, actually. The worst thing that happened was I probably left the National with chapped lips.

I was reaching out for something: the love I lost when my mother died, the love I still craved while my sisters raised me. And now the attention my father could no longer lavish on me as the baby, since he had Viola Jewel in his life.

I felt guilty about sneaking around. Ernest was one year older than I and probably wanted more from me than I could give. People at my age were already becoming sexually active. Some girls had to leave school because they were pregnant. That's not what I wanted for my life. I knew what I was. I wasn't like other girls; I was raised different. I was raised in church.

I wondered if Ernest would wait or if he would get fed up with me, his little church girl. At the same time I wondered what was right; how far could I go to hold on to Ernie, to let him know I cared, without . . . ? I was so naive. I knew nothing about my anatomy, about a man, about men and women together. I was really a little girl playing in a grown-up world. These things were never discussed in my house; I had nowhere to turn. At least Lee had the benefit of all that time with Mommy. Mommy had married very young; she'd been there, she knew just what it felt like to be me right now. I could have talked to her about anything. If only I had her now.

I knew I couldn't talk to Reebie. Things were either black or white with her. She'd cite chapter and verse to you from the Bible. Lee was a little more lenient, a little more willing to admit that life wasn't all black and white, that there were plenty of gray areas. But talking to Lee was also out of the question. If either of them suspected I was even thinking about such things, they wouldn't have let me out of the house! I had to keep it to myself, or find someone outside my house to talk to.

I found some of what I needed to know hanging around some of the fast girls. Girls I'd seen at the Green Lantern. Alberta, for one. She had a lot of style. The girl could dance, she could skate and she dressed wonderfully. She was one of the coolest-looking people in the neighborhood. And she'd had boyfriends young; I mean, very young, she started early.

You didn't even need to pose a question around girls like this. Sex was a constant ingredient in their conversation. All I had to do was grab a booth at the Lantern with one or more of them, slouch down and keep my ears open. If I was shocked or surprised at their escapades, I never showed it. I acted like I was doing the same—or more—with my man. Of course, I wasn't doing more than petting with Ernie. But the consensus around the Green Lantern was if you really loved the guy, I mean really loved the guy, you gave it up.

I loved Ernie; why shouldn't we go all the way? I fantasized about marrying him one day, having children together and being blissfully happy and in love.

Who was I kidding! I may have worked up a pretty good game face for the fast older girls at the Green Lantern—bragging that I'd done this and that with my man. Even with Ernie, I made out with him furiously, passionately. But there was something I couldn't tell him. Something I could never tell the fast girls at the Green Lantern or I'd die of embarrassment: I was almost fifteen years old and I hadn't even gotten my period yet! Who was I to daydream about marrying Ernie and having his children? I wasn't even a woman yet! Real women could have babies. Jolly, Evelyn—I looked at them as the luckiest people on earth. They'd had their periods for a few years already; they didn't have to deal with the questions, the agony I was dealing with. Maybe my accident with that boy's bike had messed me up inside. My mind was racing from one explanation to another; each one seemed more crazy than the next. But at the end of the day, they were not so crazy. For every time I went to the bathroom—at school, at home; I even went extra times just to look—hoping, praying that I would be surprised, it was always just like before. I felt no different. I would get some sad feeling in class in the middle of the day and brighten, thinking it was the "blues" that girls talked about getting just before they got their monthlies. But it wasn't. I had no one to tell, no one to talk to and it was driving me mad with worry.

I would get moody, quiet. Ernie took it as rejection and would stand me up sometimes. When we were together, he'd just badger me to go further than I wanted. When I resisted, he accused me of not loving him anymore. I wished I could tell him about the things that were really on my mind, what I was agonizing over for months now. But I couldn't. I couldn't take the chance that he would leave me because I wasn't like other girls—because I was convinced I could never have his children.

We "agreed" to break up and I was miserable. I stayed home, alone and lonely, the whole week. I didn't always see him at school and I couldn't always get out of the house at night to be where I thought he might be. We had no phone, so he couldn't call me. He certainly couldn't visit my house. But he sent no word through any of my friends or his friends. When the weekend passed with no word from him, when Jolly told me Monday she'd seen him at the National with some other girl, I thought he would never see me again.

On Tuesday, before dinner, my father told me he was moving. He couldn't take the tension in the house between us and Viola. My brothers were back in the house, the broken padlock was fresh again in Viola's mind and she didn't have to live in an environment that was hostile toward her. I thought about what it would be like living in the house without Daddy. I would miss him, but I could always walk up to see him on Livingston Street. In the meantime, I had my dear brothers, Nicky and Larry, back from Boston; I had Annie. This was home even if Daddy was living somewhere else.

Then my father lowered the boom. He felt I was too young to stay in the house without adult supervision. I had to come with him. I couldn't believe what he was saying to me. He was expecting me to leave my house, the only one I knew, the house of my mother and my brothers and sisters, and go live in some strange woman's home? Sleep in some strange bed? I could see *him* going. He'd taken a new wife: he had to think about her, her comforts. She wasn't comfortable in our house, I could understand. But why did I have to leave my house? What about the way I felt? *What about me, Daddy?*

I ran out of the house. I knew once Daddy had made up his mind there was no changing it. I wandered down Hillside Place and made a right onto Charlton Street. I passed Cookie's house looking for some of the kids who hung out by her stoop. There was no one there. I continued walking and passed our church, St. Luke's. I was almost to the next corner, when something made me turn around and walk back to church.

It was Tuesday night, there was a service starting in a half hour. I sat down in a back pew just to think for a while. There was some activity up front; the speaker was adjusting his papers in the pulpit. It was Reverend Odum; he spoke a lot at the church. I guess Reverend Warrick respected him since he invited him back so much; Reverend Warrick never gave that pulpit up to anyone. I saw Mrs. Warrick up front but I ducked my head down; I didn't really want to talk to anyone tonight.

I just wanted to think. I had a lot on my mind; too much on my mind for a kid my age. I had to think about moving out of my house now. This was my house! I was used to things the way they were; I was used to my privacy. I wasn't used to bouncing around, let alone moving somewhere strange. I couldn't bear to be separated from Nicky and Larry again; they'd only just come home. And I wasn't moving just anywhere, but with Viola Jewel. She'd probably be fussy about her food just like she'd been in our house. Only now I'd be living in her house. I wouldn't have Nicky, Larry or Annie around to back me up. It wasn't just her in the house either. She had her mother in the house with her, and a son, around my age. Oh, I'd probably get a whole lot of privacy with him around!

Why did Daddy have to go off and marry this woman anyway? Didn't he care at all for the way we felt? Didn't he care anything for me?

I looked up. Reverend Odum was speaking now but I drifted off again. I was thinking about Ernie; dear, sweet Ernie, my first love, my only love. What happened to all the dreams we had? Was I dreaming alone? Did all our time together mean nothing to him? Why was he running away from me now, just when I needed him most? Why couldn't he understand who I really was, the way I was raised, what was right and what was wrong? What I could do and what I couldn't do? Maybe he felt he'd seen the real me and wasn't interested anymore.

Well, Jolly had already seen him with someone new. He was sick of his little church girl now. And even if we were to run away, even if I were to give myself completely to him—what did I have to give? What kind of man would want a woman who couldn't have children? Ernie was right to go get someone normal.

I started to cry. I was at the end of my rope. I felt so rejected, so misunderstood, so unwanted—by Ernie, by my father, even by Reebie, who was also leaving me. I looked out through my tears at the church. I saw the Dawsons, the Millers, the Coxes, all of my friends who sat there with their mothers and fathers. I hated them all because they were normal. These girls didn't know how lucky they were, having a mother to talk to, and a father who wasn't dragging them off to live in a strange woman's house. I cried. I cried for the mother I didn't have, whom I still missed, who left me too soon. I felt so unloved, so unlovely, so bitter and unable to be loved.

"Count your blessings!" The voice startled me from the pulpit. It was Reverend Odum.

"Yessir! Count your blessings, young man, young woman, mother, dad," he shouted. "Where would you be right now if not for God? Did he wake you up this morning?" the Reverend shouted.

"Yesss . . . ," the congregation answered him.

"Did he put the breath of life in your lungs this morning?" he pressed them.

"Well . . . ," moaned an old deacon down front.

"Then give Him praise!" the Reverend shouted. "Is He worthy to be praised? Then give Him praise!"

Then the pianist started a song. The melody was familiar, but I had never paid much attention to the words. It was as if I was hearing them for the first time.

> *Count your blessings,*
> *Name them one by one.*
> *Count your blessings,*
> *See what God has done.*
> *Counnnt your blessings,*
> *Name them one by one.*
> *Count your many blessings,*
> *See what God has done!*

All of a sudden I started to think about what God had done for me—even at fourteen years old. It was almost as if I had stepped outside my body and I was watching my life unfold like a movie. I began to see the different places in my life where everything could have gone horribly wrong, like hundreds of other poor families in Newark. When my mother died, I saw how my father could have gone to pieces, lost it completely, turned to alcohol, beat us up, abused us. How my older sisters could have left our house, married the first guy—the wrong guy—who paid them the attention they missed getting from my mother. How Larry and Nicky could have run away or hung out in the streets with the wrong crowd. How I could have been abandoned and at a young age gone looking for anything that would muffle the pain in my heart—alcohol, maybe even drugs on Spruce Street.

But that's not what happened. My father was a good daddy who went to work every day and stayed active in church and loved me. And my sisters didn't run off. God had raised up Reebie, who would never have her own children but would get to raise me. Train me and watch me like a hawk and whip my butt when I got too close to the riffraff whose high style, booze and drugs would have eventually stolen my life. I had the love of family. My dear brothers, Larry and Nicky, who loved me and protected me out in the street, in school and everywhere I tagged along with them. I had dear, sweet Annie, who also looked after me, and Lee, another surrogate mother. I had friends . . . like Jolly Dean, Evelyn Nelson and Cookie Jackson.

And I had God, who met me in the woodshed; when I cried to Him that I couldn't take no more. He lifted me up and carried me through the dark days and the darkest nights. When sleep eluded me, I felt Him rock me to sleep in my own bed. I started to thank Him for everything He was to me—a father . . . a mother . . . a friend—for I saw Him in all these people, loving me through each one of them. And as I thanked Him, I began to praise Him and give Him glory. I raised my arms to praise Him and felt a glow, a warmth flow through my body that was not of this world. I was transported, high and lifted up. From inside me I felt a river of joy rising up in me, so powerful, its flow I could not stem. I opened my mouth and felt myself first talking, then singing and laughing for joy—a joy I had never felt before. I felt the Spirit coursing through my body and I just surrendered to it; I could have resisted, but why? It was the most wonderful feeling I had ever experienced.

As I walked home that night, I felt different. Something had happened to me. Everything looked different somehow. I felt God's presence all around me. In the wind that chilled my face, in the sound of the nightbirds singing, and in the millions of stars twinkling in the sky. It was as if I was seeing the world for the first time.

Was blind but now I see . . .

In the world around me I suddenly saw the hand of the Creator, busy at work creating and maintaining the wonders of the universe—yet, He was not too far off to be close to me.

God was real. I felt Him that night for myself. I wanted to serve Him now. And I wanted to sing for Him.

SEVEN

All that I've tried to do
Would not have been possible,
But through God.
He has been my dwelling place,
On this I rest my case.
—*"He Leadeth Me"*

I had grown up in church. I had attended countless services, youth rallies, revival services, but through all of this I had not felt God for myself. I was doing His work but I just didn't know what it was all about. Up until that Tuesday night, I was just coasting on the spiritual experience of my father and Reebie. It took coming to the end of my rope, the end of all my resources, to allow God to work in my life. But He did. Suddenly I could see Him leading me my whole life right to this point.

I was grateful to Reebie for running me out of the Green Lantern. I had never been a follower, but I wanted to follow those girls with their cool clothes and their great dancing. What I couldn't have known then was that lots of those girls would become junkies. Who knows where those girls would have led me and how far I would have followed?

My problems seemed to dim since that night. I went to live with my father at Viola's house on Livingston Street, several blocks from Hillside Place. Actually, it wasn't so bad after all. She had a mother who lived there and was a sweetheart. Viola also had a sister staying there who was nice to me as well. God had set a table in the midst of my "enemies." Even Ernest was not as important in my life anymore. As I rose into high school we got back together again, but couldn't seem to shake that "makeup-to-breakup" syndrome. When I finally broke down and told Annie how worried I was about not having my period yet, she told me that some girls just got it late. Especially girls that were active and sports-minded (like me). I eventually got it when I was seventeen.

I found myself feeling even closer to my father now. I had begun to live the life of faith like him. I understood the miracle of faith—believing in something unseen as if it were seen. God was no longer a mysterious thing. He was a person, in whose love I was now confident. I believed that He loved me so much that had I been the only person on earth, He would have sent His son to die for me. I learned that faith was a gift and I had been blessed with a plentiful supply. I didn't question His Word—I just believed. I grew stronger, reflecting on the role model my father was to us. How he did everything with prayer, how he prayed continually throughout the day and how he kept God prevalent in his thoughts. I realized there was no luck; there were only blessings. And most people miss out on their share, simply by not asking their heavenly Father for them.

I caught my father's vision, I now understood, why he wanted us to sing. Singing gospel was an end unto itself. You didn't have to get famous doing it or get a pile of money. There wasn't anywhere "to get," no milestone to reach. It was much more sublime than that. I'd just never had ears to hear before.

It was enough just to sing, because in singing you fulfilled its entire purpose: gospel singing was a ministry. Half of it was directed inward, the other half was directed outward. In singing, you strengthened yourself in your faith. As you sang the words, you applied them to yourself. Just like repetitive study of scripture, the Word, which is a living thing, active, "sharper than any two-edged sword," it becomes rooted in your being. God's Word is "quickened" by the action of the Spirit and grows inside you. In singing, you also bless yourself. We were created as creatures who worship. We must worship something, it's in our nature. People worship movie stars or politicians or prophets or themselves. But when we worship God as He intended us, in spirit and in truth, we are told that He inhabits the praises of His people. When we sing we feel God, and that is an unparalleled, wonderful feeling!

In singing, we convince others of the reality of God. We witness to others through our song. Many times after our programs people would come up to us and tell us how much we had inspired them. Others would be spiritually convicted and saved right while listening to us. Through our voices the Spirit had gently wooed these people until they could no longer resist His invitation.

Finally, singing is teaching. An integral component of gospel singing is teaching others to express their innermost soul to God in song. My father urged me to begin teaching choir at St. Luke's.

On a purely practical level, singing kept our family together.

"We would have all gone astray," says Reebie, "if it hadn't been for singing together."

Now that our households were split up between Hillside Place and Livingston Street, our rehearsals every Thursday night gave us an important reason for seeing each other. Of course, I would have been with my brothers and sisters anyway. I missed them once I moved in with my father and Viola. But even later in our lives, when we all worked different jobs and had our own kids, we would still get together at Lee's house to sing.

Now that I knew what and *Who* I was singing about I enjoyed singing. There was a wonderful feeling when I sang now—fire, burning—I couldn't wait to take my solo, close my eyes and praise Him. I felt like I could fly; I felt high and lifted up. Everything was different; the words meant something to me, meant something personal to me now. I didn't tire as easily. And even if they held us until last, my crankiness evaporated as soon as we started our first song and the Spirit fell.

As our priorities were put in order spiritually, as I finally recognized the ministry of our family group, the Drinkard Singers entered into its golden age.

Not coincidentally, it was also the golden age of gospel. From the end of World War II for almost twenty years, gospel found its audience.

Quartets which had always abounded in the South moved North. In Chicago, where the most famous gospel composer, Thomas Dorsey, had settled, were found the Roberta Martin Singers, Willa Mae Ford and Sallie Martin. Los Angeles, Detroit, every major city with a sizable black population had its own gospel scene. In the New York metro area, Newark was a dominant force for gospel. There was a circuit of churches and programs that could keep a group very busy.

But not make you rich. As soon as I finished high school, I got a day job and kept it just like my sisters and brothers. We were booked by Ronnie Williams on a lot of gospel concerts. We appeared with all the big gospel quartets of the day; wonderful groups like the Davis Sisters. They featured a great singer named Jackie Verdell, who was a close friend of Aretha Franklin. Both of them started their rise at the same time, both of them were equally gifted, but only one of them made it. We also followed the same circuit as the Caravans with Shirley Caesar, a powerful evangelist. We were thrilled to be often on the same stage as the Dixie Hummingbirds, a fantastic group, in that southern quartet tradition that my father came out of. Paul Simon would later utilize the Hummingbirds' genius of a lead singer, Claude Jeter, and his amazing falsetto on some of his records. The Dixie Hummingbirds, the Swan Silvertones, these were gospel groups whose records we'd been listening to for years.

We were flattered to be included on the same program with these groups, but we never did get any stars in our eyes. Singing was, first and foremost, still a ministry for us. Our meat was to go into some little church in New Jersey, sing and see people blessed, saved, even join the church that night. It was about ministry and getting together as a family: rehearsing, singing, laughing and eating together.

I was beginning to miss some of those rehearsals, living with my father over on Livingston Street. I was torn. I loved my father and wanted to be near him. I was a teenager but still a little girl at heart. I was still the same daddy's girl who marched in the Masons' parade holding my daddy's hand. Since my mother had died, I had thrown all my love over to Daddy. At the same time, I also missed my brothers and sisters. The combination of my missing rehearsals over on Hillside Place and missing Annie, Nicky and Larry convinced my father to let me return to Hillside Place "temporarily."

We continued our ministry in the churches. It had to be a ministry, because we never got paid! We would sing our hearts out all night in a church, hang around to greet the church folk, then shake the pastor's hand and leave the church with barely enough money to cover our car-fare. It's a funny thing but sometimes home churches and Christians in general don't support you. They think they've got it coming. We laughed it off, however, and went over to Cavanaugh's with our honorarium. We bought two or three hot dogs apiece, took them home to Hillside Place and had a party. The truth is, we never expected any money for what we did. We all kept day jobs—our little "tent-making" ventures like St. Paul—so we could continue to treat singing as a ministry. Annie still worked down at ODB, Larry and Hank worked at Singer with my father and Reebie and I worked in Irvington at a toothpaste packaging plant. It was clean, the money was good and my dream was to save up enough money to go to interior decorating school. I'd always had a good color sense. Somewhere inside me, I had this wild, crazy desire to take some-one's dreary apartment and make it over completely. I don't know where this came from except that maybe it was all that time I spent Down Neck at Aunt Juanita's dreary dungeon.

On Thursday nights, my brothers would ride home with my father from the foundry to rehearse. Annie, who was now the lady of the house with Reebie gone, would cook dinner. I know cooking for Daddy was a thrill for her, and my father went overboard compli-menting her fledgling efforts. I'd say it was just like old times, but even though Daddy was living with Viola on Livingston, we still thought of him as living in both places. I helped Annie with the dishes, and we went back into the living room to rehearse. Reebie had just taught us a few new ones and we were anxious to try them out on Dad. They were real gospels—hard, rhythmic, shouting kind of things. The kind of things we first heard and learned as children in the Holiness church on Mercer Street . . . so different from the old quartet stuff my father had sung. Gospel was now considered the new music.

Reebie had taken one of the anthems of the Church of God in

Christ, "I'm a Soldier for the Lord," and crossed it with one of those old spirituals. My father really lit up when he heard us do that one. As Reebie led, Annie, Nicky and Larry (in parentheses) and I trailed her in classic call and response:

> *I am (I am) climbing (climbing)*
> *Jacob's ladder*
> *I am (I am) climbing (climbing)*
> *Jacob's ladder*
>
> *I'm a soldier!*
> *(I'm a soldier of the cross)*
> *I'm a soldier!*
> *(I'm a soldier of the cross)*

When Reebie got to the "I'm a soldier" part, she'd start to clap in double time, adding a polyrhythmic feel to an already rocking beat.

> *Do you (do you)*
> *Think I (think I)*
> *Make a pretty good soldier?*
> *Do you (do you)*
> *Think I (think I)*
> *Make a pretty good soldier?*
> *I'm a soldier of the cross*

We could go on forever with this one, chorus after chorus. My daddy beamed. When we finished, he lit a cigarette. Then, leaving it pursed between his lips, he tilted his head upward to avoid the smoke, and clapped a slow, stately clap, as if to say, "My children, well done." Before he walked back in the night to Livingston Street, he would gather us around him in the living room and pray for us. He would get down on his knees and pray God would "keep his children together," that He would watch over us and protect us and bless us. He would always come up crying at times like these, when we were gathered around him like his little chicks.

We repeated this Thursday-night ritual of dinner and rehearsal with Daddy many weeks. It became a precious symbol of our family solidarity. Though circumstances had changed, though he was living with Viola in a different house, this was still our home, he was still our daddy and this singing was still the gift he had passed down to us from his birthplace.

He was also torn between us and Viola. He missed us terribly; especially me, whom he still considered the baby. He'd finish praying for us, leave us all in God's hands, but picked us right up again and worried about us as soon as he left the house. He smoked too much and he'd worried himself into some ulcers that he didn't even want us to know he had. Viola had finally told us, against his wishes. Maybe she thought we'd bother him less and she'd have that much more of him. We did begin to see less of him; whether it was Viola's demands on him to take her to various church functions and dinners, his own responsibilities at St. Luke's or his own health, I don't know. He had left the management of the group in Lee's able hands and he needn't have worried.

She carried on, in his spirit, above and beyond the call of duty. She already had two young daughters herself. Yet she was never late in picking us up, getting us to whatever church we were singing at and haggling with some church deacon for our money. In fact, under Lee's direction, we began to move on a much faster track even in spite of ourselves.

The Drinkards had come to the attention of gospel DJ Joe Bostic. He was good-looking, college-educated, fortyish and black. He had come to gospel as a curiosity, a "phenomenon" that he saw was attracting millions of black folk. It piqued his journalist's mind. He was already on the radio and soon became a literate expert on the gospel music scene. His New York City radio show beat a drum for the local artists and visiting national stars, until he became known as the "Dean of Gospel Disc Jockeys." His contacts with churches, advertisers, record companies and promoters made him a natural at managing and promoting gospel artists. Among others, Bostic became one of Mahalia Jackson's handlers. He had seen us on the church circuit and he was impressed. He thought we had prospects for a career ahead of us; recording deals, personal management contracts, road tours, radio, television . . . the list went on. Lee stopped him cold.

"Joe Bostic couldn't tell her what to do," says Joe Bostic, Jr., who would often emcee his father's shows. "They [the Drinkards] were not about making it a business. Lee had a dignity way beyond that. She wouldn't allow them to go on the road. Lee stopped them from becoming a traveling group . . . she wanted to make sure the family stayed religious."

Lee's instinct to keep us on the narrow path and our singing a ministry was, of course, learned at the feet of my father. But it was intensified as soon as Lee and our group began to venture forth from the church world to the world of big gospel extravaganzas at arenas and theaters in the New York metro area. Backstage she saw so-called church folk and gospel artists living just as sinfully as the world they were supposedly trying to save. Liquor, reefer, hard drugs—she was not about to let her family get mixed up in that. As we waited to go on, we couldn't help but hear the stories and misadventures of other gospel acts who were underpaid, if they weren't beaten out of their money by an unscrupulous promoter. They were enslaved to traveling a circuit from city to city, stuffed in a station wagon, barreling down the highway at unsafe speeds in order to make the next engagement. Hunger pangs loud enough for everyone in the car to hear, in the South they'd pass "whites only" restaurants they could only gaze at through the car window. When they would finally land in a town, they had to sleep, if they had time, in a cheap flophouse, in order to cut down on expenses. Clean clothes, showers—these were extravagances.

We were not raised like that and Lee was not about to let us get mixed up in any kind of world like that. Our usual MO was to show up, sing and leave. "In the world, but not of the world."

Not that I considered myself any kind of holy roller. By the time I reached seventeen, I also enjoyed going out with Annie to some of the clubs in Newark. There was a club scene there that rivaled New York's. In scores of places you could hear fine bebop jazz or great singers like Little Jimmy Scott, Bill Doggett and occasionally, Arthur Prysock.

My mother, Delia Mae McCaskill Drinkard (1930). *Family photo*

Nitcholas Drinkard, my father, with my oldest brother, William,
shortly after they arrived in Newark, New Jersey (1923). *Family photo*

The Drinkard Singers: (*from left to right*) Nicky, Anne, Marie (Reebie), Larry, and Cissy—aged ten (1943). *Family photo*

Marie (Reebie) Epps, my sister, who kept me on the straight and narrow (1972). *Family photo*

My brother Nicky: he gypped Annie out of her graham crackers and played organ for me better than anyone (1972). *Family photo*

One of the many gospel shows that featured the Drinkard Singers (1963).

Mitch Diamond

Classic 1950s portrait of the Drinkard Singers: (*from left to right*) Cissy Drinkard, Lee Drinkard Warrick, Marie Drinkard Epps, Larry Drinkard, Anne Drinkard Moss, Judy Guions (Clay), Nicky Drinkard (at the piano).

James J. Kriegsmann/family photo

Michael, Whitney (Nippy), and the Lincoln I jumped out of when I refused to tour (1968). *Family photo*

Below Left: Nippy and Michael: "I'm not touching you. . . I'm not touching you" (1973). *Family photo*

Above Right: John Houston enjoys the good life poolside on Dodd Street (1971). *Family photo*

Right: John and Nippy outside our first house, on Wainwright Street, Newark, New Jersey (1968). *Family photo*

Cissy and John after church on Sunday in Newark. Monday through Friday I'm still singing with Solomon, Aretha, Dionne, and a cast of thousands in New York.

Family photo

Below: The Sweet Inspirations (1968): *(from left to right)* Cissy, Myrna, Estelle, and Sylvia, pop music's first-call background group.

James J. Kriegsmann/Atlantic Records

Cissy singing "Ain't No Way" with the girls at a recording session (October 13, 1968). *Family photo*

Directing my choir as they perform for the *Face to Face* album (1996). For over forty years the choir has been my lifeblood. *James Minchin III*

Cissy handing
Whitney the second
of her three World
Music Awards, in
Monte Carlo
(May 4, 1994).
*Reuters/Eric
Gaillard/Archive Photos*

Cissy receives a
Grammy Award
for her *Face to
Face* album in the
Tradition Soul
Gospel category
(1997). *Sonia
Moskowitz/Globe
Photos, Inc.*

The Houston kids all grown up at last: (*from left to right*)
Gary, Whitney, and Michael. *Family photo.*

Reebie and Lee raised a whole lot of sand, agonizing about "these younger children today." But I think I had the sacred and the profane, if you want to call it that, distributed pretty well. I continued the spiritual pursuits in my life: I never missed a Sunday at church or a choir rehearsal. I knew the miracle that had been worked in my heart. I saw no reason to suddenly become some kind of Bible-thumper or change my personality in some phony external way. I didn't need to go saying "praise the Lord" or whatever all the time. God was prevalent in my mind. I went nowhere, did nothing without consulting Him in prayer. I knew He was always with me. I never tempted Him by putting myself in dangerous or compromising situations. God had given me an almost sixth sense for danger. It was as if I could see bad things before they happened and many times I would turn on my heel and leave a party before it ever got started. I couldn't stand the smell of reefer; it made me want to throw up. I hated drugs of any kind; hated losing control and still do. I enjoy being in my right mind.

I respected Lee for feeling she was put on this earth to pull people from the flames, rather than ease them on into the fire by putting banana peels under their feet. One of my father's dreams for our group was that it would be a beacon to other young people. That's exactly what it was for Judy Clay. My father was proud of the way Lee snatched her from the flames and installed her in our group.

We met Judy in 1950 when she was twelve years old. We were singing in Harlem at Faith Temple at 145th Street and Amsterdam Avenue. Judy was in their choir. She loved the way we sang and gravitated to us because she missed her own family down in South Carolina. She was staying with a relative in New York under not exactly prime conditions. When an older male relative in the house began to molest her, Judy told Lee. After hearing this, my sister adopted Judy, took her into her own home and treated Judy as if she was her oldest daughter. Of course, Judy had a great voice and later went on to a pop career. At the age of thirteen she was a member of the Drinkards, a wonderful asset to the group. Judy really loved to sing, and Lee put her out front, where her enthusiasm drove us even harder.

Dad's wish that the Drinkard Singers be a beacon to other kids was also what drew Freeman Johnson and his brother Carroll into our midst. They were teenagers when they too were attracted to our group. Freeman and Carroll both had great voices but they didn't join the Drinkards. Together with Larry and Nicky they formed the Four Bells. They sang pop stuff and these boys could really sing like mockingbirds. Annie thinks they sounded like the Orioles. I don't think they sounded like anybody—they sounded wonderful! They could have had a career. But then, my house wasn't particularly encouraging to its occupants singing anything other than gospel. It was kind of a shame that something that sounded so good never saw the light of day.

As Joe Bostic, Jr., said, my sister Lee wanted to make sure we remained separate from the world. Backstage at a gospel show at the Apollo, a slick twenty-something Joe Bostic, Jr., received the complete Lee Warrick treatment.

"She had them all sit around me and pray for me," says Bostic, Jr., "that I would be saved!"

The battle lines between sacred and secular seemed so cleanly drawn then. But the excitement, the feeling, the spirit of gospel could not be kept just within the church. In the early fifties, artists like Ray Charles, heavily influenced by gospel's Alex Bradford, put a heavy gospel touch on his work. Of course, anyone could tell that his "This Little Girl of Mine" was nothing more than "This Little Light of Mine." The church was outraged. They didn't name names from the pulpit, nobody wanted to get sued, but everybody in the pews knew whom the pastor was railing about. Even secular singers were annoyed (and probably a little jealous) about the way Ray was making a million from fusing gospel and blues.

"He's got the blues, he's crying sanctified. He's mixing the blues with the spirituals. I know that's wrong," said Big Bill Broonzy, an influential black blues singer. "He should be singing in a church."

If secular artists brought the church into their world it was inevitable that the opposite would also happen. In the beginning of gospel's golden age, as the music attracted a much younger audience, it was inevitable that worldly attitudes would also invade gospel. Like bobbysoxers falling out over Frank Sinatra or Nat Cole, female admirers were drawn to gospel singers who were becoming stars. In 1950, the personnel changes within the Soul Stirrers, who sang on the same circuit as we did, perfectly illustrated the problem. Long a favorite with the mature audiences, the original lead singer, R. H. Harris, walked away from the group over gospel's moral decline. Harris couldn't stand to see gospel singers behaving like pop stars with a female groupie in every port.

"I believe there's this virtue that goes along with gospel. There's more to it than good singing," said R. H. Harris. "It's a beaconing thing that other folk can see without you talking it."

And everybody said, "Amen." That "beaconing thing" was right out of my father's original design for the Drinkard Singers.

The Stirrers replaced R.H., pleasant-looking, bald and middle-aged, with Sam Cooke, young, handsome and a great singer. Sam was a singing disciple of R.H. But his appointment to the group was also a nod to the ladies who expected gospel's stars to be more than just good singers. I know about Sam's appeal. I almost wound up married to him! We dated for a quick minute back when we were both on the same circuit. We had a lot in common. Not too far apart in age, parents that came up from the South, and we were both childhood singers in family gospel groups. He was good-looking, small, well built and talked a lot of . . . Well, I wasn't even twenty years old yet. And he was living in too fast a world for me. Maybe if the Drinkards had toured as much as they wanted us to, Sam and I might have found ourselves together. His pop records are well known, but like a lot of other folk, I feel that they can't hold a candle to his gospel cuts. After Sam made his pop records, the church was critical. When he returned to a reunion of the Soul Stirrers, the church saw him as no returning prodigal. They shouted him down, called him a blues singer. When he eventually left the stage, one of the Stirrers said Sam was "tearin' pretty bad. It hurt him."

I wonder how things might have been different if that church crowd had accepted him and cheered him on. Perhaps Sam would have come back strong in the gospel field. I wonder how many gospel artists the church has discouraged simply by not taking care of its own, forcing them to go begging outside the church. Every time I hear Sam and the Stirrers sing "Touch the Hem of His Garment" I think about how good this boy could sing and how sad it was that he was taken from us so soon. The tragic way he and other phenomenal gospel talents went down, early and so full of promise, was a lesson to me about what is real in this life and what is not.

I stayed "real" at church. My father urged me to start directing choir—teaching, helping others learn to find and express their gift. I had already been a part of the choir at St. Luke's, a wonderful group of singers. I was influenced deeply by our pianist, Miss Grace Stinson. She was a delightful, lively and funny lady. She had a funny laugh, one of those goofy, country-bumpkin-type, Gomer Pyle laughs that got you laughing too. She was a simple woman, but naturally skilled as a teacher, engaging our interest and keeping our teenage attention focused on her. "What are you doing?" she would question us with an incredulity that seemed almost cartoonish. She sounded like she stepped out of a Laurel and Hardy movie; she had an almost slapstick quality. Along with Reebie, she was one of my main influences as a teacher. I took from her approach the wonderful banter she used along with humor to keep people of all ages interested in paying attention to you. It would serve me well the rest of my life. From Reebie, I took her no-nonsense approach to rehearsal and instruction. It's easy to relax and give up— teacher and student—before the job is done. Reebie taught me to stay on the case until the job is done and done right.

You can get an incredible joy from teaching, a satisfaction that goes down deep into your soul. When they finally get it right, when there are thirty, fifty, a hundred voices in front of you expressing themselves full out, they are giving something very special back to you. Try teaching something—anything—to someone. There is nothing quite like the satisfaction of watching that lightbulb finally going off over that person's head, as he or she says, "I got it!" There is great fulfillment in making disciples. For the first time, I recognized the joy my father had gotten from encouraging us and continuing to supervise us as singers. I saw the joy Reebie had also derived from this ministry.

My sister Lee let Joe Bostic take us only as far as she allowed. But one thing even Lee could not refuse him. In 1951, Joe wanted to put us on a program with Mahalia Jackson. This was not unusual; he had booked us on lots of programs with Hallie. But this time he wanted to rent Carnegie Hall. Not since 1938 when John Hammond presented his famous Spirituals to Swing concert there with Sister Rosetta Tharpe had gospel been presented at such a high-profile venue. Joe went deep into hock to rent the hall. Mahalia promoted the concert with weeks of contact with the media. In her typical earthy way she described her efforts to win the media's attention.

"I worked my butt off," Hallie growled. "I always do. No one could ever get the attention I got, because I used my own money to get attention. And that's that!"

Mahalia's work paid off. On the evening of October 7, 1951, Joe Bostic's "Negro Gospel and Religious Festival" was sold out. Mahalia broke Carnegie Hall's attendance records, even topping Toscanini and Benny Goodman. It was a wonderful night of gospel talent with Rosetta Tharpe, the Gaye Sisters and Clara Ward, Aretha's mentor. Mahalia rocked that old staid hall and people were dancing in the aisles.

"When folks, during my numbers, got to their feet, danced in the aisles and the ushers were helpless to stop them, I tried to say something, and folks cried and stamped their feet," said Mahalia. "Even I got carried away. I found myself down on my knees, yes, singing my heart out. Then, when I got to my feet, I told the crowd that had come all the way from Boston to Baltimore that we were in Carnegie Hall, and if we didn't cool it, the authorities and the police would put us in the street. I guess they heard me, 'cause most of them settled down and the program went on to near midnight."

There was a party afterward, but as usual, we didn't attend. We buttoned up our coats, piled into a cab and rode down to the Port Authority terminal, where we caught the last bus home. It was a great evening, and I was happy for Mahalia. Happy for all that she achieved as a black woman. But there was something about her success that also upset me. Mahalia became white folks' stereotype of a gospel singer. She was earthy and illiterate. When the establishment pictured a gospel singer it was Mahalia and these qualities that they expected. That expectation closed the door to scores of other great gospel artists who just didn't fit the Mahalia mold. America missed out on a whole cross section of amazing artists because this narrow stereotype ruled. And these same artists never got the satisfaction of having their message heard.

A lot of people couldn't believe my father didn't come out to see us that night at Carnegie Hall. It didn't hurt me none; I didn't expect him to come. He was busy at church or maybe his ulcers were bothering him. He was proud of us, but Carnegie Hall didn't mean that much to him. Singing was about ministry, building up your own self in the faith, teaching others and keeping his family together. He was there when we needed him; motivating us to sing in the living room at 38 Hillside Place, where he asked us to strike up a tune for him. Or just off to the side at a church, encouraging me, softly, to "sing, baby."

We were all grateful to be there that night, but Carnegie Hall hardly dented our regular routine. We still had our day jobs to hold down, church choir rehearsals, church every Sunday and our regular Thursday-night Drinkard rehearsals. When Lee couldn't get a babysitter for Dionne and Dee Dee we would move rehearsal over to her house in East Orange.

"We had an upright piano and Nicky would play and everybody would stand in the middle of the living room and they would sing," says Dionne, my niece. "And when it got to be a July afternoon or a July evening when it was ninety degrees outside, which happened frequently enough, the screens were opened and you would find, literally, an audience in the middle of the street or sitting on the curb, even sitting on our stoop, listening to them rehearse. It was fabulous, it really was. It was a free concert."

No doubt, listening to the sounds of her mother, her aunts and uncles singing togther as far back as she can remember gave Dionne a pretty good ear. Her voice developed beautifully as a teenager, as did the voice of my other niece, her sister Dee Dee. Later on, they both joined my choir.

In April, I was laid off from the toothpaste factory. I didn't run out to get another job immediately. I enjoyed spending some of my free time with Daddy. I was nineteen and had saved a few bucks, so I chipped in with my brothers and sisters and we bought Daddy a complete outfit—suit, shoes and hat—head to toe. He strutted around like a peacock, admiring himself in the mirror. I'll never forget that day.

I felt like I was growing up; my life was on an even keel and I wanted him to know I was grateful for everything he'd done for me, the sacrifices he'd made for me, how he didn't go nuts after Mommy died and how he'd kept the family together. Daddy did a lot of things for people—for his family, for men who worked with him at the foundry and church people. He mainly counseled them, taking the time to listen to their troubles. A lot of people really depended on him. But I wonder how many people actually thanked Daddy. His birthday was coming up in June and I planned on buying him something nice; I didn't know yet what, but it was going to be nice. For the first time in twenty-five years at the foundry, he'd take a day off once in a while. He said he was tired. He didn't look tired; he still looked like the same Daddy to me, just a little more gray in his hair, but at fifty-five still a handsome man. He did look a little thin and his cough had gotten worse. But I couldn't talk to him about quitting smoking; I was smoking myself. I felt bad for him; I don't think Viola cooked that much and he probably missed Mommy's cooking.

I told Annie that we ought to have Daddy over for dinner and cook some of the things he liked. He looked thin to me. Annie reminded me about Daddy's ulcers and thought it might be a good idea for him to see Dr. Goldstein for a checkup. Daddy fought us, said he felt fine, but finally agreed to see Dr. Goldstein.

I started looking for another job. Lee was working over at Tung-Sol and Annie got a job, a real good job, at the RCA factory in Harrison. The word was they were only hiring high yellows. I didn't even bother going over there.

Dr. Goldstein didn't like how thin Daddy was. He wanted him in the hospital right away. If it was Daddy's ulcers, he felt they were probably bleeding, which would explain Daddy's weight loss. Dr. Goldstein put Daddy in Doctors Hospital on Avon Avenue—convenient, because we could walk there. First they tried to bring the ulcers under control with medication. Then they tried to bring his weight up with fluids. Daddy couldn't take being cooped up in a hospital bed. Except for the ulcers, he had been pretty healthy his whole life and managed to stay out of hospitals. But now, hooked up to an IV, his own doctor and the hospital's doctors and nurses checking up on him, he knew this was a little more serious. He was also too weak to get out of bed.

On the last Monday of April 1952, Dr. Goldstein asked if we'd all come to the hospital the next day to discuss my father's condition. After work, my sisters and brothers met me at the hospital. We stood around my father's bed and Dr. Goldstein introduced us to the surgeon. He suspected cancer. He wanted to do an exploratory operation, deal with Daddy's ulcers and check the cancer's progress. Dr. Goldstein would get my father as strong as he could the rest of the week and supervise the operation on Monday morning, May 5. He forced a smile, said he had every confidence in the surgeon's ability. Then left us alone with my father.

"We were standing around the bed and Daddy was talking to us about staying together," says Anne. "He asked us to promise that we would always stay together, be close, and always sing together. That no matter where we went, we would stay in touch with each other. We promised. Then I broke down. I was kneeling beside his bed and he took his hand and cupped the back of my head and squeezed it. 'Don't worry, you're gonna be all right . . . don't worry,' he said."

My father said that he wanted to talk to Lee alone now. We filed slowly out into the hall and Lee remained by his bedside. He charged her with keeping the family together, watching over us and making sure we continued to sing together.

We visited throughout the week; then Sunday night, the night before his surgery, we gathered again at his bedside, prayed with him and kissed him good night. After we left, he called us back at the house. We were on our way to Faith Temple in Harlem, to do a radio broadcast. We couldn't come back to the hospital but we told Daddy to listen to the broadcast; we would dedicate a song to him. We caught the bus and rode over to New York that night in silence, each of us in our own little world. We were worried about Daddy. On the broadcast, we weren't ourselves. But as we dedicated one of Daddy's favorite hymns, something deep came out of us as we sang. In his hospital room, my father must have heard that "something." The nurses told us he cried when he heard us.

> *I will guide thee with mine eyes,*
> *All the way from earth to heaven,*
> *I will guide thee with mine eyes.*
> *If you cannot sing like angels,*
> *If you cannot preach like Paul,*
> *You can tell the love of Jesus,*
> *Tell the world he died for all.*
> *I will guide thee with mine eyes,*
> *All the way from earth to heaven,*
> *I will guide thee with mine eyes.*
> —*"I Will Guide Thee"*

They took my father down to the operating room early Monday morning. My brothers and sisters had gone to work. So I was the only one waiting for him in the room when they wheeled him out of surgery after lunch. The grave expression on the surgeon's face said it all. The cancer had devoured my father's lungs. The doctors couldn't do anything for him; they just closed him back up. When my father regained consciousness, he just lay there in bed, too weak to utter a sound. He never said a word to me, just looked at me with his eyes. I was alone with him. I put my hand over his and prayed for him, inside, that he would pull through. I felt small and helpless. I was no longer his little girl as he was no longer my big, strong daddy. He was frail and weak, his eyes dull and uncomprehending. I was the strong one now. And oh, how I would have given up my strength at that moment so that he would come to life.

I turned away for a minute to pray; when I met his eyes again, he held my gaze for one more moment, then closed his eyes. He became so still, I was frightened. I walked out to the nurses' station. From the look on my face, they just came out from around that counter and followed me back into the room. They took my father's pulse, then pulled the white curtain around his bed. My father was dead.

I was supposed to call the others but I couldn't. I lost it; I broke down and they had to take me home.

It was the biggest funeral St. Luke's had ever seen. My father knew a lot of people—he'd helped so many—at church, at his job and at all the churches he would take us to sing. "There were so many cars lining the streets," says my cousin Honey, "you would have thought the President had died."

From my father's job, Bill Hart, the future mayor of East Orange, remembered my father.

"I had three influences in my life," Mayor Hart says. "My father, my high school principal, who was white, and Mr. Drinkard. That's a pretty high rating.

"I think that he had the same dream that Dr. King had—that one of these days we would look at him like a man, rather than a black man. I think he had the dream that maybe one of these days, his grandchildren or his great-grandchildren would be down at that foundry as leaders— maybe run the plant, maybe even own it."

In his own family, Daddy was a leader. His father and mother, his sisters and brothers all flocked around him. Not because he had so much, but he just had a way of looking out for you. Like the way he took us children to the bathroom in the middle of the night, turned the light on for us and waited until we were back in bed. The way he stopped my uncle from giving my cousin Honey the beating of her life because she uttered the word "pregnant." And the way he spoiled his baby sister Flossie, who was old enough to know better.

Daddy's death hit me worse than Mommy's. I was older. I was closer to him, and after Mommy died, I had given him all my love and devotion. I was devastated. There was no one left to turn to.

I walked around in a daze the next few years, just going through the motions. I lost all incentive. I gave up my dream of going to interior decorating school. I was nineteen but I had lost the zest for living.

One day, on a lark, I went out and got a job. "Let's go get a job," I said to my friend Effie. She was really looking for a job, I just wanted to get dressed up for the interview and see some new faces. I purposely picked the RCA factory in Harrison because I knew they hired only high yellows and I would never get the job. Guess what? They hired me and sent my friend Effie, who really needed a job, home. In 1952, televisions were selling like hotcakes and they hired me onto their assembly line. With my small hands, I was a whiz at putting together cathode-ray tubes. It was a good job, with good pay and benefits, and I got to go to work every day in a dress and heels. I liked it and ended up staying there eleven years. Deep inside, however, I was still drifting, unhappy and restless.

I partied with Annie and my brothers for a few years. We danced until the wee hours at Newark's nightspots, giving Lee and Reebie fits but never missing a choir rehearsal or a Sunday morning at church. After my father died, Reverend Warrick left St. Luke's and we were no longer comfortable there. The Drinkard family was not the kind of family to be without a church. Though we were brought up AME, we had sung a few times at New Hope Baptist Church across town on Sussex Avenue and liked it. We joined New Hope and, as at St. Luke's, I began directing a choir there.

I was thankful for that choir. The interaction with friends there and the rehearsals kept me busy and my mind off how much I missed Daddy. My sisters and brothers were all married now, starting to raise families, so I didn't pal out with them as much as I used to. I was lonely, but I felt too unsettled to get involved in any relationship. Then my cousin introduced me to Freddy. He was attractive and had a good job in construction. We started going out. Freddy respected me, seemed to understand me and loved me. After we had been dating for several months, he proposed.

I thought marriage would cure my restlessness, that unsettled feeling I had. Marriage seemed to be agreeing with my brothers and sisters, so I figured I would try my own hand at it. I put on the white dress and Freddy and I had a big wedding at New Hope Church. Reverend Walters married us. Reebie, Lee and their husbands cooked. It was a beautiful wedding. Freddy was a good provider and treated me wonderfully. I just had no business marrying him. He respected me, he didn't beat me, but only months into the marriage I knew something was very wrong. I didn't love Freddy—not the way a wife should love a husband.

All the things he could give me, all the things that everyone around me thought were so important meant nothing if I didn't love him. My friends thought I was nuts.

"But, Cissy . . . ," my friends would say. "The guy's good to you; he makes a nice living, he doesn't beat you . . ." Yes, that was all true—but it wasn't enough! I wasn't in love; there was no romance. It wasn't easy facing up to this realization. What would people think? I had gone and had a big church wedding—all my family and friends had participated. Now just a year after my wedding, I was ready to up and leave. I could have stayed married—lied to my family, my friends, even my husband—and told them I was happy. I could have lied to everyone but myself. "To thine own self be true": I don't know where I picked it up, but it's been part of me so long, it doesn't matter. I believe there is truth in that old saying. As far as worrying about what other people thought—I've never much cared. I don't mean that in an arrogant way. I always try to be courteous. I guess it's just common sense. Hey, why should I worry about what you think, when I'm the one that has to live my life. Of course, I could have stayed like so many people I knew. I could have stayed and been like one of those old biddies who come up to me and brag, "I've been married for fifty years." *Yeah, and for the last forty of those years, you've been miserable!*

Deep inside, I was deathly afraid of living my life never having truly loved. Freddy and I stayed together about two years, then I left. He didn't deserve what I did to him. I've got excuses, but none of them are adequate. Freddy was a good man. I was just too young. My sisters hated what I did and told me so. All three of them married and would stay with their first (and only) husbands their whole lives. Besides their scorn, there was another reason why January 1957 was a particularly difficult time to leave—I was pregnant. But I was working at RCA, getting faster at threading those little filaments into the bottom of those cathode-ray tubes, and getting rewarded with regular raises. I was determined to support myself and my new baby even without a man.

I moved in with Lee to cut expenses. When I wasn't working, I was usually directing my choir at New Hope. We had some people who could sing in that group we called the eight o'clock choir. I recruited most of them from the people I used to party with in the clubs. But I didn't half-step with them about the commitment. If you joined the choir, you had to show up on time for a midweek rehearsal, and please don't stay out so late Saturday night that you're nodding in my choir stand at 8 A.M. Sunday morning. Forty-one years later, I still have a lot of those old recruits. That ragtag bunch was the motliest crew you ever saw. But their commitment was like iron; if you called a rehearsal, they were there. Those "sinners" had something to praise God about. I guess it has something to do with that scripture, "Him who is forgiven much, loveth much." I also directed the young people's choir.

"We had the best choir in New York and New Jersey," brags Judy.

Well, we did have some wonderful voices in that choir and our young people's choir, the Reverend C. H. Walters Choir. We had Judy and her sister Sylvia; my seventeen-year-old niece, Dionne, and her younger sister, Dee Dee. I also had a girl in my adult choir we called Chicken. She was my right hand; all I had to do was look at her and she'd follow me with the right note. She used to crack me up; when we marched up the aisle she'd syncopate her step just a little to try to throw my time off. She was always doing something crazy. She lived fast and died very young at twenty-four.

Singing together was never quite the same after Daddy died. He was our great inspiration. Reebie tried to pick up where he left off, motivating us, cheering us on. In the summer of 1957, I was twenty-three and round and pregnant when Joe Bostic took us, Mahalia Jackson and Clara Ward to the Newport Jazz Festival. This was to be a first. Never had gospel been presented before so many people; so many white people.

"As we were going up we were quite nervous," remembers Annie. "We had never faced anything quite of this magnitude. We also knew that the Jazz Festival was mainly to white audiences, so that sort of unnerved us a little bit.

"As we were singing and the spirit was moving through us, the audience picked up the spirit and rose out of their seats and came swarming down to the front of the stage, reaching out for our hands."

"It looked like the heavens were coming down," Reebie says. "There were people everywhere. I was singing 'My Rock' and I jumped down off the stage to where the people were . . . the spirit was moving . . . you just had to move with it!"

I wished Daddy could have seen Newport. Carnegie Hall was one thing—pretty much preaching to the choir. But reaching a group this huge, seeing the spirit fall on such a large unsaved multitude would have reminded Daddy of the day of Pentecost!

On October 12, 1957, I delivered a beautiful five-pound-six-ounce baby boy! Gary was a wonderful, dark tar baby with the biggest eyes you ever saw. I stayed in the hospital a few days and brought him home to Lee's house. He became everybody's favorite baby, especially his little fifteen-year-old cousin, Dee Dee.

Bostic helped negotiate an album deal for us comprised of live recordings made at Newport. In 1958, we had the distinction of becoming the first gospel group ever signed to the RCA-Victor label. We recorded "Make a Joyful Noise" down at Webster Hall, one of RCA's old studios in Manhattan. It became a popular album, especially when Joe Bostic opened his radio show with one of its cuts, "Rise and Shine." One of our label mates at RCA, another gospel fan, also loved the album. Elvis Presley tried to get a hold of us either to record or tour, but Lee refused to cooperate. Elvis didn't give up. Ten years after "Make a Joyful Noise" debuted, I had the pleasure of meeting and working with him.

Lee helped me take care of my newborn. But the time came when I had to return to work. I was twenty-four and determined to be totally self-reliant. I had my own job and my own car and was proud that I would not rely on a man to support me. But my self-reliance came with a heavy price tag. In order to hold down my job at RCA, I had to make a hard decision—to board my baby out. I agonized over it, rethought it a thousand times, but I kept coming back to the same conclusion. My father had an expression, "If you make your bed hard, lie in it until it gets soft." I suppose this was his way of talking about what the Furnace of Affliction had taught him: You had to walk through it. You had to go through your problems. There was no easy way around them. If you avoided the "work," you didn't grow. Without the struggle, true change wasn't possible. I had certainly made my bed hard. I had divorced Freddie and left a promising life of relative ease to raise my son alone. Now I would have to lie in that hard bed until it got soft. No one could watch Gary at home: we all worked. Lee and Judy both had factory jobs. Dionne and Dee Dee were big girls already going to high school.

I heard about a lady who watched kids in her house, Miss Hardy. She was a sweet older woman, and after meeting her I felt a little bit better about the whole thing. I had few options. Every day I had to be at work at seven o'clock. There was no way I could get up early enough, to feed Gary, dress him, get myself dressed, get him over to the babysitter and still get to work by 7 A.M. I worked out an arrangement with Miss Hardy where I would drop off Gary every Sunday night. She would keep him the whole week; he would sleep there Monday through Thursday and I would pick him up Friday afternoon and take him home for the weekend.

I missed him terribly. After work every day, I'd run over to see him at Miss Hardy's. I'd play with him, feed him and kiss him up. But there always came that horrible time when I would have to leave my Gary and go home to Lee's. As a baby he would fuss and cry when I had to walk out the door. But as he grew, he got used to our inevitable separation. He learned as early as a toddler that a tantrum did no good; Mommy would always have to go. He adjusted because he had to. He wouldn't holler and he wouldn't scream when I had to go. He would push his face to the window and watch me go down Miss Hardy's walk, with big tears rolling silently out of his eyes. He was hurting, but what could I do? I had to work to take care of him. Later on, Miss Hardy adopted a little girl who was a hateful little heifer. She burned Gary on the face with a hot fork. I almost went crazy. I was going to take him out of there, but Miss Hardy pleaded with me not to. She really loved Gary and I realized it wasn't her fault; it was this bad little girl. I wanted to kill her.

Boarding Gary out was a sad time in my life. I found solace only in my Lord. I didn't talk to anyone about my problems. I've found that real friends, true friends, who will keep your confidences and not put your business in the street, are very rare. Further, I was in a position of leadership in the church, directing my choirs. I couldn't get too friendly with people I needed to be a teacher to.

But even as a teacher, I received so much satisfaction, so much healing and nourishment from my choirs. This was and is my existence—giving and getting in that teaching role. To see them learn what I'm teaching, to see them learn to express their innermost soul to God in song—this blesses me.

I missed my little boy. The memory of Daddy passing was also still fresh in my mind. Though I was staying with Lee and had the support of my family, sadness would sometimes overtake me. I wondered if I would ever experience a true love. I reckoned I didn't deserve to, after what I had done to Freddy.

Then, when Gary was six months old, the Drinkard Singers began appearing on a gospel television show broadcast from Symphony Hall in Newark. During one Saturday-morning broadcast, a tall, good-looking rich kid from Newark sat in front of his television set staring at me.

"Who's that one, Bernie?" said John Houston to his musician friend, pointing at me during my close-up. "Can you introduce me?"

I was about to meet John Houston, a self-confessed gospel groupie. Neither Lee nor Reebie was in favor of my seeing him; but as far as I was concerned, my knight in shining armor was about to ride into my life. Unfortunately, because of the big ideas John had for my career, my sisters, at least for a time, hated my knight in shining armor and the horse he rode in on.

EIGHT

There's always somebody talking about me,
Really I don't mind.
They're trying to block and stop my progress,
Most of the time.
The mean things you say don't make me feel bad,
I can't miss a friend I've never had,
I've got Jesus and that's enough.
— "That's Enough"

John Houston wasn't really a rich kid, but in my neighborhood he was about as close to being rich as you could get. Both his parents were professionals; his mother had a master's degree and taught school over in New York. His father was an electrical engineer. He grew up in the old First Ward, a combination of middle-class blacks, Italians and Jews. He said he was a "good little Catholic boy" who had graduated from Seton Hall Prep and served during the war in Europe. He was much older than me, my sister Lee's age exactly, thirteen years my senior. He was thirty-seven and I was twenty-four when we met. My sisters weren't in favor of my seeing him, because they thought he was robbing the cradle. But when I saw him standing with our pianist Bernie, out of camera range, on our Symphony Hall set, I wasn't think- ing about age. As a matter of fact, I wasn't thinking about anything except who was that good-looking guy. He was tall and handsome enough to be a movie star with his light skin and fine features. He told me later his dad was part Indian, which explained his features and his complexion. He made a point of telling me the name of the tribe, the

Lenni Lenape, the original nation from which all tribes in the East came. Iroquois, Algonquin, Mohawk, Hackensack—even the Indians who sold Manhattan Island to the Dutch. Right then, John could have sold me the Brooklyn Bridge. I loved listening to him, he was so interesting and funny, so sophisticated without being a stuffed shirt. I was falling in love with him before I even knew it.

"I was a gospel groupie," says John. "I just loved that music, I don't know why."

You liked that music, John, because the spirit of God was talking to you through it. John loved to get into lofty theological debates with me and tease me. But beneath his cynical pose, he had a deep reverence for God. John believed in God. He'd just had enough organized religion to last him several lifetimes.

He took to my son Gary right away, which further endeared him to me. His mother was a sweetheart, "cultured" John would say, and roll his eyes. All about books and plays and museums. She still taught over in Manhattan. I admired her to have taught and then gone on for that master's. John's dad was more of a neighborhood guy, funny and wise at the same time. After work, he liked to hang out in a bar not too far from Hillside Place.

After John had come out of the service, he held a number of different jobs. Among other things he had gotten a City Hall job in Newark, through political appointment. He didn't stay with that one too long, the bureaucracy and the paperwork bored him. John liked to be on the move, in the middle of the action, looking for a big break. He liked to drive, and at night he'd drive a cab in Newark. He also drove those big trucks; eighteen-wheelers with loads of beef he'd pick up in Chicago and drive all night back to Jersey.

We had a small wedding on May 24, 1959, and by 1960 I was pregnant with Michael. We set up housekeeping on Eighth Street, on the top floor of a three-story tenement. I was still working for RCA. We were happy, very much in love, but struggling. I still had to pay Miss Hardy to keep Gary, there were doctor's visits for my pregnancy, insurance, utilities, rent, and the bills were piling up. John was driving a cab at night to pick up a few bucks.

One day, a new girl moved into the apartment across the hall. John kept trying to invite her in for a cup of coffee and to meet me. But she kept refusing him like he had the plague.

Bae later explained. "I was a single mother and I had four children. My husband had left us and I was struggling. My sister and I moved in together; my sister would watch the children and I worked. My sister said, 'Did you see the guy next door?' My sister was a very big flirt and I said, 'Oh, no, please don't. I'm sure the guy's married. I don't wanna see.' One day, John Houston was standing in the hall and he said, 'Hi, how're you doing?' I happened to look up and I thought, oh, this is real trouble, 'cause the guy is an extremely handsome man. And he said, 'Did you just move in?' And I said, 'Yeah,' real gruff. 'Would you like a cup of coffee?' he asked me. 'No!' I practically yelled at him.

"I guess it was a few days later and we met up in the hall again. 'Why don't you come on in and have a cup of coffee, my wife's inside.' I went inside and there was this woman, pregnant, with her belly from here to around the corner and the most glorious smile I had ever seen. We hit it off immediately."

That was the first time I met Bae. She has been my best friend ever since. My kids call her "Aunt Bae" because she has been a constant in their lives. Her kids grew up with my kids. She is the only person I ever trusted completely with my children. Like John, she was a lapsed Catholic. Like John, she grew up in the old First Ward, in the heart of Little Italy. Her mother was Italian and her father was black and I can't tell where one picks up and the other leaves off in Bae. She makes the best lasagna I've ever had; her ribs are wonderful. Bae is short for "baby"; her real name is Ellen White. Over the years, I've cried so much on her shoulder, I just call her a big water closet. But back on Eighth Street, we were just struggling together, trying to move up a little higher.

"I remember going over there at night; there were just the two of us," Bae notes. "We'd do each other's hair, we'd watch *American Bandstand* or we'd just talk. We were so young, with young children, watching *American Bandstand,* eating a bologna sandwich with a Pepsi. Sometimes, we split the Pepsi.

"My first husband had left me with twin babies in my stomach—

two little girls. I should have been a welfare mother, a junkie, an alcoholic. That's part of the common bond that Cissy and I shared: 'Uh-uh, it ain't gonna take us down. We're gonna stick it out.'

"We were working poor. Women, black women in those days didn't aspire to be biochemists. We took jobs at factories like RCA and they were considered good jobs, like being a secretary. You went to work in a nice dress and high heels and you put that little apron on at work. You almost felt middle-class. We shopped at Lerner's, at Macy's and Orbach's, where if you were lucky, you found a leftover from Bloomie's. But there was always that drive to move ahead, move on up.

"Cissy taught me to pray . . . And she used to bug me about going back to church. She knew I was Catholic, she knew I had a good heart, but she used to say, 'You've got to honor thy Father. You better get your narrow little butt back in church.' "

In August 1961, Michael was born. I took a few weeks off from work, nursed him and then introduced him to Miss Hardy. Now I had two children in day care on top of all our other bills! I picked up a few extra dollars directing another church's choir in addition to New Hope's and I continued to rehearse and sing with the Drinkards. John always came along, traveled with us to churches, because he couldn't get enough of us singing.

"You have no idea how good they really were," says John. "Their harmonies were absolutely off the wall. You couldn't understand how anybody could do the things they did with their voices. They could sing and change harmony parts as they were singing. They could hold their own with the 'stars' of gospel—Bradford, Clara Ward, Mahalia, all of them. If Lee would have let them travel, if they would have given up those day jobs, they could have been just as big as Bradford, Clara and Mahalia. Bigger."

Of course, Lee wasn't hearing any of John's glamorous ideas. She knew he genuinely loved the Drinkards, and respected her; that's why she let him come along to hear us sing in churches. But she still kept him at arm's length. She felt he was a loose cannon waiting to go off. At least once that I remember, she even threw him out of a church!

We were singing at a church in Hackensack, New Jersey, sitting up in the choir stand. In the pulpit was a woman evangelist with a healing ministry. John's Catholic backround had never prepared him for a Pentecostal healing service with people falling out and getting "slain in the spirit." John didn't know how much was for real and how much wasn't. Ever the cynic, he suspected there was a lot of sanctified theatrics going on. Every time a supplicant was slain and fell backward, into the waiting arms of a nurse, John and Sonny, Reebie's husband, found it so hilarious, they just sat in the second-row pew and giggled like two little kids. Annie had a bad headache and when the evangelist invited those who wanted to be healed to come forward, Annie started down from the choir stand. Already I saw John following Annie with his eyes. In the first pew, I saw Lee; well into a slow burn about John and Sonny giggling in back of her. Annie waited her turn at the end of a line that went up the aisle. People were falling out in front of her, apparently healed. Annie's turn came; she was the last one. She closed her eyes and the woman evangelist anointed her with oil and prayed over her in tongues. Annie "received" her healing and reverently made her way back to her place in the choir stand. The church was quiet, only the organist playing softly. But John was following Annie like a hawk with his eyes. He was dying to know if her headache was healed—maybe he and Sonny had money on it. Judy also wanted to know if Annie had been healed. Even down in the pews, without hearing a word, John knew exactly what Judy was asking Annie. All John had to see was Annie slowly shaking her head "no" and that was it. He couldn't control himself; he hollered, he screamed, he busted out laughing. Loud. Down in the first pew, Lee had about all she was going to tolerate from irreverent John Houston. She stood up, in front of the whole church, looked right at John and pointed to the door. John and Sonny got up and slunk up the aisle, right out of the church.

John had a fascination with the world of gospel music performers. They were the raggediest crew you ever saw—they lived out of a suitcase, said and did some of the most hilarious things. Some had a problem with alcohol. But in their hearts, they were sold out to God. Sometimes they even appeared to be fools for Christ. We were playing a gospel show in Connecticut once with the great Alex Bradford. Alex was such a great songwriter and singer, it was never any secret that Ray Charles was deeply influenced by him. Bradford combined drama with his shows, complete with other singers, actors and even dancers. Alex and his troupe portrayed events from the Bible, the resurrection of Lazarus, the Easter story. During a show in Connecticut that John and I were watching from the wings, one of Bradford's young male dancers fell, injuring himself on the piano. John and I both gasped. Concerned for the young man's condition, we both asked if he was all right when we saw him later backstage. "Oh, that was nothing. I was dancing in the Spirit," he said beaming extravagantly. "When I'm dancing in the Spirit, the Lord always protects me." The next day John and I were picking up a few things in town when this particular young man turned the corner. His head and his leg were wrapped up in bandages, and he was hobbling on a couple of crutches. John and I fell out right on the sidewalk. We still laugh about that guy. Characters like this and much worse antics convinced Lee she was right to never let us tour. No one else in the family ever gave her an argument about it.

"When I met Cissy," says John, "she was cemented to that family. They meant everything to her."

John had no chance to manage the Drinkard Singers. But he began to take the Gospelaires around. They were a group that my nieces Dionne and Dee Dee had formed with a few other girls from New Hope's young people's choir. John drove them to churches and arena-type gospel programs. One day, when we were playing the Apollo again with Alex Bradford and the Davis Sisters, Abie Baker, a musician, came backstage. He was a trumpet player trying to put together a recording session and he needed some background singers.

"Anybody know where I can get some singers?" he asked, standing in our dressing room.

Though John was sitting right there on a folding chair he didn't catch the drift. Then Davis Sister Jackie Verdell nudged John. "You have background singers," she said.

"I do?" said John.

Jackie told him he could use the Gospelaires, Dionne and Dee Dee's group. None of us remember what ever came out of Abie Baker's session. All John remembers is that Abie taught him his recipe for chicken fricassee. But right there in that Apollo dressing room, at least four careers were launched: Dionne, Dee Dee and the other girls in the group—Judy's sister Sylvia Shemwell, Carol Harding and Myrna Smith.

"John became kind of our manager," says Dionne. "He was the one who would get up in the morning and get on that bus with us, or get us in the car and drive us into the studio. And Cissy played a very important role in that—in allowing him to do that, because we took him away for many, many long sessions at night."

John seemed so happy taking Dionne and the girls into New York I didn't mind. He was right where he wanted to be—in the middle of the action. He would catch a bus with them in the afternoon and take it over to Port Authority. John would shepherd the girls north through Times Square and the myriad of recording studios that lay beyond. On Forty-seventh Street, in the lobby of the dumpy America Hotel, was Mira Sound, where Phil Spector liked to work. Further uptown was A&R Studio, Bell Sound, Associated, Regent Sound, Scepter Records on Fifty-fourth Street and on Fifty-seventh Street and later Columbus Circle, there was Atlantic.

They all loved John: the engineers, the musicians, the producers and the money guys behind the producers. He had the common touch and the gift of gab. He hung out in the control room hobnobbing with the movers and shakers of the record business: label owners like Jerry Wexler, who had a piece of Atlantic. Morris Levy, who owned Roulette Records and the Birdland nightclub, and Scepter Records' boss, Florence Greenberg. He bantered back and forth with talented producers who were just coming into their own making the hit records of the day. Jerry Leiber and Mike Stoller, who did the Coasters and the Drifters. Luther Dixon, who worked on the Shirelles hits, and Henry Glover, who was especially good at cutting bluesy records for Morris Levy. John's always been a people person. He genuinely enjoyed the contact, and he loved sitting there in the booth soaking up knowledge.

John's easy manner with executive and musician alike got Dionne and the group a string of good sessions. Jerry Leiber and Mike Stoller used them behind the Drifters; Henry Glover called on them for backgrounds on some rock-and-roll records. They were making money. It wasn't long before John thought that I could be doing the same thing. He thought my voice was better than them all. He'd listened to me sing with the Drinkards; he'd heard me just goofing around the house singing something from *West Side Story* and he was convinced I could do it all—gospel, pop, show tunes and cabaret. John had big ideas, but frankly, my dear, I wasn't interested.

"My biggest challenge," says John, "was getting Cissy to do something other than gospel."

John always had a lot of things he wanted me to try. But I've got a pretty strong head myself. I'm initially suspicious; I guess it goes back to losing my mother so young, thinking people were holding out on me, keeping information from me about how sick my mother really was and how she died. Until I get comfortable with a new idea, I'll resist you.

I had a million reasons why I didn't want to go over to New York and sing pop music for John. For one thing, I had a good day job at RCA. Coming up in the tail end of the Depression, my father really drilled it into us how much of a blessing a good, steady job was. I'd been at RCA for ten years and I'd reached some kind of seniority. Plus, there were benefits, a credit union. Why should I leave that kind of security? And for another, I had enough pride that I just didn't want to go do something because John wanted me to. I hadn't resolved it in my own mind. That was probably because I knew how my sisters felt about pop music. My father never allowed it to be played in the house. Even when he'd go over to visit his sister Tiny, my cousin Honey knew to "cut off the Victrola and stop all that mess."

"It was never talked about," says Anne. "But you knew how he felt about it. Secular music had a taint on it. It wasn't kosher and he never steered us in that direction."

Those who the church felt had left gospel, like Dinah Washington, Sam Cooke and the Staple Singers, were branded "blues singers," renegades, apostates, backsliders. They were booed if they ever tried to stand in a church or on a gospel program.

"In those days, everybody who sang gospel believed that if you switched over to popular music, something bad would happen to you," said Sam Cooke's guitarist, Bobby Womack. "I grew up believing all that and I was afraid to make the change. See, the gospel world used to be a lot more sacred than it is now. Our parents put us out of the house when we started singing pop music."

Dionne's involvement in pop illustrated a curious double standard. It was okay for the youngsters to do it, went this line of reasoning. They were the next generation; they weren't raised like us. We knew better, they didn't.

I decided I wasn't going anywhere with John. The whole thing raised too many questions, too many dark thoughts, and made me uncomfortable. Besides, my first priority was my new baby and my day job. If I didn't keep that going, we'd be on the street.

Then one cold autumn night—September 13, 1961, to be precise—when Michael was only a few weeks old, John got in a terrible jam. He'd promised Henry Glover he'd bring Dionne and the girls into New York for a session. At the last minute, Dionne got a call from Scepter, who needed her for a Shirelles session. Dionne took off for the Shirelles and John was stuck for a top voice.

John didn't want to disappoint Henry Glover. Henry liked John, but you could coast just so far on friendship. As a manager, John was obliged to producers like Henry for continued work. If it got around that you were unreliable, other producers would stop calling you; there were fifty other guys waiting in line to pick up the work you blew.

John didn't want to mess Henry up with his boss either. Morris Levy was, as John used to say, "a renegade of the first order." He was Alan Freed's manager, owned Birdland and had lots of ties in the underworld. He had a sign on the wall behind his desk that said: "Please God, Send Me a Bastard with Talent." Morris was a gangster—a lovable gangster, but a gangster nonetheless.

I told John I'd be his top voice.

"Are you sure?" he asked.

"Yeah, I'm sure," I said.

I left Michael and Gary with Bae and we got in the car.

"I bundled her up," says John. "I was afraid. It was cold; she'd just had the baby . . . I think she did it just to help me out; just to make sure I was straight."

Maybe I did. John was doing so well booking the girls for sessions. He seemed so happy in the middle of the action. He was doing something he liked. I didn't have to worry about him driving a load of beef on some rain-slicked highway between New York and Chicago.

Henry Glover wasn't too happy to see me.

"Henry wanted to cancel the session because Dionne wasn't there," says John. "So I got him back in the control room and I talked to him. I told him, 'Listen . . . just listen.' And when Cissy started singing in the backgrounds, he changed his mind fast. Then he didn't want anybody else but Cissy back there."

The session went on until 6 A.M. Henry called us back in for the next three days and every one of the sessions ran late. The artist was Ronnie Hawkins, a Roulette Records star, a good old boy from Arkansas that Morris Levy was trying to turn into the next Elvis Presley.

"Elvis is in the Army, and Buddy Holly is dead," Morris used to say. "Ronnie's the only one left."

I guess Ronnie was good-looking enough and he could sing some, but he wasn't no Elvis. His band sounded good; four Canadians and a blond-haired drummer from Arkansas. On one of the breaks, Levon Helm, the drummer, asked John where they could eat. John started to point him to the nearest Child's, where you could get a reliable cheeseburger. "No . . . no," the drummer interrupted. "We're lookin' for some good southern cookin'. You know, ribs and collard greens!"

I learned much later that Ronnie's band went on to great success, first as Bob Dylan's band and then on their own. That little drummer was even in a few big movies. But at the time I couldn't have cared less. I barely spoke to anyone during those three days of sessions. Part of the reason was that I wasn't used to talking to white people, even musicians, on a casual basis. I was probably a little suspicious of them too. Except for my teachers in school, I didn't have much contact with white people. I didn't think anything of it, I just wasn't used to it. My father never expressed any kind of racism in our house—that wasn't Christian. Mostly, though, I was there to work, not socialize. John could run his mouth all he wanted; I just wasn't interested.

I really didn't feel all that comfortable there. I knew I had to be in that studio, but I couldn't wait to leave. I wanted to get my work done, and get it done quickly. I was there, but I didn't have to be part of them. I was in the world, but I wasn't of the world, as St. Paul put it. I knew what my coming here would mean to my sisters and I didn't want to think about it.

John helped me over bad feelings like this. At church, I had to fight my own battles. No one ever said anything to my face, but people would talk. Serving two Gods? Please. How can you serve two Gods when I know there's only one, okay? At times like these, I thought about the words to one of my favorite gospels, "That's Enough," written by Dorothy Love Coates.

There's always somebody talking about me,
Really I don't mind.
They're trying to block and stop my progress,
Most of the time.
The mean things you say don't make me feel bad,
I can't miss a friend I've never had,
I've got Jesus and that's enough.

Besides, I was only singing backgrounds. I wasn't a pop singing star. I was doing a job, performing a function, that didn't make me less faithful than anything else I did.

"Cissy always had that attitude 'as long as you don't become part of it,' " says Annie.

My filling in for Dionne renewed John's relationship with Henry. And Morris Levy always paid us and paid us on time, something that confounded my husband for years, given Morris' reputation.

I went back to my job at RCA and took a session when it didn't interfere with my day job. A few months later, however, Annie and I would leave RCA at lunch and work an afternoon session in the city. We sang on a few things together, but Annie bowed out early in the game.

"Somehow it just didn't set right with me. The atmosphere was not congenial for me," says Anne. "There were things going on that made me uncomfortable. Also, I couldn't always get babysitters and juggling the sessions with RCA started to get hectic.

"Cissy was always more outgoing than me. And she always had that attitude of not letting it become part of you."

After I got my feet wet with Ronnie Hawkins, Dionne, Dee Dee and I started to do a lot of sessions together. We sang behind the Drifters for two young Jewish guys from LA, Jerry Leiber and Mike Stoller. At first, it was a shock to realize that these two had written songs for the Coasters and some of my favorite artists, like Ruth Brown and Jimmy Witherspoon—they had such a great handle on black slang. Jerry was the wisecracking half of the team who usually wrote the lyrics. Think of the Coasters' "Charlie Brown" and you'll get a picture of Jerry Leiber's sense of humor. He had the strangest eyes—one brown and one blue. It used to spook me every time I looked at him. Mike Stoller was more studious and the musical brains of the outfit.

"We knew about the Drinkards, so we were already fans," says Mike. "We couldn't do a lot of overdubbing then, so you really had to catch it on the mix the first time. You could always count on them to get it right every time.

"They had this amazing rapport between them. They breathed together, they felt each other, they knew where they were going to go. If they didn't breathe together on the first take; they did on the second . . . they were almost as one voice, except that they were actually singing three different parts."

We had that "rapport" because Sylvia, Myrna, Dionne and Dee Dee had been in my choir at New Hope. My experience with my choirs and just singing for so long had given me a good ear for harmonics. Jerry and Mike appreciated that. But I did something else with the voices that won us a lot of admirers, and as a result, got us a lot of work. At the time it was an innovation, but few people ever realized what I had done and why it made my groups sound different. Most groups had three members—I added a fourth. But I used the fourth voice in an unexpected way. I had Estelle, the bottom voice, double the part that I was singing on top. It made for a much fuller, richer sound. But nobody ever figured out why we sounded so different.

I admired the way Jerry and Mike used our voices. They always knew exactly what they wanted. I was kind of amazed how much they knew and appreciated gospel, even claimed to be Drinkards fans. But I was more amazed at how expert they were at making records. For many months I just watched them: How they took a song apart, broke it down and improved it. How they went to an arranger next, who translated the sounds they heard in their head to paper. The arranger's "charts" included a part for every instrument in the rhythm section— and strings, brass, woodwinds and voices if requested. Then Mike and Jerry or the arranger would select the right musicians to transform the chart into a great record. I really had no idea that so much work went into a song that ran three minutes and fifty-seconds!

"On Broadway" by the Drifters, produced by Jerry and Mike in 1963, illustrates perfectly the many hands it takes to make a great record. It started as a great song written by Barry Mann and Cynthia Weil. First, Mike suggested modulating up and changing the key. Another one of Mike's ideas vastly improved the song. Barry originally sang the line, "They say the neon lights are bright on Broadway," going down on the word "Broadway." Mike had the word sung higher and changed the whole mood of the song. Once Leiber and Stoller had hammered the song into shape, they called in an arranger. One of their favorites was Gary Sherman.

Gary has earned Pulitzer prize nominations for his symphonic compositions, arranged thirty number one records and masterminded a long-running series of Coke commercials, one of which I sang on. But back in the early 1960s, he was brand-new to R&B; his experience was strictly orchestral. Next to hipsters like Leiber and Stoller, Gary looked like a fish out of water. He wore those clunky "space shoes" (from his days as a podiatrist), loose-fitting, comfortable clothing and had frizzy red hair. But it was not for his personal style that Jerry and Mike hired him. Sherman was a genius at orchestration. Writing parts for strings, brass, woodwinds and percussion, he was able to create the mood and drama that Leiber and Stoller were searching for. When he returned with his chart, Jerry and Mike sat down at the piano and examined every nuance of Gary's score.

"We would have major discussions about everything," laughs Sherman. "We would discuss violas, cello lines—even rests!"

Next, the artist entered the picture. The Drifters were great singers, many sharing gospel roots. But even their wonderful sound was just another color on Leiber and Stoller's palette. For "On Broadway," Jerry and Mike had these great singers just riffing the same rumbly bass unison into a mike for an hour—sounding like some kind of chain gang from the 1920s. The moody undertow of cellos, percussion and metallic guitars created a New York City night that went on for eternity. In the break, we girls, singing as high as the heavenly host, offered the song's battered hero the only salvation he'd ever know on Seventh Avenue's rain-slicked asphalt. The scenes Jerry and Mike crafted were so vivid they stopped being records—they were movies. The first fifteen seconds of the Drifters' "Some Kind of Wonderful"—the boom of an oriental gong and a choir shimmering with so many layers of voices it is no longer of this earth—sounds like a combination of *The Ten Commandments,* and *The Inn of the Sixth Happiness.* These guys raised pop music to a whole new level. I was glad to be able to contribute whatever I could to their records, but more often than not, I was like any other musician or artist on a Leiber/Stoller date—a tube of paint in Jerry and Mike's hands.

We would sometimes rehearse for upcoming sessions in Jerry and Mike's office on the ninth floor of the Brill Building on Broadway. One day, during a rehearsal for the Drifters' "Mexican Divorce," the writer of the song, Burt Bacharach, wandered in. He took an immediate interest in Dionne. After we left, he asked Jerry and Mike if he could use Dionne on some of his projects. Shortly after that, Dionne began recording demos, demonstration records of a songwriter's compositions, for other artists to study and mimic when actually recording the song.

In the months after Michael was born, Jerry and Mike kept us busy stacking our voices on top of the Drifters, giving them some "choral height," as Mike liked to say, on records like "Some Kind of Wonderful," "Please Stay," also written by Burt Bacharach, "Sweets for My Sweet," and "When My Little Girl Is Smiling."

Things got so busy in the studio that I was forced to quit RCA. I had been there eleven years, and it was time to go. More to the point, in two full days of sessions in New York, I could earn what it took me a week to earn at RCA! Of course, it wasn't as easy as it sounded. Three back-to-back sessions in New York could eat up practically your whole day. Sessions ran from 10 A.M. to 1 P.M., 2 until 5 P.M., 7 until 10 and then 11 to 1 A.M. Of course, some sessions ran late into the morning. Eventually, I joined the union and made a little more money as the contractor—one who contracts and "hires" the background voices for the session.

Dionne didn't last long as Burt's demo singer. She fought for and won the right to record some of Burt Bacharach and Hal David's songs. The last demo she recorded was "Make It Easy on Yourself," which Jerry Butler got the hit on. The first one she recorded for herself, with me, Dee Dee and Sylvia singing background, was "Don't Make Me Over." Dionne was barely twenty-two years old when the record went into the Top Ten in December 1962. As the story goes, the record pressing plant mispelled "Warrick" for Warwick and the mistake was just never corrected.

"Don't Make Me Over" started a steady flow of work from Scepter Records and Burt Bacharach, who also produced Dionne's records. Some weeks I spent more time in the studio than in my own home. But the work also opened up to me a wonderful world of musicians, producers, arrangers and songwriters. Some of them were funny, creative souls so absorbed in their craft they hardly realized how hilarious and endearing they really were. If not for the recording studio, our ships would have passed in the night. But as I worked with these people every day, I gradually let go of some of my normally suspicious nature. I came to respect some of them and even love others.

My day of work in the studio began at 10 A.M. for a morning session. By the time John dropped me off, there were already people working there, getting the room ready. In the booth, a tech person was cleaning the tape machines. Out in the studio, a piano tuner was tinkling away. The engineer and the assistant engineer were busy setting up microphones. Depending on the job, there could be as many as forty-five players on a session that called for strings, brass, woodwinds and percussion. The girls and I made our way through the control room, through the big room already being set up with chairs and music stands for the soon-arriving rhythm section and orchestral players.

One of the most important people on the date was also there early. The arranger was usually checking his master arrangement against the individual parts that the copyist had duplicated for the various musicians. Three arrangers in particular worked on most of the records I sang on: Bert Keyes, Teacho Wiltshire and Gary Sherman. Bert and Teacho were more "street," more "feel" arrangers, working on their charts right up until the session began, and sometimes still feeding pages to the copyist while the session was in progress! Bert did a lot of Shirelles records. Teacho was wonderful—a tall, light-skinned black guy with a great smile. His arrangements were simple and melodic, with a nice uptown feel that included some good little hooks. He and John became thick as thieves. "I'm worried about your health, little brother," John would say, hooking an arm around Teacho's shoulders. "Let me buy you a nice piece of meat." John would take Teacho down to Gorman's on Forty-second Street and buy him a hot dog! Teacho wrote the funky chart for the Isley Brothers' "Twist and Shout." As I mentioned already, Gary Sherman became known as one of the most brilliant arrangers on the scene. His first big record was Jay and the Americans' "She Cried," another Leiber/Stoller production. Gary was able to translate the intent of songwriters like Barry Mann and Cynthia Weil and Carole King and Gerry Goffin into first-class charts. One of the key players responsible for blending the black R&B sound with pop. In the beginning of his career as an arranger and still fresh from the symphonic world, he listened to us as singers, learning the R&B/gospel feel.

"She never made me feel like 'I'm black, you're white,' " Gary recalls. "She never made me feel like a 'honky' who didn't understand the R&B idiom.

"Gospel harmony is a diatonic kind of thing. I never had them singing anything that wasn't appropriate [out of the pure triad] major sevenths, ninths, thirteenths. Nor would we ever have them sing a line that they felt uncomfortable with, a blasphemous or off-color line. Once there was a word they were a little upset about. We changed it immediately. She was a real strong church person, very moral. She believed in the teachings of Christ, I knew that instantly. It was no act."

Fifteen or twenty minutes before the session began, while the arranger was explaining his chart to the producer—Leiber/Stoller, Jerry Wexler or Jerry Ragavoy—and the artist—Solomon Burke, Freddie Scott or Lorraine Ellison—the "guys" would start filing in. The musicians would hang up their coats, take out their axes and warm up their instruments. One of our favorite engineers, Brooks Arthur, explains the unique mix of talent that had entered the room.

"Sure, Gary Sherman was a great arranger," says Brooks, "I was a great engineer, Leiber and Stoller, Mann and Weil were great songwriters, but now you had to sprinkle in the black guys with the white guys, the Latin percussionists, so when you cross-pollinate, you get a real sound, a real record incorporating natural feels, things you can't describe or put down as notes on paper."

There were guys like pianist Paul Griffin and guitarist Eric Gale, now unpacking his instrument. In the corner, Gary Chester, a blondish, all-American was warming up on drums.

Paul Griffin, a little black gospel piano player was one of the first musicians I remember meeting on the sessions for Scepter Records. Paul looked like an elf who always had a smile on his face. He was a few years younger than me and had grown up in Harlem. In Paradise Baptist on 135th Street, where his mother took him to church, they sat, for no particular reason, behind the church pianist. Paul would drift off during the service and find himself watching the pianist's hands. This went on for several years. One day after church, Paul was just doodling around on the church piano and he found he could play it. Like my brother

Nicky, he just picked it up. When the church's pianist died, Paul took over. The saxophonist King Curtis gave Paul his first opportunity to record around 1959. But Paul went on to play piano not only on all of Dionne's and the Shirelles' records but also on most of the records released by Scepter. He became an in-demand session player, adding a gospel touch to Bob Dylan's "Like a Rolling Stone" and Don McLean's "American Pie." To give you an idea of the caliber of musician Paul is, Burt Bacharach, who is a very capable pianist, trusted all the piano parts on his records to Paul while he conducted.

"The sound that you hear on those records is the sound of gratitude," says Paul of his early session efforts. "Being thankful for being able to play . . . grateful, as if I'd been saved from something horrible. If it wasn't for music, I don't know what would have become of me. I'd had a lot of jobs—I was a cutter in the garment district; I delivered groceries for a supermarket, but nothing with any kind of future.

"I'd grown up in Harlem with no male role models except the junkies, the pimps and the numbers runners. John Houston was a revelation to me as an African American, a sharp, intelligent, wonderful guy.

"I really liked Dionne's voice. In the studio sometimes I'd get so hung up on it, I'd forget to play! But the first time I heard Cissy's voice, I heard that gospel thing and it felt like home. I was filled with instant love for her and her whole family. If they call Aretha the Queen of Soul, then they should call Cissy the Queen Mother. She'd come into a session sometimes and she'd say, 'Hi, Paul.' She'd gesture toward the control room and say, 'Let's forget about them today. Let's just do this next one for me and you.' That used to knock me out."

One of Paul's friends—tight ever since they first played that King Curtis date in 1959—was Hugh McCracken, another rhythm guitar player on our sessions. A talented, "blue-eyed soul" brother, Hugh was an exceptional player who also doubled on harmonica. That's Hugh's tremelo guitar that opens Neil Diamond's "Girl, You'll Be a Woman Soon" and his funky harmonica on Neil's "You Got to Me." His bluesy, soulful touch is all over countless hits from Neil Diamond, Van Morrison, B. B. King and Aretha Franklin.

Some of these guys were fun to watch—someone should have had a camera. Like Carl Lynch, a little brother who played "chicks"—that chick-chick guitar sound ticking away on most 1960s pop records. Just think of any of the medium-tempo Shirelles records and you'll hear Carl. Carl would sit back with a big smile, close his eyes and open and close his mouth with the beat. Gary Chester, a phenomenal drummer (Burt Bacharach's first call drummer), also blinked with the tempo.

Eric Gale was a legendary guitarist. He played on hundreds of sessions for artists like Aretha Franklin, Solomon Burke, Frank Sinatra and Paul Simon. Eric was so unique as a player that he was able to play the "chicks" and at the same time incorporate a figure. Other guitarists would try to look over his shoulder to copy his fingering and Eric would get pissed off.

The session's contractor would take the parts from the arranger and hand them out to the musicians. During the quick run-through that followed, the arranger would have the opportunity to explain the chart further to the producer or artist and give input to the musicians. During this rehearsal, Brooks, the engineer, would set his record levels so as not to waste valuable time during the session. Time was our enemy. It drove us to complete at least three to four songs per each three-hour session. We learned to work quickly and make good takes the first time. The producer would call for a run-through, then sometimes play it back for us immediately—"like a Polaroid," Brooks used to say—so everybody could see where we were at. Then we'd start going for takes. If we hadn't nailed our expected three to four songs and the budget allowed, we might go over an extra half hour. If the client was "rich," we might work an additional hour.

After the rhythm section and orchestral players went home, the producer and the engineer would often take us out of the smaller vocal booth into the main studio.

"You could always hear a background that was recorded in a booth," says Brooks. "It was kind of squared off at the top."

We would overdub our previously recorded parts, trying to put some more teeth into our background. Sometimes some of the fellows would come out of the booth and add their voices to ours. I remember Brooks and Jeff Barry singing with us when we did our background part for Van Morrison's "Brown-Eyed Girl." Gary Sherman also used to love to come into the studio and sing with us.

"You can't imagine the thrill of singing in the middle of them," recalls Gary. "To inbed yourself inside of that gospel voice, to have such pleasure, what could be better in this world?"

The studio had emptied out and things were a little more relaxed now. Brooks would come out and take a break with us. We'd have our coffee and danish together—Brooks would turn a music stand flat so we could rest our coffee on it. He was a nice dark-haired Jewish guy, with great engineering chops.

"It was a special privilege to be able to share that coffee and danish with them," Brooks recalls. "You got to know them as friends and colleagues; you got a better feel for them—it was a special bonding for all of us. There were life lessons to be learned in that studio every day. And it was as much about hearing those girls yakkin' between takes as it was about hearing them sing. You'd hear funny things about their families, their clothes, funny private things, jokes. They'd tell you about records you'd never heard, so you went out and bought them. And you, too, might share something with them. You might play something back for them that you'd recorded from another session. If they liked it, you'd feel honored. The coffee and danish with Cissy and those girls was as valuable as college, maybe. You learned about being cool, being hip. About not being a *yenta* [busybody] and knowing your place."

In 1964, Jerry Leiber and Mike Stoller stopped producing the Drifters. They were picked up by a Jewish whiz kid originally from the Bronx: Bertrand Russell Berns, a.k.a. Bert Berns. No comet streaked across the music business in the early 1960s faster—or more brilliantly—than Bert. In a few short years, he had written or produced a pile of top ten hits by Solomon Burke, the Isley Brothers, Van Morrison, the McCoys and the Exciters; started a successful record company; and discovered and launched some important artists. Like few others, he was able to make records that were so soulful, they appealed to both the black R&B community and the white pop audience. He brought people together—black, white, Latin—in the studio, making his records and in the audience, buying them. Bert used me and the girls almost exclusively as his background singers; he wanted the passion he heard in gospel always driving his records on.

Jerry Wexler met him around 1961 when Bert was a fifty-dollar-a-week song plugger, demonstrating his own songs on guitar and piano in the Atlantic Records offices. Silently, Bert watched Wexler and Phil Spector butcher his song "Twist and Shout" as they tried to record it with a male duo, Derek and Howard. When the song was cut properly a year later on the Isley Brothers, it was a smash. Only months after they first heard it, the Beatles added it to their repetoire. When they recorded it in 1964, it went to number two on the charts, making Bert a very rich man at thirty-five. He started looking for property in New Jersey, eventually building a house with a guitar-shaped swimming pool. Even with a wife and a couple infants, it was hard to visualize Bert as a family man. He was moving so fast, covering so much ground—songwriter, producer, label executive, talent scout—all with such passion and intensity that you had to wonder how long he could keep up the pace.

The same month Dionne's career took off with "Don't Make Me Over," December 1962, I also got pregnant. This would be my last child; I was getting tired of babies. I'd had two boys and I wanted to believe I was carrying a girl.

Whatever it was going to be, it would be the first child I ever carried that spent the first nine months of its life in the recording studio! Whether I was singing on a hard-preachin' Solomon Burke record ("Can't Nobody Love You," March 1963), a man they said had such deep gospel roots he could be loved equally by rednecks and blacks as long as they both were Baptists . . . or we were wailing like banshees in the cool asphalt jungle of the Drifters' "On Broadway" (January 1963), this was bound to be an interesting child. One thing I know for sure. That baby never stopped moving inside me or making me feel ill.

John squired me back and forth from Jersey to the city. After he dropped me off, Tom Dowd watched over me.

Tom, or the "kid," as Ray Charles used to call him, was Atlantic Records' chief engineer. He was a genius. Tom could make terrible singers sound good and good singers sound fabulous. He started with Atlantic in the late 1940s as a kid fresh out of Columbia University. In those days, in an office on West Fifty-sixth Street, he would push the desks of his two bosses, Jerry Wexler and Ahmet Ertegun, to one side of the room and record Big Joe Turner, Ray Charles and Bobby Darin. He engineered all of Atlantic's sessions through the 1970s, but by then he was really producing too.

"First time I met her? Wexler hands me a box of tape with a chick singer," says Tom. "Says fix it up—quick! I called in Cissy, Dionne and Dee Dee. They nailed their parts and we overdubbed the background in one take. The record? "Just One Look" by Doris Troy—not a record you'd ever notice had a background. They were so close to her, they breathed with her."

While I was pregnant that year, I used to scare Tom to death. The baby was overdue, I was huge and I'd get these false labor pains. Tom would stop the session, petrified I was going to have the baby right in the studio.

In Tom's forty years with Atlantic, he presided over several eras of popular music. From its beginning, Atlantic always leaned toward black, rootsy music. But in the 1960s, it became the home of soul music, which was really just gospel music with secular lyrics. Three of Atlantic's greatest soul singers came out of a gospel background: Wilson Pickett, Solomon Burke and Aretha Franklin.

"We were coming up with more records that we recorded in the South, out of Memphis and Muscle Shoals, that had more of a gospel or a religious feel than the records you would make in New York, which were inclined to be more bluesy, jazz," says Tom. "Cissy and her group particularly liked singing on those kinds of songs.

"And when it came to getting somebody to sing with Aretha, we had the ideal solution—because we had these girls that had the same basic musical root as Aretha, which was a church root. And that chemistry just worked beautifully. They knew each other on eye contact."

I'd heard Aretha's father, Reverend C. L. Franklin, on the radio as far back as I can remember. He was a very popular minister from Detroit. Aretha's mother abandoned the family when Aretha was a child. Her father's church and especially her home became a way station for some big names in gospel, like Clara Ward, Mahalia Jackson, Sam Cooke and James Cleveland. Clara Ward was her mentor. Aretha traces her desire to sing back to the funeral of an aunt when Clara Ward sang Thomas Dorsey's "Peace in the Valley."

All of the foregoing is a matter of public record. Anything else I know about Aretha is private. She's had her troubles like everybody else and I don't feel it's my place to talk about her. She feels like a little sister to me.

I'm very proud of Aretha. When you look up "soul singer" in the dictionary, her picture ought to be there. Her records defined "soul" because she never stopped singing like a gospel singer. Of all her records, though, I keep going back to the first time I ever heard her. In 1956, when she was fourteen years old, singing "Never Grow Old" in her father's church.

I have heard of a land
On the faraway strand,
'Tis the beautiful home
Of the soul.

Built by Jesus on high
Where we never shall die,
'Tis the land
Where we'll never grow old.

We'll never grow old,
We'll never grow old,
There is a land
Where we'll never grow old.

Every gospel singer worth their salt knows this hymn. But Aretha made it her own. In 1972, she rerecorded it, live, like the first time in church. There is an ecstasy she reaches that pulls the whole church along with her. You can hear them shouting as one voice, the congregation and the singer. When I hear it now, I still feel the same way I did the first time I heard it. It always ministers to my heart. It's the ultimate reality check. No matter what happens to me on this earth, no matter how bad things get, no matter how poor, how friendless, how bankrupt of spirit, there is coming a day when God will wipe away every tear. And there will be no more weeping and no more sorrow, and the former things will pass away. This is my hope. If I didn't believe this, I simply couldn't believe.

Between calls from producers like Bert Berns, Jerry Leiber and Mike Stoller, and Burt Bacharach, I continued to be in the studio more than I was in my own home. There were sessions for Aretha, Solomon Burke, Wilson Pickett, Gene Pitney, and Dionne. I marvel at how I ever had time to deliver a baby. But on a hot August night in 1963, I awoke from a deep sleep. As I climbed over John to get to the bathroom, my water broke all over him. John dried off, put on his pants and drove me to the hospital.

After I did all that pushing and the baby's head was out, they gave me some anesthesia and knocked me out. When John came into my room later to tell me it was a girl, I thought he was playing one of his bad jokes on me. I was convinced it was a boy.

"I'm telling you, it's a girl," John protested.

"John, stop your lyin'," I told him.

When they brought her to me, I stopped doubting. She was the most beautiful thing I'd ever seen. A headful of hair, eyelashes, fingernails—she had everything. I named her Whitney Elizabeth; Whitney was a name I liked from a TV show and Elizabeth was John's mother's name.

Three weeks later, I sat in the living room nursing Whitney. On television, I watched 200,000 people mass in front of the Lincoln Monument for the largest peaceful demonstration in our country's history, the March on Washington for Jobs and Freedom.

I am not a political person; I'm not a "causes" person. But I was deeply touched by Dr. King's speech. I thought about what my father had been through in the South; in Newark, how the cops used to bother my brother just because he was black. Look at what people were going through in the South, just trying to integrate a lunch counter. Even John. He was back out there having to drive again. A man that smart had no business driving for a living. My father was the type of guy who never used his color as a crutch. But the sorry fact was that if John's complexion was four shades lighter he wouldn't have had any trouble finding an executive position in some blue-chip firm. Things weren't right in our society; things still aren't right. We are so suspicious of anyone who is different than us; and from suspicion grows fear; then fear becomes hate. That hot August day I prayed that the world would change, if only for Whitney's sake.

"I have a dream," Dr. King addressed the multitude in Washington, "that one day . . . sons of former slaves and sons of former slave-owners will be able to sit down together at the table of brotherhood."

At that moment, something made me think of the recording studio. I had taken several weeks off to be with my new baby. In three years singing on sessions, this was the longest I had ever been away. I had to admit I missed my buddies over there. It occurred to me, in that moment, that our little mixed group of kooky Jews, soul brothers and Irish engineers had, in a sense, already fulfilled Dr. King's dream of brotherhood. In just a few more years, we would literally fulfill his dream when we recorded in Muscle Shoals and Memphis—making music with white Southerners named Oldham, Allman, Cropper and Cogbill. If their great-grandfathers didn't own slaves, they probably had some rich cousins who did.

At least in the recording studio we were living together as God intended us to. Some days, we spent twelve to fifteen hours together there. The skin-deep barriers of race seemed to fall away as we toiled side by side creating our little pop masterpieces. There was an optimism in the air. People were coming together. Even my old friend Sam Cooke, after hearing Bob Dylan's "Blowin' in the Wind," was inspired to write a song that captured the way we all felt. Sam titled it simply "A Change Is Gonna Come."

> *I was born by the river, in a little tent,*
> *And oh, just like the river I been running ever since.*
> *It's been a long time coming, but I know*
> *A change is gonna come!*

NINE

He changed my life,
He changed my life,
Everything's all right
Since He changed my life.
—*"He Changed My Life"*

A new baby always feels like a brand-new start. Whitney intensified our feeling that things were going to break wide open for us—for everyone, very soon. The worlds of art, music and literature were changing, beckoning statesman and common man alike to follow. The old ways were not the best ways. A new spirit was blowing across the land; a young "can-do" President and his wife were in the White House.

I really liked John F. Kennedy. The Russians never backed him down during the Cuban Missile Crisis. His brother Bobby didn't look like he'd walk away from a fight either. President Kennedy was also pushing the most important civil rights legislation this country had ever seen. We'd had race problems in this country for so long, all I hoped was that one day, we'd get somebody in the White House who would at least make things better for our kids. I guess I was hoping that Kennedy was the man.

Even in the music business, a progressive thinking industry, there was new blood. In England, the Beatles were poised to capture America's heart; they already had number one records there. In November 1963, their manager flew to New York to book them for their first appearance on *The Ed Sullivan Show*. New writers in the old Brill

Building like Carole King, Neil Diamond, and Paul Simon were already capturing the new spirit in their songs; some imitating the most influential writer of the day, Bob Dylan, whose biggest song said it all: "The Times They Are a-Changin'."

In the closing months of 1963, we sang background on a session for Burt Bacharach that produced two hits for my niece Dionne and launched her career: "Anyone Who Had a Heart" and "Walk on By." In 1964 and 1965, as English records dominated the charts, the records we made held their own.

I'd always wanted a girl. And just because I wanted one so badly, I figured I'd never get one. Now, everything was different. I wanted her to be a special kind of little girl, different—that was my whole thing. I wanted her to be raised in a real home, not an apartment. John found a reasonably priced house on Wainwright Street in Newark. But we needed five hundred dollars to put down on it. Our friend, the arranger Teacho Wiltshire, lent us the money. Within a month after we closed on the house, I had John breaking down walls to create that new open kitchen and living room I'd always dreamed about. And what's a house without a dog? We bought a German shepherd for the kids and named him Thor.

John was also crazy about Whitney. He would put her in the carriage, put a blanket over her and wheel her out to the porch. She was so feisty that despite the cold she would kick the blankets off and keep John running back and forth, trying to keep her covered and warm. She reminded him of a comic strip character from the old *Journal-American,* a character that was forever getting into trouble. "Nippy—seldom right," the slogan went. The nickname stuck.

Gary was seven years old and adorable. He was a very quiet kid; not unhappy, necessarily, just quiet. Throughout his life, I would worry about him and purposely draw him into conversation to make sure he was okay. By the age of five, he could pick out his own clothes and dress himself. But he had a one-track mind. Even as a toddler, when you asked him what he wanted for Christmas, he said, "Ball, ball." Early on, he proved himself to be a natural athlete, good in all sports.

He could also sing like a mockingbird. But he wanted other kids' acceptance so badly he sometimes let them take advantage of him.

One day, I went to pick him up from school and found a boy beating him up in the schoolyard. Gary was taller than him and could have pulverized him. But he just stood there, silently, his head hanging, getting whupped.

"Gary," I screamed, "hit him back!"

Gary didn't move. My temper flared; I wanted to run in there and kill the boy who was beating up my son. I was wild with rage—if I'd started in on this kid, they would have had to take me out in a straitjacket. I also knew how important it was for Gary, for any man, to defend himself. I ran into the schoolyard and brushed the other boy aside. I was inches and seconds away from knocking him down with the back of my hand. I glared at him, then instantly turned back to Gary.

"Hit him back, Gary," I demanded.

Gary just hung his head. I put my hands on his shoulders and shook him.

"What's wrong with you?" I said. "Look at me, look at me!"

I was acting like a madwoman. He finally began to lift his head and meet my wild eyes.

"If you don't hit him, you're gonna get whupped twice: once from him and another from me!" I said.

Gary flinched at my threat. But he made no move toward the other boy.

"You don't believe me?" I howled. I grabbed him by the arm, spun him around and started whacking his butt with my free hand. By the third or fourth swing, he was crying, crying from the injustice of it all—getting beat up by one boy, then whupped by his mother. Suddenly he felt the boy's eyes upon him, watching him cry. Now he was embarrassed and shocked into the present. He fell on the boy like an animal, pounding him with his fists.

A few days later, when John was walking Gary to school, he heard two boys talking.

"Don't mess with that kid," said one.

"Why?" the other asked. "Is he tough?"

"Yeah," said the first one. "But his mother is really bad."

John said he felt about an inch tall. He said he felt like turning around and asking them, "Hey . . . what about me?" I just laughed.

Early on, as we established our family, I made John the gentle, more lenient parent. I tended to be the disciplinarian, so I told him to be the softie. He looked confused and couldn't understand why I was doing this. "They need somewhere to go after I whip their butts. Let 'em run to you." I wanted John to be their safety valve. I thought it best that they run to one of us for solace rather than go outside our house for a sympathetic ear.

As it turned out in later years, when Whitney couldn't get her way with me, she went around the back door to John. Likewise, when John put his foot down, the boys came running to me. Either way, John was never too far from the kids—he was spending more time at home as work got harder and harder for him to find. At least that's what he told me.

"Cissy and I had many a bitter argument over whether I was working or not—and sometimes I wasn't!" remembers John. "There came a time when I got sick of beatin' my brains in, driving for a living. Cissy was making good money singing backgrounds—a heck of a lot more money than I could make—so my thought was, I'll stay home and watch the kids.

"Nippy was so bad . . . Nippy was terrible! And I loved her to death. I had waited all my life it seemed for a girl child and when I got her . . . she was something, boy, she was something else. I think Cissy sometimes resented the fact that I was home and she wasn't. But I was doing the one thing that necessarily had to be done—I was watching those kids. I don't think she saw it that way, though. We argued about it a couple of times but not where it was any big thing."

Neither was Michael immune to childhood trauma. As a young tyke, he split his head wide open, riding his tricycle down the front steps of our house because John was too slow in taking the bike and Michael down the steps. I'm glad we lived just down the street from the hospital. Aside from the usual stresses of raising a young family, we were happy—very happy. If I knew there was something I wanted for the house or the kids, I worked some extra sessions. To cover the mortgage, John would sometimes pick up some extra money on a Saturday morning, driving a big truck for someone.

A month after my little girl was born, my heart broke for the four little black girls who died in church when a madman placed a bomb there in Birmingham, Alabama. If the times were a-changin', they weren't changing without some terrible resistance. Each new push forward, each new peace march was greeted with two steps backward of violence and hate.

Then one day in November, the girls and I boarded a bus for Manhattan and another session with Solomon Burke. Just before we entered the Holland Tunnel, a man listening to a transistor radio said the President had been shot in Dallas. It had to be a hoax. I looked at Estelle stunned and dumbfounded. When we reached Port Authority, I already saw people and policemen dazed at the news. I thought it would be a good idea to call the studio before we made another move. It was true—our session with Sol, all sessions were canceled.

Like the rest of the nation, we stayed home and watched the grim events of the next few days unfold. As we watched the state funeral for John F. Kennedy, his young wife, his little girl and John John, saluting his father's coffin, I thought of the song we had just cut with Dionne, "Anyone Who Had a Heart."

Just a year later, we were saddened again when Sam Cooke was shot to death. It sounded like one of those "wrong time, wrong place" episodes; at least that's what I think Sam's old friend Bobby Womack said. The lyrics of "A Change Is Gonna Come," Sam's last big record, now took on a greater significance with him gone.

> *It's been too hard livin'*
> *But I'm afraid to die*
> *'Cause I don't know what's up there*
> *Beyond the sky.*
> *It's been a long time comin'*
> *But I know a change is gonna come.*

It was harder now to believe that change was coming. But we pressed on, thinking that perhaps this violence was only the birth pangs of a better day being born.

As Dionne and Dee Dee began to work almost exclusively with Burt Bacharach, I got a lot more calls for background work. I put together combinations of voices until I found what I was listening for. I added to Sylvia Shemwell the voices of Myrna Smith and Estelle Brown, both of whom I knew from either church or gospel circles. I was the top voice, Sylvia was usually below me, Myrna was right in the middle and Estelle hit bottom.

We worked well together; if I was leading, these girls could sense where I was going and follow me intuitively. "Singing with her, you can't just sing your part straight," says Sylvia. "She's not going to sing it straight. And when she moves, you've got to go with it—and you gotta feel what she does—and through the years we feel it without looking at each other. We change the background with the flick of an eye. I mean that's a gift." We became the producer's first-call background group— referring to us simply as "Cissy and the girls."

"She taught me a lot about recording voices," says Brooks who engineered most of Bert Berns' sessions. "She taught me to keep my eye on the chord and not on the chick."

I guess Brooks was referring to Myrna, who was very attractive and even ended up as the "love interest" on the cover of a Freddie Scott album during those days.

I loved working with Brooks and, of course, Bert. He asked for my input and gave me great freedom to make my own contributions— harmonically and lyrically—in the backgrounds. First and foremost, Bert was a musician—a guitar player who often came out of the booth carrying his acoustic to demonstrate a particular lick or just play along with us on the track. He was not a distant executive; he understood all of us. He was no "suit." As a matter of fact, for a guy who was making hundreds of thousands of dollars every month from his songs and the coowner, along with Jerry Wexler and the Ertegun brothers, of Bang Records, he was the unlikeliest-looking of executives. Bert was a good-looking guy, tall, with big, sad eyes and a crazy smile. He funked-up his classic good looks with a long tail of hair down his back and a pompadour. His one concession to proper executive attire was a sharp sports jacket or blue blazer worn over an always open-necked sports shirt. Still, he thumbed his nose at society by mischievously topping his crazy hairdo with a yachtsman's cap—white, with shiny black bill and captain's gold braid. As a streetwise record producer, at the top of his game, Bert may have alienated key executives—and even important artists, like Solomon Burke, who Jerry Wexler wanted Bert to produce.

"I remember I introduced him to Solomon," recalled Jerry Wexler, "and Bert was a real freaky guy to look at, with a long wig down his back, you know—and Solomon didn't say anything to him, but took me to one side of the studio, and said, 'C'mere, c'mon out in the hall,' where he says, 'Are you kiddin' me with this paddy boy?' I says, 'Just be cool and listen to what he does, okay?' "

Sol had totally misjudged Bert—and with one of the most cutting racist epithets blacks reserved for whites: "paddy boy," derived from the rivalry between blacks and the Irish early in the century. What Sol didn't know about Bert was that he was an encyclopedia of soul. Almost singlehandedly, Bert had schooled the symphonic-minded Gary Sherman on what R&B was all about. By the time Bert was finished, Gary was able to write arrangements for some of the grittiest records of the 1960s, including "Cry Baby" by Garnett Mimms and the Enchanters and "If You Need Me" by Solomon Burke, and go on from there to the Drifters' "On Broadway."

"He was the funkiest producer I ever encountered," remembers Gary. "We'd spend hours listening to records, Bert pointing out trumpet sounds, guitar sounds—'You hear that drum figure?' he'd say. 'You hear that bass? *That's* what I want!'—he taught me what soul was. Bert was my favorite."

What Sol—and very few others—also didn't know about Bert was that he was sick. He was born with a congenital heart defect. His parents probably spent their lives cursing God for their son's condition—that is, if they even believed in God. They had named their son after the twentieth century's most famous philosopher—and atheist—

Bertrand Russell. Instead of letting his condition make him an invalid, Bertrand Russell Berns did a 180. He became an adventurer—his love of music, which began with the classical piano lessons of his childhood, became his ticket out of the Bronx.

Bert, the adventurer, collected soul wherever he found it. As a young man, he first found it in pre-Castro Cuba, while working as a nightclub musician. He found the baion there, a sensual Latin rhythm he also heard upon returning to his native New York in the burgeoning Puerto Rican neighborhoods of the early 1950s. Bert incorporated the baion into his records, as did producers Leiber and Stoller, Phil Spector and Burt Bacharach. Bert based "Twist and Shout" and "Hang On Sloopy" on the baion. He also discovered a phenomenal, soulful blind guitarist in Cuba named Arsenio Rodriguez.

In his twenties, Bert worked as a session pianist and a song plugger out of 1650 Broadway, the mecca of music publishers. Here he joined other young writing teams in the same building, cranking out pop songs on upright pianos in tight little office cubicles. There were teams like Carole King and Gerry Goffin, Barry Mann and Cynthia Weil, Jeff Barry and Ellie Greenwich, Neil Sedaka and Howie Greenfield.

By the time he was thirty, Bert had lost most of his hair. He turned the loss into a personal trademark. Bert grew a long tail in the back and got a funky piece for the top of his head. A few years later, in the middle of the British Invasion, Bert was invited to produce some sessions in London for Decca Records. His personal style was not an issue with Carnaby Street–suited musicians. While cutting a new band called Them, Bert collected another soulful artist—the band's lead singer, Van Morrison. In 1964, Bert was thirty-five, sixteen years older than Van and most of the other musicians he was working with in London. But Bert's passionate songs bridged the age gap. Bert wrote Them's biggest hit, "Here Comes the Night" and also loosened up Decca's staid English recording studio.

"I remember him coming out of the console," Them guitarist Billy Harrison told *Wavelength* magazine. "He walked over to the drum kit, grabbed a stick, started beating on a cymbal, saying, 'Let's get this thing cooking,' and created an atmosphere. Suddenly everybody went 'Yeah, we're not sitting here tied to these seats, we're allowed to express ourselves. Berns just created a whole freedom of atmosphere within the studio. The guy was magic."

Van Morrison also thought highly of Bert. "Except for Bert Berns, I felt that those people who said they were producing Them didn't have a clue."

At Them's studio dates Bert also befriended a twenty-year-old session guitarist, Jimmy Page. Bert championed the young blues player, brought him back to America with hopes of him playing on some Solomon Burke records. Immigration prevented this, but in only a few years, Atlantic would reap the reward of Bert's discovery—Page's band, Led Zeppelin, would become one of Atlantic Records' biggest-selling rock acts.

Bert's love of the blues, the biaon, gospel and pop all found their way into the records he had us sing on. As a result, his records—"A Little Bit of Soap," "Twist and Shout" and "Tell Him"—communicated to both black and white listeners.

"Bert was the king of that crossover black music," says Brooks Arthur. "He had a way of capturing a feel that cross-pollinated white and black America. The records he made were right in the pocket for the black community and perfectly in the pocket for the white community. Bert Berns's records had a way of crossing that line in a real sweet and wonderful kind of 1960s way."

Solomon Burke changed his mind about Bert as soon as Sol started working with him in the studio. Bert's handpicked musicians, our churchy backgrounds and Brooks on the board created a string of hits for Sol: "Cry to Me," "Goodbye Baby (Baby Goodbye)," "Everybody Needs Somebody to Love." Bert's emotion-charged songs and Sol's gospel delivery was a marriage made in heaven.

At the core, it was the intensity of Bert's songs that distinguished his records and his art. Writers Carole King and Gerry Goffin could only wonder what the hero of their "Some Kind of Wonderful" was thinking, in the end leaving him mute:

There's so much I want to say,
But the right words don't come my way.

Whereas Bert had all the right words. His songs expressed the pain of loneliness ("Cry to Me"), regret ("A Little Bit of Soap"), of losing love ("Here Comes the Night") and begging for it to return ("Baby, Come on Home"), of missing someone ("Are You Lonely for Me, Baby") and also pleasure ("Am I Grooving You," "Twist and Shout"). They were simple songs—not sophisticated like a Bacharach/David tune or funny like a Leiber/Stoller song. But whether they were about pain or pleasure, they were sensual. They were about feeling. They were about being *alive*. But always, in Bert's songs, the night also encroached. Bert's songs were howled or shouted or screamed. They were the songs of someone living on the edge, so far out that only a prayer—howled or cried—could bring deliverance. A prayer was the only thing that could hold back the night.

Baby, my heart is breaking
And there's no hope—no hope in sight.
The sky is in a shower of darkness.
No one, no one to hold me in the lonely night.
—"Heart Be Still"

Even Bert's "Tell Him," a simple pop tune, has the same urgency, the same intensity of his grittier, more R&B titles. He never comes out and actually says it, but the message is clear: Let's cut to the chase; life's too short.

I know something about love.
Gotta want it bad.
If that guy's got into your blood,
Go out and get him!
If you want him to be the very part of you
That makes you want to breathe,
Here's the thing to do.

He Changed My Life

Tell him that you're never gonna leave him,
Tell him that you're always gonna love him,
Tell him, tell him, tell him, tell him right now.
—*"Tell Him"*

You could always "tell" Bert; he was always there to listen. As you made your point, your suggestion to improve the record at hand, his eyes would lock on you. "I hear what you're sayin' . . . I hear what you're sayin'," then he would shake his head slowly, pondering what you had just said. He was dead serious. Bert's sessions were fun. We kidded around with him and he kidded us back. But when we got down to cutting a record—that was serious business.

"His sessions were cutting edge," recalls Brooks Arthur. "The musicians came to play for him and you played a little bit better, a little sharper for Bert. You played on the edge of your chair—you didn't sit back. Some people command that kind of respect. It was a 'performance' from you because it was all going down live: The artist was in the vocal booth, Bert was in the control room and things had a little more fire in them because he was there. He had that power."

When good things started to happen in one of Bert's sessions, when the artist, the musicians and we girls gave Bert that natural feel he liked—slightly gritty, kind of bluesy—he would start to scratch the back of his head and run his hand through that tail of hair.

We never socialized outside the studio. Given the chance, I suppose my husband, John, light-skinned and raised in a white world of prep schools and Catholic colleges, might have found good company in Bert or Brooks. But I rarely socialized with anyone outside of John, we were our own best friends. The close camaraderie Brooks, Bert, Gary Sherman, the arranger, the musicians and I had in the studio however was enough to make us all believe in our hearts that black and white were coming closer together.

I guess I was still trying to separate who I was from what I did: a Christian singing secular music. In the world, but not of the world. I was also still rehearsing and directing my choir, still very active in church. During the day, I missed my kids and would rather have been with them. But I loved working regularly with these funny, super-talented people.

We even had our mascots, Judy and Billy. Of course, Judy was our Judy, Judy Guions, whom my sister Lee had adopted at twelve years old and we had recruited to sing for the Drinkards. Judy, now going under the name Judy Clay, already had a few record deals by the mid-1960s. Billy Vera was a little white guitarist and singer/songwriter from White Plains, New York, who led the Shirelles' road band. Billy had written a song called "Storybook Children." On the surface, it was just a sort of star-crossed-lovers thing: two people in love, condemned for it and yearning for a place they can be free to love. But once Billy and Judy, an "interracial couple," sang it the song took on a new meaning. Of course, Billy and Judy were not a "couple." But some industry people were still afraid to touch the record. Others of us welcomed the record as a symbol that prejudice and intolerance were finally disappearing.

"It was amazing," says Billy Vera. "The record was such a symbol of brotherhood that I could walk down the streets of Harlem and black people were so happy to see me. The reason it worked, the reason black men didn't think I was a white guy 'stealing their woman' was mine and Judy's body types. Judy was a big woman, taller than me, heftier than me. I was this little shrimpy white guy. Everyone could see I was no threat."

There were lots of songs written then with a distinct message of brotherhood. From 1965 to around 1969, the air seemed to be full of great songs and sentiments like my friend Felix Cavaliere's "People Got to Be Free," "He Ain't Heavy, He's My Brother," "Reach Out in the Darkness," and "Get Together." I loved the lyric for Jackie DeShannon's "Put a Little Love in Your Heart" (which we sang on). The Beatles broke the message down to its most basic: "All You Need Is Love."

Even Bacharach and David caught the spirit. "What the World Needs Now" was initially offered to Dionne but she passed. Burt cut the song on Jackie DeShannon and this great lyric saw the light of day. Of course, we backed up Jackie on the record.

> *Lord, we don't need another mountain*
> *There are mountains and hillsides enough to climb.*
> *There are oceans and rivers enough to cross,*
> *Enough to last 'til the end of time.*
> *What the world needs now is love sweet love,*
> *It's the only thing that there's just too little of*
> *What the world needs now is love, sweet love,*
> *No, not just for some,*
> *But for everyone.*

It wasn't some hard-preachin' gospel record, but God *is* love after all. Dionne's "I Say a Little Prayer for You," on which we sang, also had its heart in the right place. Perhaps all these records cleared the way for a young man from Newark who grew up in the Church of God in Christ. By 1968, Edwin Hawkins was already working on a new arrangement of a gospel standard that would soon land at the top of the Hit Parade. It didn't happen before and it hasn't happened since. But I'd like to think that the massive popularity of "Oh Happy Day" by the Edwin Hawkins Singers had something to do with when it was released. The record's appeal cut through all ethnic and religious groups. All the Jewish producers and arrangers who used me and the girls because they liked our "churchy" sound went ape, as we did, over the record.

> *Oh happy day*
> *Oh happy day*
> *When Jesus washed*
> *He washed my sins away.*

I don't know if the producers, arrangers and half of the people who bought the record understood what the record was talking about—but I sure did! It was the joy of salvation that they were singing about, pure and simple. That record reminded me once again what this life is really about, and what it isn't. It isn't about making hit records or a pile of money. Money is nice but I don't want to worship it. Life is about getting up in the morning, and thanking Him, praising Him for the breath He put in my lungs. Thanking Him for keeping me in my right mind, thanking Him for my precious children and my brothers and sisters. But most of all, life is about thanking Him that my name is written in the Lamb's Book of Life. Whenever I get down, depressed or on my sickbed, I think on these things: how wonderful He's been to me.

People responded to that record because those singers felt that joy of salvation for themselves, and that joy was coming right back out of their voices onto the record. I hoped that one day I too would be allowed to make a gospel record.

The great records we made for Bert, arranger Gary Sherman, especially those for Solomon Burke brought us further within the fold of Atlantic Records. When they bought Aretha's contract from Columbia Records, they tapped us immediately to work with her. If Aretha's records didn't have the sophistication of a Bacharach/David original or the crossover potential of a Bert Berns production, they made up for it in gospel fire. I loved singing with her.

"Cissy and myself," says Aretha, "we groove together so good because we come from the same place—different churches, but the same place. Whenever we got together, we knew that we were going to sing, that we were going to do some good singing here today, wherever 'here' was."

"Here" was in Atlantic's studios in New York, Memphis or Muscle Shoals. We recorded in all those places with Aretha.

"They'd come into the studio," says Atlantic's Jerry Wexler, "she'd listen to the tape and they'd gather around the microphone and start working out. It was a collaboration; it was a communal thing. Most of it came from Cissy Houston and the girls, most of the ideas, most of the lines and most of the parts."

Aretha, the Sweets and I made some great records together. I guess my favorites are "Natural Woman"; I spent a lot of time working out those background parts, and "Ain't No Way," a bluesy dirge with a sparse background. While we were recording that one, we were stumped for a background idea. As usual, "Ree" gave me plenty of freedom to create and put my two cents in.

"Why don't you try the obbligato?" my husband, John, suggested.

I thought he was nuts. But when I tried it—a high, octave-tripping solo behind the lead voice—it was the perfect, victorious counterpoint to the resignation in Aretha's voice. I am very proud of that record. Some months later, when we performed "Ain't No Way" with Aretha at New York's Philharmonic Hall at Lincoln Center, the audience rose four times to give Aretha and me a standing ovation.

Something about the chemistry of the southern white musicians in Memphis and Muscle Shoals, where many of the original tracks were cut, Aretha's fabulous voice and piano and our amen corner background vocals put those records across. For a solid year, starting in February 1967, when Atlantic released her first record, Aretha was just unstoppable. Her first record was "I Never Loved a Man," the flip side was "Do Right Woman," her second, "Respect," was released in April, her third, "Baby, I Love You," her fourth, written to order by Carole King and her husband, Gerry Goffin, "(You Make Feel Like a) Natural Woman," entered the charts in September 1967. In the next months, "Chain of Fools," "Since You Been Gone" and "Ain't No Way" followed—all becoming big sellers.

Singing with Aretha was a wonderful experience—she inspired us and we, as singers, inspired her. On the road, even after the curtain went down, we'd gather around the piano and keep singing. "I love this tune," she said one night and started playing Dionne's "I Say a Little Prayer for You." We jumped in with a background and it sounded so good that when we got back to New York, we recorded yet another big hit with Aretha.

There was talk of a tour with Aretha, something I personally dreaded since the first tour I took with Solomon Burke in 1966. It was the first time I had flown and it was in one of those puddle jumpers that couldn't get above the turbulence. I wanted to cancel the rest of the tour but I couldn't. I missed the kids, I missed John and I was miserable.

I cut a one-off single for Kapp Records, then Jerry Wexler, one of Atlantic's partners, reeled me in. I guess he didn't want me wandering to other labels, so Atlantic signed "the Group" and called us the Inspirations for our gospel influence. But there was already another group with that name, so they dubbed us the Sweet Inspirations. Our first single, "Why Am I Treated So Bad?," was released in 1967. It was a slow, languid blues written by gospel singer Roebuck Staples, of the Staples. It was so funky it sounded like it was recorded down in a Louisiana bayou complete with tasty blues licks, a walking bass and seductive horns.

That same year, we also played the Apollo Theater. We were not only backing up our old friend from Scepter, Tommy Hunt, but Atlantic thought it would be a good idea to start exposing our name, the Sweet Inspirations, to the record-buying public. In the Apollo that day was a young Luther Vandross playing hooky from school to see Tommy Hunt.

"At that point, I'd never heard of the Sweet Inspirations," says Luther. "The quality of all of their voices devastated me and in particular Cissy Houston's voice, tone, range and emotion reached out to me. When the show was over, I waited by the backstage door. I saw them get into a limo and I ran over to the car. 'Y'all are the best singers I've ever heard ever ever!' I said."

Atlantic wanted us to tour with Aretha for her first big tour and open all her shows. I reluctantly agreed but was more excited about the carrot they dangled to make my time away from home more palatable: Atlantic would give me and the Sweets the opportunity to cut a gospel album!

I hated to leave John and the kids but you do what you have to do. John was having trouble finding work, so, with my session work and the tour, we thought it best for him to stay home with the kids and pick up some work, driving at night and on weekends when I was home. Michael and Whitney took my leaving the worst, especially Michael.

"When she went away," says Michael, "I would cry and my father couldn't do nothin' with me. As soon as she came to the door, I stopped."

Whitney was only five and even then had all the answers. "I'm gonna make a lotta money one day, Mommy," she said, "so you won't have to go away and work."

I wasn't in California a week with Aretha when I woke up crying in the hotel one night. I knew something was wrong with Whitney. The Lord gives me these things—visions, I guess, to prepare me for things. Sure enough, Michael and Whitney had been jiving around, playing with a wire clothes hanger. She had her arm inside the hanger and the hook part in her mouth. When Michael jerked her arm, the hook cut into the roof of her mouth, way back in her throat. Whitney pulled the hanger out of her mouth, saw the blood and went running for John. John rushed her to the hospital. The doctors said the hook had just missed her vocal cords. They put some stitches in the roof of her mouth and filled her mouth with surgical packing. She was okay but she could hardly talk with all the packing. That's when I called home. John picked up. He didn't tell me anything, then I asked to speak with Whitney.

"I could see the panic in my father's face," says Whitney.

John covered the receiver so I wouldn't hear. "He said, 'Now, Whitney, your mother's in California working and I don't want you to upset her. Please talk as normal as you can.' "

Of course, as soon as I heard her muffled voice I asked to speak with Daddy. John gave me the blow-by-blow and I died a thousand deaths. But there was nothing I could do; I couldn't leave California. I just had to trust that God would continue to protect Whitney while I was away.

The tour with Aretha went well. By the time I got back, Whitney's stitches were ready to come out.

We recorded a few more things for Dionne in the early months of 1967. Then in March, Bert got an overseas call from singer Van Morrison in Belfast. Van's band, Them, had seen some success since Bert had produced "Here Comes the Night," but after a frustrating tour of the United States, they returned to England. Van left Them, but the band hired a new vocalist and went on without him. Downcast, he returned to Ireland. Bert made arrangements for Van to fly to New York.

"Van was suspicious of us," laughs Brooks Arthur. "Like, who were all these Bert Berns people?"

Van had already felt burned by the English record company that had originally recorded Them. They had packed the date with session players and purposely changed the band's sound for commercial purposes. Later, the record company manipulated the band's image for the press, giving them a phony street tough image. When Van looked around our studio and observed all the players that had been hired for the session, he probably thought he was revisiting the London studio where all the trouble began for his beloved Them. Maybe Van had misunderstood Bert; maybe he thought the session was going to be just him and his guitar. It was too late to do anything about it now—A&R studio was booked, the players were contracted and Gary Sherman had already written a basic arrangement for "Brown-Eyed Girl." For the date, Gary had hired two guitars: Hugh McCracken on rhythm and Al Gorgoni on lead. McCracken, twenty-four, was already a favorite player for Neil Diamond, who also recorded for Bert's label, Bang. Herbie Lovelle would play drums and Sherman himself would later overdub organ. The surprise hire was the bass. Eric Gale was an exceptional guitarist, but he convinced Gary to hire him to play bass.

"You've never heard me play bass, man," Eric told Gary. "I'm a dynamite bass player." Sherman would take a chance with Eric.

Sherman needn't have worried about Eric—or any of the other players. They each took his charts—the charts he purposely wrote just loose enough for every player to express their own style—and created a head arrangement that blew everyone away. Eric plucked the bass strings with a pick; unusual but not for an unusually gifted player like Eric. Gorgoni devised a guitar figure that became as memorable as the song's hook. And McCracken drove the song on with a jangly, percussive twelve string. The only problem was Van Morrison. Before the session began, he was a shy, withdrawn twenty-one-year-old, hanging in the back of the studio. But once Brooks and Bert rolled the tape, he was a live wire, so full of ideas and improvisation that every take sounded like a different song! He was straying so far from Gary Sherman's charts that Gary, in desperation, ran out into the studio and was cuing the musicians like an umpire—holding up two fingers, then three fingers to signify the section Morrison had suddenly landed on.

Brooks looked over at Bert. Sure enough, he was scratching the back of his head like a maniac. But neither of them knew if Van Morrison would survive the session. He was scatting toward the fade like a madman, his eyes closed in the vocal booth, wringing wet after each of the twenty-two takes!

Do you remember when we used to sing,
Sha-la-la-la-la-la-la-la-la-la-la-ti-da,
Flip-flop-flip-flop-flip-flop-flip-flop,
Sha-la-la-la-la-la-la-la-la-la-la-ti-da.

"He was exhausting himself after each take almost orgasmically," recalls Brooks with wonder. "This guy was electric; he was magic. He changed the ions in the air."

When the rhythm section left for the day, Brooks set up some mikes for us to overdub a background part. Brooks played us the take they liked; we clamped on headphones and went for it. Bert smiled, but we took it again anyway, just to see if we could make it any prettier. This time Brooks and Jeff Barry, Neil Diamond's producer, came out to add their voices to ours. I loved singing that song. The chorus gave me the chills. Why? This may sound silly, but it always felt like my father was singing to me in that chorus: "You're my brown-eyed girl."

I never had an experience like that before or since. Van's a great artist; I loved what he did with "Brown-Eyed Girl." As we gathered up our things to go home, Brooks played a very rough mix of the song he'd done on the fly. It was one of those records you knew was a hit as soon as you heard it. Bert was uncharacteristically quiet. I think he knew that besides making another hit record, he had another artist in his stable. An artist with the kind of passion and intensity he enjoyed writing for. I could hear the wheels spinning inside his brain. By September, "Brown-Eyed Girl" was a big hit. Bert toasted his new artist with crazy free verse on the album's back cover:

Van Morrison . . . erratic and painful . . . whose music expresses . . . the right now of his own road, his ancient highway. Born and raised in Ireland . . . with few but precious fragments of South and Soul . . . Mother England and Muddy Waters . . . for Morrison it was an infinite yearning . . . for Morrison it was and is the uncanny drive to hum of pain and women . . . He's on the golden heels of success and his recordings are ubiquitous "baby please don't go" from the down home weed country of the United States of Negro America. This l.p. is Van Morrison. We won't explain it to you . . .

—Bert Berns

In November, Van returned for another recording date with Bert. I couldn't wait to hear what Bert's next session with Van would sound like.

Of course, after November there never was another session between Van and Bert. Perhaps you have been reading between the lines—the intensity and the passion in Bert's music, the threat of darkness and night that he purposely wrote into many of his songs and his heart condition—and you know what I am leading up to. On the next to the last day of the year, December 30, 1967, Brooks Arthur and Bert Berns knocked off early, for a change, at 6 P.M. They planned on quietly celebrating New Year's Eve, the next day, with their wives at Bert and Ilene's place on the East Side. They shut everything down at Century Sound, Brooks's studio, and agreed to meet the next day at Bert's. On the street, Bert waved at Brooks, flagged down the first cab and disappeared inside the taxi. That was the last time Brooks Arthur saw Bert Berns. Later that night at 9 P.M., the phone rang in Brooks's apartment. It was Ilene Berns, crying. Bert was dead. He had just suffered a massive heart attack. He was thirty-eight.

What is that old saying about trouble always coming in pairs? Barely three months after Bert died, the Sweet Inspirations and I were recording our first gospel album. As we were singing "Guide Me, Oh Great Jehovah" I saw Tom Dowd, our producer, take a phone call in the control room. Then he hit the talk-back.

"You may want to come in here, Cissy," said Tom.

A cold shiver went through me. Who had called for me and what bad news couldn't Tom tell me over the studio talk-back? I thought of the kids and immediately went into prayer as I walked into the control room.

Tom looked up from the console. "Cissy, Martin Luther King was just shot in Memphis," said Tom. I had no reaction at first. It was not the news I was expecting. I was prepared to hear that one of my kids was lying in a hospital somewhere or worse. The sensation of relief washed over me, then the news sunk in. Tom gave us the option to leave the studio immediately if we wished. I went out and talked to the girls. We had some prayer, we shed some tears and we decided to pick up where we left off:

> *Guide me, oh thou great Jehovah,*
> *Pilgrim through this barren land.*
> *I am weak, but thou art mighty.*
> *Hold me with thy powerful hand.*

> *Bread of heaven,*
> *Bread of heaven,*
> *Feed me till I want no more.*

> *Bread of heaven,*
> *Bread of heaven,*
> *Feed me till I want no more.*
> —*"Guide Me, Oh Thou Great Jehovah"*

Bert's death shocked me so badly, I don't know that I ever really grieved. Then Dr. King's murder and, two months later, the assassination of Robert F. Kennedy opened up some kind of floodgates in me. I wept for King and Kennedy, both young men, leaving widows and young children. Men of peace, reconciliators on whom I had pinned some kind of hope, cut down in their prime. I wept for them both, their images ever before me in the newspapers and on television. But in my heart I was really grieving for Bert, for his wife, Ilene, and their children, two toddlers and Russell, the newborn. Bert, too, through his music was a peacemaker. I think he knew he was living on borrowed time. He acknowledged that fear with the many foreboding images of night that haunted his songs. That's why life—the pain as well as the pleasure—was all precious to him. The heroes of Bert's songs were never afraid to experience pain—they nearly reveled in it, handling it with such gusto they overcame. Still, I was afraid to think about how many dark nights of soul, Bert himself had spent wrestling with God.

> *Baby, my heart is breaking*
> *And there's no hope—no hope in sight.*
> *The sky is in a shower of darkness.*
> *No one, no one to hold me in the lonely night.*
> *—"Heart Be Still"*

Some people say "Heart Be Still," sung by Lorraine Ellison, is one of the greatest R&B records Bert ever wrote. Of course Bert heard it first as "Peace Be Still," by gospel artist James Cleveland. It is a magnificent hymn; no one who hears it can fail to be moved—as I'm sure Bert was. The original words concern the plight of the disciples as they find themselves on the Sea of Galilee in the middle of a ferocious storm. In the boat, Jesus lies sleeping. As I remembered the words, I couldn't help thinking how much the disciple's pleading resembled the cry of Bert's heart in "Heart Be Still." I wondered how many times he had played "Peace Be Still" by James Cleveland, what he thought as he heard the following words and how many times he had made these words his own anguished prayer.

> *Master, the tempest is raging.*
> *The billows are tossing high.*
> *The sky is o'ershadowed with blackness.*
> *No shelter or hope is nigh.*
> *Carest Thou not that we perish?*

He Changed My Life

How can Thou lie asleep?
When it seems each moment is threatening
A grave in the angry deep.

"Carest Thou not that we perish?" In the summer of 1968, as I mourned a friend, a politician of great promise and a minister of peace—as I saw unrest and riots break out all over our country, I found myself meditating on this question.

TEN

Savior, you are more than life to me
And I am clinging, Lord, close to thee
Just let thy precious blood apply
Just keep me, Lord, ever, right by your side.
—*"Every Day Every Hour"*

In the spring of 1968, I stood in the wings at the Apollo Theater watching Judy Clay and Billy Vera, our "mascots." They were singing their hit, "Storybook Children." I had once told Billy how much I loved their song, but how it used to make me cry because it was so sad. He used to tease me about crying every time I heard their record. Billy looked over at me; he saw me crying and smiled. But I wasn't just crying for the song's tender lovers. I was crying for all of us. The assassination of Dr. King touched off riots, looting and vandalism and a new black militancy that further divided this country. Seventy-two years after the words "separate but equal" ushered in the segregated schools, restrooms and public transportation of my father's day, a national commission investigated the black violence of 1968. "Our nation is moving toward two societies," the report concluded, "one black, one white—separate and unequal." The murders of Martin Luther King, Jr., John F. Kennedy and his brother, Robert, now seemed to snuff out the hope and dreams we had for racism to finally end.

Bert Bern's death too, was the death of a reconciling spirit. A spirit we needed so badly at the time to bind us up in our brokenness and division. Bert bridged the black and white worlds with his music. Who knows what he would have gone on to. I regretted that John and I had never gone out together or socialized with him and his wife.

"If it wasn't for Bert, I wouldn't have a career today," says Brooks Arthur, who has engineered hundreds and hundreds of sessions and today owns his own studio. Bert was the first guy to give Brooks a chance to engineer. "After he died so young, I kept his memory alive for thirty years by incorporating his favorite expression, 'I hear what you're sayin',' into my own speech. When Bert died, one of his sons was only three weeks old. He's about thirty now and I met him recently. When he asked me to tell him about his father, I was able to tell him his father's favorite expression. I had a great peace about keeping that expression alive in my own life all these years, until I happened to meet his son and was able to give it to him."

Atlantic continued to release Sweet Inspirations singles and albums. The label insisted that we tour to support their efforts, and though I hated being away from the kids even more now, I had to cooperate if I was to continue working. Eventually I wanted to move us out of Wainwright Street; Newark was changing. Drugs were coming into the neighborhoods.

But buying another house would cost money. Money we didn't have. John was working weekends, driving nights, when I was home, and taking care of the kids while I toured or did sessions.

Late in the summer, the girls and I went to Memphis to do backgrounds on a Dusty Springfield session. I admired her for being a very exacting singer, one who, like me, had been singing with a family group since she was a child. Though Dusty gave Jerry Wexler and Tom Dowd fits, the sessions yielded a much-talked-about album and the popular "Son of a Preacher Man." I also found out later that a Bert Berns song I sang on had actually changed her career. Early in 1963, and still a folksinger, Dusty visited the United States for the first time. She was on her way to record a country record in Nashville but landed first in New York. Walking up Broadway, she stopped dead in her tracks in front of Colony Records, dumbfounded by the sound of the Exciters' "Tell Him" blasting out of the store's speaker. "*That's* what I want!" she shouted, abandoning her plans on the spot both to visit Nashville and record any more folk/country records.

Sometimes my dear friend Phyllis Hardaway would watch the kids and John would take the Sweets and me out on the road. I couldn't ride the bus with the rest of the acts on the tour: they smoked reefer and I couldn't stand the smell. I'm afraid of drugs, period. I've never wanted anything or anybody to control me. Habits determine character and character decides your destiny. So, Atlantic bought a Lincoln for me and the girls which John drove; the band usually followed us in a station wagon. We took Bernie Durant (the guy who introduced John and me) along as a kind of valet. In the South, the old attitudes still prevailed. We'd all be starved somewhere in Georgia and I'd make John stop the car. The "We Serve Whites Only" sign wasn't posted but the message was clear: we don't serve your kind. John wouldn't go in the store; he refused to subject himself to the indignity of it. I was hungry and I didn't care. I marched in the store.

I placed my order at the counter. The older white woman looked at me, I guess, for being so nervy.

"You from up North?" she drawled.

"Yes, I am," I shot back, in my proudest Newark accent.

I paid for our food, turned on my heel and walked out. As I handed John a cheeseburger, he just looked at me and shook his head.

Other times we weren't so lucky. There was an incident down in Georgia and another in Kentucky I'd just as soon forget. Guns drawn; escort to the town limits, the whole bit. Lots of times the promoter liked to get funny with our money or try not to pay us at all. I'm glad we had John along to take care of us. Of course, we girls were no hothouse flowers either.

I remember two episodes on the road that seem funny in the re-telling but were frightening while they were happening. It was 1968, just above the Texas line in Oklahoma at some roadhouse in the boon-docks. It was a big dance and we'd just finished the first of two shows, and were waiting in the dressing room. Our contract stated that John would collect our fee from the promoter after the first show—which is exactly what John was trying to do. The promoter had different ideas.

"This little short-armed bandit, walking around with a gun hanging out of his back pocket, said he wasn't paying us," recalls John. "And who did I think I was, anyway, he wanted to know. Oh, you'll pay me, I told him."

The house was filling up for the second show when John entered our dressing room. He instructed us to grab our garment bags and follow him out. John folded a garment bag across his arm, too, and started for the parking lot. As this crooked promoter saw the featured attraction of his second SRO show fading into the sunset, he followed John out the door, swearing and cursing. As John turned sideways to face him, there was something about the way the garment bag was draped over his forearm that made this creep think that John had a gun under it. "Aw shoot," he groaned. "You got the drop on me, don't you?"

"I never heard anything so funny in all my life," laughs John. "I almost fell out right there in the parking lot. And here comes Cissy and those badass girls right behind me. They had broken up those big heavy chairs in the dressing room, and each one of them had a leg. I never had to worry about anything with them."

We were right there backin' John up. Hey, we were tough women—heads of families—and if one of us went down, we were all going down. We got paid and did the second show without a hitch. The other incident during the same year I'll never forget could have left me a widow. We were playing a dance in Annapolis, Maryland, in the middle of nowhere. A big shed with a corrugated tin roof. Again, we met up with some clown who wasn't inclined to pay us our money. This latest "attempted robbery" must have come at the end of a series of similar misadventures because John was at the end of his rope. He was stressed out and he did something he'd never done until then or since. Had I known what was going down, I would've pulled the plug on the whole situation, but I was gathering up my things after the gig, getting ready to leave with the rest of the girls.

John was arguing with the promoter in the parking lot trying to get our money. It was pretty typical—the guy kept stonewalling John, refusing to pay up. The language got nastier, the threats and accusations getting more serious. So serious that Bernie sidled up behind John and slipped him a pistol.

"I was crazy," recalls John, "absolutely nuts to have taken it from Bernie in the first place. But I was so pissed off about getting stiffed again, I lost my head. I stood up with that pistol in my hand and I told this guy, 'Look, I want my money. We played the gig and you guys are screwin' around with our fee.' "

Bernie got me and the girls into the Lincoln and had the engine idling, ready to roll. In the meanwhile, John's Humphrey Bogart act had finally convinced the promoter to cough up our money. I turned around in the car and saw John, gun still drawn, backing away from the promoter. He finally made it across the parking lot and jumped in the driver's seat as Bernie slid across to the passenger side. John floored the gas pedal, steering toward the parking lot's exit.

"As I got to the fence I noticed they had a chain across the exit, which they dropped just before I came through," John remembers. "I'd have gone right through, I didn't care. I'd have torn that Lincoln up. As we drove down the road, I was shaking like a leaf. After a few miles, I pulled over to the side of the road and took the pistol out of my pocket. When I examined the gun more closely, I really got sick. That pistol had no firing pin! God forbid, that joker had drew on me, they would have been giving me last rites in the parking lot. 'Bernie,' I screamed, 'you gave me a gun with no firing pin! Are you crazy?' I almost murdered Bernie for his nonchalant response: 'Better than nothin', little brother.' "

In 1968, we got a real plum assignment in Las Vegas. Elvis Presley was making his return to the stage and wanted the Sweets to provide background vocals. They flew all of us out, including John, and put us up in a suite of rooms. Elvis was gorgeous, drop-dead gorgeous. This was before he gained all that weight and he looked wonderful. The first day he showed up to greet us, our jaws just dropped. John liked him too. After a while, John became a regular, one of the boys, with Elvis' buddies and Vernon Presley, Elvis' father. While we rehearsed with Elvis for a few weeks, John would meet the boys every day in the hotel coffee shop. They were good old boys, but had been living on a certain level, a very high level of the entertainment business for ten years already, while Elvis had become an international star. John sat there and kept his ears open.

"You'd be surprised what you heard, what you could pick up about the business at that table," remembers John.

The boys all liked John and so did Elvis.

"I used to call him, Elvis Pretzel," says John. "And I used to watch him rehearse. I used to kid him: 'Are you sure you're not part black, Elvis?' He'd act kind of 'aw, shucks, John' about it. 'I don't know about that,' he'd say. 'You do look kinda like my uncle. You'll have to ask my daddy.' Used to crack me up."

When we first arrived for rehearsal, John thought our dressing room was kind of small for the four of us. He went up to the Colonel, Elvis's manager, and asked if we could get a bigger dressing room. The Colonel said we were only going to be there for a couple of weeks, and advised us to just tough it out. But John wasn't satisfied. He kept right on going and knocked at Elvis's suite. "John, why don't you take the comedian's dressing room," Elvis told him. "He ain't doin' nothin' for me." We exchanged dressing rooms with the comedian on Elvis's show, Sammy Shore (Pauly's father).

I'd call home every night, allowing for the time difference and timing the call to be near the kids' bedtime. Gary was a little bit older and kept his feelings in check. Nippy was always into something—busy playing or watching her favorite performer, Michael Jackson, on TV.

Michael took my absences the worst.

"I hated it," remembers Michael. "It would take about a week to get accustomed to her being gone. She'd have the timing of her telephone call down, it'd be just before we were going to bed. She'd make sure we knew what we had to do for the next day. She'd tell us she loved us and to make sure we prayed before we went to bed."

Michael would cry sometimes on the phone and it broke my heart. My friend Phyllis, who was watching the kids, said she heard Michael praying once before he went to sleep.

". . . and oh, God," Michael prayed, "why'd you make my mommy a star?"

Elvis was fun to work with, but I thought he was squirrelly and told him so. I'd get bored doing the same show with him every night, so I'd occasionally throw in an obbligato. He would look back and smile his great smile and I knew he liked it. So I'd do it again. He'd tease me about it in the dressing room later. I guess something about those obbligatos made him think I was squirrelly, and he used that to come up with his nickname for me: Cissy Squirrelly. He was very sweet to us and I think he genuinely enjoyed us. After the show, we would jam with him for an hour, singing gospel. He really loved gospel, had a feel for it and was tickled to have four "church sisters" backing him up. At the end of our engagement with him, he gave me a bracelet inscribed with my name on the outside. On the inside of the bracelet he had inscribed his nickname for me: Squirrelly.

Seven weeks away from home, even if it was with Elvis, was too long to be away from the kids. I had people taking care of them, either Bae or Phyllis and both sets of their kids. My children never had to come home to an empty house. But seven weeks is a long time in a kid's life and I felt like I was missing them growing up.

Singing with the Sweet Inspirations was also getting old. Myrna and Sylvia were younger than me and wanted to start wearing more revealing costumes onstage. I wasn't in favor of that. I was a mother and a role model to my kids. Going out on the road, I was also forced to give up directing my choir at New Hope. That hurt too. This was something that had been part of my life for over twenty years. It was something my father had urged me to do when I was a teenager. The road tours also made it impossible for me to sing with my brothers and sisters, something I'd promised my father I would do. We sang on holidays, of course, Thanksgiving, Christmas, when we'd all get together at Lee's house. But this was only a once-a-year thing. I was losing touch with the things that kept me grounded—my family, my church, my choir.

"We missed Cissy when she was out on the road," says Anne. "Lee, Reebie and I used to get off our jobs on Friday, meet at my house and fry up a whole mess of chicken. We sat on my porch, just ate chicken and talked. We missed her at those times."

That same year, 1968, I realized how much I'd already missed, how much time I'd never recover to spend with my brothers and sisters. That summer, my brother Larry suddenly went into a mysterious coma that put him in the hospital for months. As Larry lay in this coma, running a really high fever, the doctors could not determine what was wrong with him. I came off the road and stayed at his bedside praying for days. He was unconscious so long that every adult family member took a shift at his bedside praying for him—even John. I was hysterical. Larry was my closest playmate growing up. He was only two years older than me and I loved him dearly. The thought that someone might have slipped him some poison or shot him up with drugs made me crazy. I was so wild, searching for some explanation for Larry's mysterious coma, that I even thought for a time some evil person had put him in a spell. The church elders came to his bedside, anointed him with oil and prayed for him. I visited healers on Larry's behalf, talked to doctors and prayed. Finally, the doctors caught a break in Larry's case. They determined that Larry was suffering from encephalitis. Larry was a garbageman in Newark. Unbeknownst to him, he had probably been stung by a mosquito that was carrying the disease. The prayers that had gone up for Larry finally broke his fever. He came out of his coma but he was never the same again. The fever had fried his brain. My once vibrant, funny and talkative brother was now only a shadow of the Larry I used to know. He would ask you the same question repeatedly, forget things and was sometimes afraid to go outside. My once independent brother now depended totally on the people around him to care for him. I always had looked up to him as an older brother. I now found it too painful to be the strong, "normal" one in our relationship. I know it's wrong, but I don't visit him as much as I should. His wife, my beautiful sister-in-law, Summer, has faithfully taken care of Larry since the day he fell ill in 1968. That's commitment—love in its purest form.

I realized my time out on the road had prevented me from spending time with my brother while he was "normal." I could never recover those years.

Always lurking in the back of my mind was another personal demon. I was closing in on the age mother was when she died. Each time

I came back from a road trip with the Sweets or Aretha, I felt like I'd missed something in the kids' lives—a school play, or a Sunday school presentation at church. They were growing like weeds now; Gary was shooting up seemingly overnight, as were Michael and Whitney. I'd look at Whitney and realize I wasn't too much older than she when I lost my mom. My being away so much was beginning to make them more independent. I didn't have to be dead—I was already gone from their lives! What was I going to do? I couldn't just stop working—I was the main breadwinner in the house. I had to keep working, and the best work, the most lucrative work, was in the recording studio. Session work was great but you were basically punching a clock; you got paid for what you worked and not a dime more. No opportunity to earn royalties, record advances or personal appearance fees. My only shot at that kind of money was with the Sweet Inspirations. We had a few albums, some singles, even a Grammy nomination. But to sell records, to become an act, I would have to tour! What was I going to do? I couldn't free myself from this trap—either I could starve and see my kids or support them and never see them. I also wanted to move out of Newark. My back was against the wall. The working-mother syndrome was tearing me apart inside. I saw no way out, no solution.

Then one night I went into my room and lay down on the bed. My situation was impossible, I thought. I began to cry, and pray, trying to sort out my impossible situation.

"With God, all things are possible." I heard the scripture inside me. All things? What about my situation? How could I even think about moving out of Newark, buying another house, when we could barely cover expenses on this one! At last I began to focus on God, instead of my problems. I thought about His attributes, the way He had been mighty in my life, in my father's life, in my mother's life. I meditated on His goodness. I realized my problem was with my focus. I was concentrating on my own resources, my own skills, my own limited power. I had to take my eyes off self and put them on the unlimited resources and wisdom and power of my heavenly Father. I was hung up on "me," when I needed to be thinking about "He."

> *He . . . can turn the tide*
> *And calm the angry sea*
> *He . . . alone decides who writes a symphony*
> *He . . . lights every star*
> *That makes our darkness bright*
> *He . . . keeps watch all through*
> *Each long and lonely night.*
> *—"He"*

The song "He" isn't generally thought of as a gospel tune but it has always ministered to me. We tend to forget that the same God who set our world in motion, who governs the seasons, the ebbing and flowing of the tides, the same great God who placed the planets in their orbits and set the stars in the heavens to light our way, is the same God who cares for us, is interested in our welfare, if only we will invite Him into our midst.

The next morning was Saturday. I got up, showered, dressed and packed a bag. I had some out-of-town dates with the Sweets that would take me away for about a week. It wasn't too long, I told myself, I would call every night, John was home, the kids would be all right. I had a cup of coffee with Bae in the kitchen. The kids were already outside playing. John was warming up the car. As soon as Michael saw my bag he started to cry. It was Saturday and I usually left for gigs on weekdays. Michael thought Saturdays were powerful enough to keep even Mommy home. I reached down to hug him but he pulled away.

"Okay, be like that, Michael," I said, while John put my bag in the trunk.

Knowing he'd hurt me made Michael cry even more. By the time I got in the car, Whitney and Gary had joined their brother on the sidewalk.

"I remember we were all sitting on the curb—me, my brother and my sister," says Michael. "We were all crying and my mother was pulling off in a Lincoln—and the car stopped. We were all crying and the car stopped.

"All of a sudden she got out and my father was hollering, 'Get back in the car, Cissy.' And she grabbed her bag and stuff and she said, 'I can't go no more.' She walked back in and we all followed her into the house and she stayed home."

I told John I was quitting the Sweet Inspirations. I wanted to get off the road. I was missing the most important years of my children's lives and no kind of money was worth that. I told him to get me a deal somewhere else. I'd worked almost seven years as a background singer; I was known in the studios and I was known in the industry.

John took what he learned sitting every day with Elvis' entourage in the hotel coffee shop and got me a new record deal. Charles Koppelman was a veteran record man who would later develop the career of Tracy Chapman. His new label, Commonwealth United, was interested in giving me a record deal as a solo artist. John and I took the fifteen-thousand-dollar advance they gave us and started looking for a house outside of Newark. In June 1970, Commonwealth released my first single, "I'll Be There." The "B" side, I picked myself: "He"/"I Believe."

The kids were thrilled with the house we found in East Orange on Dodd Street. It was a small Cape Cod style where they each had their own room. But best of all, the previous owner had installed an in-ground swimming pool. From June to September, Nippy rarely came out of the pool. The basement was fully finished. We put a pool table down there. Even Thor had a nice backyard to run around in.

I resolved to do only sessions work, and even these I limited.

I was still the main breadwinner, which kept John at home with the kids. We were pioneers in alternative parenting long before it was popular, long before anyone knew "Mr. Mom." I still spent quality time with the kids—I took them skating, bowling and to the movies. I usually cooked them breakfast, too. When I had to work, John picked up the slack. He did everything—he cooked, cleaned, did the laundry and drove me over to the city. I didn't have to ask him to pick me up either; he wanted to do it. He was the man of the house whether he worked a nine-to-five job or not and I gave him that respect. If we were short of money to pay the bills at the end of the month, John got it;

whether he had to drive a truckload of beef from Chicago to New York or drive a cab nights. I give him credit: a lot of men wouldn't have been able to handle working in the house, taking care of the kids. Their egos would have been bruised. John wasn't like that.

"I was in love with my kids," says John. "It wasn't work; it was fun. Big fun. Especially taking care of Nippy. I used to do her hair, get her dressed, the whole bit."

"My father did the cleaning, he washed the clothes, did the ironing and made us breakfast," says Michael. "I mean, he taught me to cook. His chicken fricassee—I'll never forget it; the meat would fall right off the bone. For breakfast, he would do whatever we wanted. My sister and I liked Cream of Wheat, but my brother wouldn't eat that. Gary liked Wheatena, so my father made him that. My father did everything that a mom would do, we didn't miss a step. My friends used to laugh at me sometimes when we would leave for school, because my dad would kiss all of us. They'd say, 'Ahh, your father's kissing you on the mouth.' Yeah, that's right, y'know. Because their fathers—they didn't have no fathers—so my father was like Uncle John to the whole neighborhood."

It should be no surprise that our house became the most popular house in the neighborhood. There was a pool in the backyard, a pool table in the basement and John Houston, chef extraordinaire, barbecuing hamburgers and grilling hot dogs in the backyard.

"Guys I knew, friends of mine, could feel comfortable around my family," says Gary. "My friends didn't have the kind of love in their families like we did. They knew they could come and get a meal and they could sit and talk and be free around the Houstons. But they could only go so far. They knew my mother didn't take no mess. My mother would want me to bring my friends over, but she would feel them out and then she would let me know."

As in the house I grew up in, we all ate together as a family. Myself or one of the kids blessed the food. Unlike my father, I believed it was okay for brothers and sisters to fight. Nippy and Michael proved that to me every day. They were only two years apart and fought like cats and dogs. When John and I came in from work every afternoon, Whitney usually met us at the door with a long list of grievances against Michael. It got to the point where we made a rule that there would be no discussion of grievances during the week. On Saturday, we would have a "beef session" or a family meeting where the kids could air their grievances against each other. At the same beef session, we also allowed them to air any grievance they had against us. Later on, when Michael got older he guessed the hidden purpose of the beef session. Michael guessed that if he and Nippy had to wait all week, until Saturday, to air their grievances, they would either forget or consider the problem unimportant. He was right.

But Nippy took the meetings very seriously. She would call a meeting on Michael and come prepared with actual lists of grievances. If you made light of her or her grievances in any way, or if you tried to inject humor into the meeting, then she would get up and stomp away from the table.

"I would be complaining and very serious," says Whitney. "I was very, very serious about these meetings; I would jump up, say what I had to say and sometimes I'd get angry and leave. I was the outspoken one at the meetings . . . I was like Michael's shadow . . . We were two years apart . . . There were things that Michael got into that I thought my parents should know about . . . I was a tattletale. But he used to pick with me so bad, man. Constantly. Pull my hair . . . With his fingers in my face he'd go, 'I'm not touching you . . . I'm not touching . . . I'm not touching you.'"

Whitney also came to resent the authority that we gave Michael over her. We had house rules about her being home before the streetlights came on. As her older brother, it was Michael's responsibility to bring Whitney home before those streetlights came on. Wherever he was, he had to find her and bring her home. Whitney hated being under Michael's surveillance. Even worse, in Nippy's mind, he had the authority to make her leave her friends and come home. She would fight him all the way to Dodd Street.

"I would go find her and her girlfriends and I would be like, tough," recalls Michael. "She wanted to stay with her girlfriends and some of them stayed out until 2 A.M. My mother wouldn't have that. Most of those girls turned out to be, y'know, hoochies."

I worried about my kids, I admit it. It used to drive John nuts. He'd take me out to dinner at some nice restaurant and I'd get up three times during the meal to call the baby-sitter. "Those kids are fine," he'd bellow. I guess I had a heavy burden to be for my kids what I never had after I was eight years old—a mommy. I was particularly concerned about Gary. He rarely spoke up during family beef sessions or brought a grievance against anyone. This was consistent with his personality.

"I always wanted to be liked and accepted," says Gary. "That's something that I had a problem with growing up. People would say, 'Oh, yeah, your cousin Dionne' . . . or 'Your mother sings here and there' . . . or 'You have this or that.' But I wanted to let them know that it wasn't like that . . . so you lower yourself in order to be accepted. My mother never wanted us to lower our standards or to lower ourselves to someone else's level just to make a friend."

Gary got in with the wrong crowd for a while. I tried to tell him that the people he was surrounding himself with didn't have his best interests at heart.

" 'I'm telling you this because I love you,' she used to say," recalls Gary. " 'I'm telling you because I don't think anyone else is going to tell you. But you're going to find out for yourself.'

"She always knew exactly what was going to happen, whether it was me or my brother or sister. And she'd tell you before it happened. I would hide things from her, do things in secret, but she knew automatically, with my character, my personality, that something was up. Things never slipped by her. Even if people never told her, it was exposed already, because she knew through her spiritual life.

"My mother put me out one time in my life. I was about fourteen and she put me out because I didn't come home at the right time. She said be home by eleven and I came home at twelve or twelve-thirty. I knocked at the door, which was locked. She said, 'Go back where you came from.' Okay, I did; I stayed out for two days. She was out looking for me 'cause she couldn't sleep. And I was right around the corner.

She didn't know and I didn't want anyone to tell her. She couldn't sleep; she couldn't rest . . . a mother's love is a different kind of love."

There were many times that Gary came back to me and said, "Hey, Ma . . . you know, you were right about such and such a person. You were right and I'm sorry." I could never resist an "I told you so," but I'd also grab him up and hold him tight for coming back to me with the humility to say he was wrong. I love that boy.

Gary could sing. I had him and Nippy in church with me, in the children's choir, whether they liked it or not. Even if they turned a deaf ear to the sermon or looked out the window during Sunday school, the Word became part of their life, singing it Sunday morning and during the week at choir rehearsal. Michael didn't get the benefit Gary and Nippy got being a part of the choir. He went through a phase where he didn't like church. When John stayed home from church, Michael stayed with him. He was shy about singing in public. I was concerned about his spiritual education. I didn't want my own spiritual experience to overshadow his own.

"We always sat in one area in church and my mother always watched her children," says Michael. "When she would feel God—she would cry or whatever and she would always look at us.

"I was scared when I saw her get excited . . . But we talked about it and it was all right. I didn't have to be ashamed for being afraid. She told me that one day I would feel Him for myself, and when I surrendered to it, I would also know the feelings she felt.

"As I think back now, I think I felt God every time I went to church. I just didn't know then what it was. But we were able to talk about it, because she made it easy to talk about God. And especially back then, talking about God wasn't easy. Everybody in the neighborhood wasn't into Jesus. Most of my friends were going to the mosque and there I was, the little church boy. They laughed when they saw me going to church. But it got to the point where representing Jesus, you know, was something I was proud of doing. I learned that I didn't have to fight for Jesus. You know, God could handle Himself—you just be a light that shows, that's all you got to do; people will see."

I tried to teach Michael about prayer—not to pray for himself but to pray for the people he loved and they in turn would pray for him. I taught him about luck—there is none; there are only blessings. You just have to keep your hands open to receive them. And I warned him about hate. How hate will consume you . . . how hate will prevent you from loving.

Most of all, I wanted my kids to know that God was there. There were so many distractions that were part of their lives, so many diversions vying for their attention. The separate reality that movies, music videos and television promoted made it easy to forget God even existed. I wanted my children to know they could always call on Him . . . and count on Him.

> *Do you despair?*
> *Do you think God's not there?*
> *Do you move on your own,*
> *Without consulting the throne?*
> *He's always there,*
> *Call Him in prayer*
> *He'll guide you*
> *Just you wait right there.*
> *Stop, look and listen*
> *And know He cares.*
> *—"Stop, Look and Listen"*

I know He cared for the Houstons. He made it possible for us to move to Dodd Street and provided in wonderful ways so that we could take care of the kids. There always seemed to be money to send the boys to basketball camp for a few weeks during the summer . . . give Michael guitar and piano lessons (he ended up playing congas with his Uncle Nicky at New Hope) or buy some little special dress I wanted for Whitney. If there wasn't enough money, I worked some extra sessions or leaned on John to pick up some extra work on the weekend.

Life was good on Dodd Street. I was off the road and able to resume working with my choirs at church. The boys were happy, plugged into athletics, and I was finally able to spend the kind of time with my daughter I'd always hoped for. John and I were close, even if we didn't always share the same interests, we preferred each other's company.

"They were like Tom and Jerry," says Bae. "They did everything together. She trusted him implicitly. They had a fantastic relationship, the kind of long-lasting relationship I last saw in my grandmother's generation. They gave me stability, they were so loving and demonstrative. And not in a syrupy, phony kind of way. There was always this wonderful affection between them, just below the surface. They deferred to each other; they pleased each other. We might have been sitting there watching television, talking about some sexy guy or something on the screen, and John would come in from the backyard. Cissy would say, 'Hey, you gonna fry up some chicken?' And he'd say, 'Yeah, why don't we go down to the supermarket and get some.' I'd cook up a pot of beans and we'd eat, just the three of us."

During the summer, Dionne often invited the kids to fly with her to one of her concerts. The boys got the biggest kick flying in Dionne's chartered jet. But Nippy really enjoyed watching her cousin Dionne sing from the wings or a front-row seat. Dionne had two sons and she really enjoyed Nippy's company. Dionne would bring her back to me and couldn't stop talking about her—she was so ladylike, so inquisitive and so cute.

Nippy was also smart as a whip. By third grade, she was so bright they wanted to skip her a grade. I refused. When she was in fifth grade, they asked me again if they could skip her. Again, I wouldn't allow it. My friend Bae got all over my case.

"Why not, Cissy?" Bae demanded. "Nippy will graduate high school at sixteen or seventeen. That'll be great!"

Great? Who will she hang around with in school? A bunch of kids faster and older than her? No, thanks. She'll graduate when she's supposed to. I didn't need to look at any educational studies showing the benefits of skipping grades. I knew what was right for my daughter. I didn't want her experiencing life any sooner than she needed to.

I had to admit she was bright. I took her everywhere with me—to the bank, to the supermarket and to New York and the recording studio. Even as a third grader, she was so inquisitive she talked to everyone a mile a minute.

"But, Mommy," she'd start one of her questions, "so and so and so and so, don't you know, Mommy?"

The "don't you know, Mommy" coda she attached to all her queries really tickled me.

"No, Whitney, Mommy doesn't know," I told her, holding that cute little face in my hands.

She talked to everyone on the bus. I told her she just couldn't do that. "But why, Mommy, why . . . ?" she would ask. Of course, everyone, old and young, male and female, also wanted to talk to her. The little suede bucks and plaid skirt I dressed her in accentuated her studious, inquisitive air. First, I thought she would make a good teacher or a doctor. My ob/gyn for my pregnancy with Nippy was a black woman who really impressed me. First Whitney wanted to be a teacher. At school, the teachers loved her so it was no surprise she had aspirations in this direction. Then she went through a stage where she wanted to be a veterinarian. That was fine with me too. Then a few years later she changed her mind again. This time she wanted to be a singer. I hoped that was a stage she would also pass through. I didn't want her in the business. I'd seen how the music business treated people, especially women. The knocks you took from label executives, musicians and the public had a way of making you old before your time. I wanted to keep my little girl a little girl as long as I could. I loved to dress her in the morning, comb her hair and fix it up with pretty ribbons. I used to go through the children's department at Bloomingdale's, combing the racks for something cute for her to wear. Everybody loved her. When I took her to a session at Atlantic, everybody made a fuss over her. One minute, she was eating french fries with Aretha. The next, she was jumping into Myrna's lap. Everybody thought she was delightful.

Everybody but the other little girls at Dodd Street School. I knew something was wrong one day when she came home for lunch and claimed she didn't have to return to school that day.

"What do you mean, you don't have to go back to school today?" I asked her.

"Yeah, Mommy, the teacher said I did so good today, I don't have to go back," she announced.

I finally dragged it out of her. Some girls in class had picked on her and threatened to beat her up after school.

"I don't have to go back, do I, Mommy, do I?" she asked.

Nippy was petrified. I kept her home that day. The next day, they chased her home again. And the next, and the next. When Michael heard about it, he wanted to take up for Nippy. He waited for the girls outside class and glared at them.

"Michael, you can't do that," I told him. "You can't beat up girls."

"They're beatin' up Nippy," he sulked.

I went to see the principal. I demanded satisfaction from Henry and probably got a little too upset and loud in his office. He promised he'd take care of it.

"Make sure you do," I reminded him, "or I'll take matters into my own hands." Henry knew I wasn't playin'.

"I was more inclined not to tell her a lot of things that occurred in school," says Whitney. "I was her daughter, Dionne was my cousin. Both my parents were live-in parents, in a day when there were a lot of single parents. We had a household that was very much family and all the kids kind of drew to us. At the same time, there was a certain amount of jealousy. We had a pool, y'know. My mother and father worked very hard so that we would be self-contained, we wouldn't have to go out in the streets to find or do anything. That was difficult for neighborhood kids who didn't have the same things or the kind of parents that sacrificed. My parents worked very hard. I think that's what people missed. They saw our lives as something that was almost like a fairy tale, instead of something that was really worked for."

Whitney wouldn't tell me things that happened to her in school because she knew I would rush to her defense. But I was angry. Angry and hurt that Whitney was being persecuted. And for what? The blessings in her life? A nice family, a nice home, pretty dresses to wear? I understood but I didn't want to.

"These girls don't want to be with you because . . . why . . . because you have things?" I asked Whitney. "I comb your hair? What? I don't understand. Because Mommy dresses you nice? Whitney, sometimes you're better off being by yourself. Sometimes, you just have to be your own best friend."

I hated having to say that to her. Our house was the most popular house on the block. Kids came to eat at our house; my kids let friends with nowhere to stay sleep in our basement without my even knowing. Was this how we were paid back for our kindness? How was I supposed to explain this to my daughter?

Now, every chance I got, I took Whitney to church with me. New Hope Baptist Church became Whitney's second home. She didn't like going at first; she fought me. Then, after a while, she began to like it. No one was looking at her clothes; no one was jealous of her. New Hope became her second family, the way it had become mine. Through the choir, Anne's daughter Felicia and Whitney became close friends, besides being cousins.

Church became so ingrained in her routine that when she wasn't at New Hope, she attended a little Holiness church in our neighborhood. I never went there, but I suppose it wasn't much different than the Holiness church I went to as a child on Court Street.

"I was about thirteen or fourteen," says Whitney. "I can remember being in church—a church on the corner of Dodd Street, where we lived. That's how much I loved going to church; I would find a church to go to that I loved, that had the same kind of spirit as New Hope. I can remember the Holy Spirit coming into that church and just taking over. I remember just crying and accepting the Savior in my life and in my heart . . . knowing that He was real . . . it wasn't fake. And things were happening! I could see things, a vision of myself . . . I could see things that He had in store for me. Things I never knew before I met Him. I just remember crying, purging, just purging and crying, thanking Him for what I didn't know then, but I do now."

As I reflect back now on the girls who "chased" my daughter into church, I'm reminded of Joseph and his brothers.

"Ye thought evil against me," Joseph said to his brothers as he forgave them for persecuting him. "But God meant it unto good . . ."

Joseph was forsaken by his family. His brothers hated him so much, they sold him as a slave into Egypt. Then he was thrown in jail when his master's wife maliciously accused him of rape. But wherever Joseph landed, he always landed on his feet. In whatever circumstances he found himself—even jail—he prospered because God was with him. That is the kind of God we serve. Even in our own despair and misery, He is working His plan for our ultimate good.

This was a tremendous lesson for me. While I was anguishing over my daughter, while I was confused and hurt that anyone would disrespect her, God was working His plan. If those girls had never persecuted Whitney, she never would have made church her second home. I finally understood the reason why we are told to praise the Lord for everything, the good and the bad. Had I been doing that, I would have been able to flow along with God's plan. For, in only a little while, and according to His plan, they chased her right into the arms of the Lord.

When Nippy was thirteen years old, she announced she wanted to sing professionally. I wasn't happy about her decision. I had worked so hard to get off the road for my family's sake—now Nippy was contemplating a career in show business. But I told her if she really wanted to sing, she would have to learn how to do it correctly. That meant rehearsing every week and singing every Sunday with the choir. She agreed. I moved Nippy up to my eight o'clock choir; now she was sitting at the grown-ups' table. This is where she really began to learn a great deal, because I utilized her as a leader.

"Some nights, Nippy and my mom would come in from choir rehearsal mad at each other," says Michael. "Mommy might have thought that Nippy didn't sing with enough emotion that particular night."

My own early training under Reebie had made me a cruel taskmaster. I didn't take no foolin' around, and God help you if I caught you talking during rehearsal.

"She could embarrass you so badly," says Whitney, "you'd feel like you just wanted to slide under the chair and crawl away. She's real good at that."

I feel bad about that now; I cry about it. I wish I hadn't been so rough on Nippy. But she learned what she had to learn.

Nippy was determined. She accepted the roles in our relationship; I was the teacher, she was the student. I have to give her credit—the kid had guts. At twelve or thirteen years old, it's pretty tough to dedicate yourself to something. Whitney was a very pretty girl. She could have been out socializing, getting all the dates she wanted. But she didn't. Now, part of that was me, not allowing her to date at what I thought was a young age. If I said no, she would often go around me to her father, who was a little more lenient with her.

The point is, she could have rebelled, but didn't. She gave up lots of weeknights for choir rehearsal. She couldn't stay out late Saturday nights; she had church early the next morning. But besides my voice of discipline, Whitney was listening to another voice. A voice I did not become aware of until after her first solo at New Hope.

It was a "humble" solo. It was no full-out gospel standard, no big, emotional Thomas Dorsey number that might have been associated with Mahalia or Clara Ward, or one of us Drinkard Singers, for that matter. It was just a small piece of scripture that I had set to music. Whitney would step forward after the announcements, look at me for her cue, I would raise my hands to cue the choir, and she would begin singing.

> *Let the words of my mouth,*
> *And the meditation of my heart,*
> *Be acceptable in thy sight,*
> *O Lord, my strength, and my redeemer.*
> *—Psalm 19:14*

It was a psalm of David, the last four lines of a beautiful psalm extolling the works and the word of God. Like no other psalm, it deserves to be sung. David starts out considering how the heavens declare the glory of

God; the beautiful skies and exquisite cloud formations, pouring forth testimony . . . the night, rich with the wisdom of a million stars . . . all silent. "There is no speech, nor are there words." I imagine David's voice rising here, full-bodied, as he sings of the miraculous properties of God's word—the scriptures that are able to make wise the simple, enlighten the mind and restore the soul.

> *More to be desired are they than gold*
> *Yea, than much fine gold:*
> *Sweeter also than honey and the honeycomb*
> *Moreover by them is thy servant warned:*
> *And in keeping of them there is great reward.*

As David considers the holiness of God and his own imperfection, God's impossible standard and his own tendency to sin, I see him, in my mind's eye, falling to his knees.

> *Let the words of my mouth, and the meditation of my heart,*
> *Be acceptable in thy sight, O Lord . . .*

It was a humble prayer, a prayer that considered the greatness of God and the humility of the singer. I taught it to Whitney; we practiced it and rehearsed it until she knew it well enough to sing it on Sunday.

But I never got to see her sing it. At the last minute, something happened. I was called out of town for a gig that weekend. You do what you gotta do, I told myself to ease the pain of not seeing Nippy sing her first solo in church. When I called home that night, John was beside himself. Nippy had got up there and sung her heart out. She had made everyone cry: my sisters, Nicky, even John.

The first Sunday I was back at New Hope, I scheduled Nippy to sing the solo again. When I heard it, I did something I don't do very often: I changed my mind. I wasn't against her singing anymore. I had a peace about her choosing this as her life's work. There was something in her voice that no one, not even I, could teach her. Of course, it was in the genes; all the way back to her great-great-grandmother, Victoria

Drinkard, her grandfather Nitch Drinkard, her aunts, her cousins and me. But there was also something else I heard beyond just her ancestors.

"When I opened my mouth to sing," says Whitney, "it was there, a feeling and a spirit that would come through me and out of my mouth. It wasn't anything I could control. I didn't fight it, it was just there. At first, I thought it was just hereditary, something that God said, like 'Here, your mother's got it, you've got it.' But after a while, as I got to know the Savior, I began to realize what He had given me, the greatness of what He had given me and where He wanted me to go with it. From that point, I started to prepare myself for this . . . for this life."

Once I heard Whitney sing in church that day, I knew there was something there that had nothing to do with show business. There was a call on her life.

We got much closer after this. A lot of typical mother/daughter stuff fell away. Our relationship changed in some subtle ways. We were able to enjoy each other in a different way. There was an ease with which we related that wasn't there before. We laughed together, more like girl-friends. I was still Mommy; I still had to discipline her. But there was now an added dimension—we shared a sense of purpose, a call.

One night in September 1976, we shared an "experience" I would just as soon we hadn't. I was already sleeping when the phone rang. Whitney picked it up in her room and thought the caller was "prank-ing" her.

"We think we have your father here, in the hospital," they said. "We believe he's had a massive heart attack."

"Yeah, right," said a thirteen-year-old Whitney. "My father's sleep-ing in the bedroom," and she hung up.

They called right back.

"Please, wake up, we have to talk to someone," said the caller, this time more alarmed. "We think we have Mr. Houston in the hospital." Nippy told them to hold on. She went to John's bedroom and didn't find him in his bed.

"I freaked," says Whitney. "I went back to the phone and I said, 'You *do* have my father.' "

"Yes, we do. He's had a massive heart attack," said the caller. "We need to talk to your mother."

Whitney woke me, then handed me the phone.

"Mom, Daddy is in the hospital," said Whitney. "Something's wrong."

I took the phone. They told me John had suffered a massive heart attack.

Whitney says I hung up the phone, put my head in my hands and started screaming, crying loud enough for the neighbors to hear. Two minutes later, just as suddenly, she says, I straightened up, said, "We have to go," and got dressed. I remember none of this. If John was dead, then I didn't want to live either.

ELEVEN

There are times we complain
And we cannot explain
Why the things in our lives
Don't go as planned.
—"Count Your Blessings"

Whitney and I ran out of the house only to find that we had no car. John had apparently driven himself to the hospital! I ran back into the house to call a cab and Bae, who met us at the hospital. I wasn't prepared for the scene at the hospital. There was John laid out in the emergency room, white as a sheet, hooked up to a million wires, tubes and monitors. John had always been strong as an ox, healthy, so full of life, always there for me, the kids and his own parents. To see him helpless like this was too much. Whitney started to cry. I had Bae grab her and walk her out of the emergency room; if John saw his baby crying that would have destroyed him. I grasped his hand and he managed a weak smile. There was no gutsy John Houston bravado—cursing a blue streak and laughing. He was scared. I'd only seen him like that one other time. It was while we were on tour in Europe with Aretha around 1968 or 1969. Me, John and the Sweets were flying from Madrid to Lisbon. The Sweets were sleeping in back of us, John and I were sitting together when I noticed something strange. We were descending rapidly, too rapidly. I looked at my watch. We were nowhere near Lisbon. Across the aisle, I noticed other people stirring, worried looks on their faces. I looked out the window and saw lights—not airport lights—coming up fast. I turned to John.

"John, this damn plane's gonna crash," I snapped, ready to write a nasty letter to Lisbonair.

John had no tough-guy comeback, no smart one-liners. His face was ashen. He had also felt the plane descending too fast and saw the lights.

"Cissy, how's the rest of 'The Lord is my shepherd . . .' go?" John asked, dead serious.

I almost bust out laughing, half because I seldom saw John so serious and half because for a guy who read the Bible as much as John did, raised a good Catholic, he should have known one of the most popular passages of scripture.

We bowed our heads, held hands and prayed, reciting together the twenty-third psalm.

The Lord is my shepherd
I shall not want.
He maketh me to lie down in green pastures:
He leadeth me beside quiet waters.
He restoreth my soul:
He leadeth me in the paths of righteousness
For His name's sake.
Yea, though I walk through the valley of the shadow of death,
I will fear no evil: for Thou art with me;
Thy rod and Thy staff they comfort me.
Thou preparest a table before me in the presence of mine enemies:
Thou anointest my head with oil;
My cup runneth over.
Surely goodness and mercy shall follow me all the days of my life:
And I will dwell in the house of the Lord for ever.

Amen. When we lifted our heads, the plane stalled for a second, then began to pull itself out of its steep dive. I looked around at the relieved faces, the nervous smiles of the other passengers. Estelle, one of the Sweets, who had somehow slept through the whole hair-raising episode, now awoke.

"Cissy, Cissy, I had a dream that the plane almost crashed," she said.

"That was no dream, honey," I told her.

After that, John and I rarely flew together. We reasoned that if one of our planes went down, we wouldn't leave the children parentless. Of course, that was my worst fear, the first scene that flashed before my eyes as I felt that plane to Lisbon go into its nosedive. My kids, motherless and fatherless, having to fend for themselves, alone in this world. I wasn't afraid for myself; I even had a peace about dying: "To be absent from the body is to be present with the Lord." I guess John, even with all the Bible he knew, had no such assurance. I saw it on the plane that day and I saw it on his face again as he lay helpless after his heart attack.

I was no tower of strength myself that night in the emergency room. I was terrified I'd lose him right there in the hospital, the same way I'd lost my father. But I had to be strong—for John, who always relied on my prayers during a crisis, and for the kids.

In the next few days, my sisters joined me at the hospital. We prayed for John around the clock. By the end of the week he began to get his color back. The doctors said that at his age, fifty-six, John had an excellent chance for a full recovery. I was happy just to be able to take him home. But John was pretty shook up. He still had both his parents and, unlike me, he hadn't yet experienced the death of a loved one. Now, death had come very near. In the months following his heart attack he realized how close it had come. Depression is common after a major heart attack. Understandably, John was less like his old self. He became a little more inward. At fifty-six years old, his life could have ended. What had he accomplished in his life? he asked himself. The heart attack forced John to take stock of himself. Always a deep thinker anyway, John now put his life under heavy scrutiny. Where had he been . . . where was he going?

I tiptoed around John, tried to keep the kids quiet; I was just happy to have my husband alive and home. As we entered the Thanksgiving and holiday season, I found many things in addition to John's recovery to be thankful for. Gary had been rewarded with a full scholarship to play basketball for De Paul in Chicago. I was so proud of him, and even happier that he would know the satisfaction of paying his own way through college. I had been trying to impress on the children the importance of paying your own way through life, depending on yourself. I had refused to allow Dionne to buy Gary a new car for his high school graduation. Of course, he wanted it and was at first annoyed with me. When De Paul notified him that he'd won the scholarship, he understood what I was talking about when I said, "God bless the child that's got his own."

Whitney had also made me proud. I had entered her in the Garden State Competition, a talent contest that drew five thousand contestants. Nippy had finished as one of the five finalists.

Michael had met a wonderful girl. Donna Jackson was a sweetheart, originally from North Carolina. She'd met Michael in middle school but started getting serious with him in high school. I was happy for Michael; he was so tender and emotional, he needed a nice girl by his side. His previous girlfriend was literally unable to stay by his side. She was a track star, and was not his emotional speed. We used to kid him about her: "Michael, where's that girlfriend of yours?"

"Aw, Ma, I can't catch up with her," he'd mope.

I also had cause to be grateful for my own career. In 1976, Luther Vandross, the young high schooler who'd played hooky and saw me and the Sweets at the Apollo, was rising in the ranks. He'd proved himself as a capable backup and jingle singer and our old friend, the brilliant arranger and producer Arif Mardin was responsible for signing Luther to Atlantic's Cotillion label. He sent me his first album with a long letter. He wrote that I had inspired him to go on in the business and asked if I would consider supervising the voices on his next album. Of course, I did and in the process made a good friend in Luther.

During this time, I also had the pleasure of working with producer Joel Dorn at Atlantic. I sang on lots of great sessions for Joel—Bette Midler, Yusef Lateef, the Neville Brothers—too many to mention, but all memorable if just for Joel's creativity. Joel was my friend, my good friend. In the following years, Michael Zager, another talented producer and arranger, cut "Tomorrow" and a bunch of jingles with me, for products like Bounce and R.C. Cola. Michael also proved to be a wonderful friend.

I was so caught up in an attitude of thanksgiving that I wrote new lyrics to the old song "Count Your Blessings." It was inspired by one of

John's friends, a man who had diabetes, and we visited him in the hospital. As the disease progressed, he suffered the loss of each of his limbs, until he was just a stump.

There are times we complain
And we cannot explain
Why the things in our lives
Don't go as planned.

If we just look around and see
All that God has done
Not just for me
But also for you.

We complain of no shoes
While there's a man with no feet
We have eyes
While the blind cannot see

So amid conflict great or small
Remember God's still over all
Count your blessings
See what God has done.

Count your blessings, name them
One by one, claim them
Just be thankful
For what God has done.

John had no such attitude of thanksgiving. He was grateful to be alive but fearful he could have another heart attack. He examined his life for the cause of the attack and decided it was stress. As the years went by, our bills and our spending had only escalated. I sent Gary two hundred dollars a week for his entire four years at De Paul. I guess this was the protective mother in me. I didn't find it easy to let my baby, my first child, fly so soon from my nest. Even though Gary's scholarship paid for everything, I couldn't bear the thought of my son being so far from home and going hungry or lack money for clothes. I suppose the money I sent him was just a way to hold him in my arms a little longer. We also had incurred an added debt by placing Whitney in private school. She had taken enough hard knocks up until fifth grade; when East Orange decided to create a middle school for grades six through nine and bus kids in from other neighborhoods, I drew the line. John's mother and I went shopping and found a good private school for girls. My solution for these added expenses was to work harder: book more sessions for myself and take on some private voice students.

I think this probably frustrated John. He saw the sessions as an inefficient use of my talent. John was always very ambitious. He thought I could go much further as an artist, a solo artist. He loved the work I did behind artists like Aretha and Elvis. Loved the contributions I made to all those hit records. But in the end, I think he saw the sessions as punching a clock, making a few record company executives very rich, while I was paid by the hour. The only way to beat the system, he thought, was to use the same system to build yourself as an artist. Then you could set your own price. I had a few problems with becoming a "star." First, I had a bad taste in my mouth from the Sweet Inspirations. I don't think we got the kind of support from the record company that we should have gotten. And not just in terms of promotion. Our records should have had a proper arranger, a producer and everything else they throw on a record or act the company wants to see make it. I was very proud of the solo album I did for Commonwealth United. There were all kinds of great songs on that album. But when Commonwealth United went bankrupt, another company inherited the record and let it die on the vine. You don't forget that kind of stuff. You work very hard on a record and then some fool in the executive suite sabotages your dreams. While they tee off on a game plan for their company, you're expected to put your life, your career, your family on hold. At the time, I also saw the music business as somewhat racist. If you were black you were expected only to sing rhythm and blues. They didn't want you singing show tunes, cabaret or certain kinds of pop. Oh, every so often they'd let a few in—Sammy Davis, Jr., Lena

Horne—but for the most part, non-R&B was run like an exclusive white country club. The stereotypes made me angry. Second, I didn't want to be a star. I had seen too many people just get beside themselves; get too grand until they forgot what was important in life.

"She hated leaving her children," says Bae. "She always wanted a girl. Finally, she gets a little girl and there's this opportunity for a solo career and what do you do? Theoretically, I know what I would have done. I would have said 'go for it' because the end will justify the means—you'll have the money, you'll be able to stay home with your child. Not Cissy."

My resistance to John's grand designs must have been a rewind for him back to the days when he'd first tried so hard to get me to sing anything other than gospel.

Of course, as I worked harder, booked more sessions, took on more students, I too got more stressed. At least a few times, I blew our money for the monthly bills on a dress or coat I just had to have. I felt justified; I was working harder, I deserved it. John never said anything. But he did get a job on the Planning Commission at City Hall down in Newark. He managed that nine-to-five job and still kept up with me: taking me to my sessions, picking me up in the city, sometimes late at night, after a club gig at Reno Sweeney's or Mikell's and then having to get up early in the morning for his regular job in Newark. He was burning the candle at both ends.

John decided stress was responsible for his heart attack. At fifty-six, he was certainly too young to die. He felt cheated, having to go through the rest of his life looking over his shoulder, being careful, watching his health. He resented whatever and whoever had put him there. He decided I was to blame.

I felt bad for John; I loved him. But I wasn't taking the blame for his heart attack. I even thought it was funny at first. One of those typical off-the-wall John Houston notions he'd try to fly by every so often. But he was serious.

We'd always bantered back and forth our whole marriage. John liked to tease me, mess with me, get my goat. It was part of his love affair with me. He used words to draw me out of my shell. He had such an active mind, he needed someone to engage him intellectually. I wasn't the brainiest person in the world, but I kept up with him. I was hip to his little games and that tickled him. We fought and he'd curse me out. But just before he went over the edge, he'd smile with that twinkle in his eye and reach out for me. "Come over here, girl," he'd say. "You know I love you." Before we got in that bed at night, we always made up. We made up some more in bed too.

Now when we fought, it took a little longer to make up. First, a few days; then it was a week. John could stay mad at you for two weeks and not talk to you. John had a hard head and I accepted him just the way he was. Besides his mother, I was the only one that could do anything with him. I just let John blow off steam; he'd come around when he was done.

I stayed busy in New York with sessions and with my choirs at church. I took Whitney with me everywhere. She would watch me at various recording sessions; I could see she was learning, just soaking everything up like a sponge. Everyone liked her and before too long they were inviting her to sing background. I let her do a few sessions when she was twelve or thirteen, which I supervised. I determined that I would give Nippy all the encouragement I never got to go on and get a career for herself. She was attractive and sweet and she could sing. But one of her first outings could have been a disaster.

At thirteen years of age, Whitney had made me proud when she was picked to be one of the five finalists in the Garden State Competition. But there was much more to the story. We had spent months finding the right dress and selecting her repertoire, Barbra Streisand's "Evergreen." Whitney had been in contests before but nothing this big.

The pressure mounted as three more finalists fell away. It was just Whitney and another young lady. There was a strict time limit on the contestant's performances. I'd been careful to coach Nippy on pacing her song correctly. She'd done beautifully in the preliminaries, finishing her song well under the time limit. Then something happened during the finals. Her pacing was off. In the closing bars of "Evergreen" Nippy ran out of time. One of the judges told her that if she hadn't run overtime, she would have won the competition. As it was, she came in second. Ironically, the girl who came in first sang "The Greatest Love," a song my daughter would practically make her theme song six years later.

"I remember my mother looking at me," Whitney recalls. " 'Are you disappointed?' she asked me. 'You came in second, that's a good spot. Your mommy doesn't mind. If you're discouraged, it's okay because it makes you work harder. You should be encouraged by the fact that you can be better.' That was my mother's thing: 'Whitney, you're good, y'know, and one day you will be best.' And then you get better. You don't ever think that you've arrived. She would never let me think that I'd arrived. No, she was like, 'You're still gettin' there honey' But in my mother's eyes, I can see the pride and the love she has for me."

Whitney would only build and grow stronger from that early disappointment. In 1978, I took her onstage with me at Carnegie Hall during a benefit for the United Negro College Fund. She remembers "almost peeing on myself" she was so nervous, but she did a great job taking a verse and chorus of "Tommorrow" from *Annie* with me. While she sang with me that night, a photographer from *Vogue* invited her to stop by his office; he thought she'd make a great model. She wasn't particularly interested. Nippy was very beautiful and plain; she didn't even wear makeup. She wasn't aware of her own beauty because that wasn't what we were about. Beauty means nothing if you're hateful and mean inside. Pretty is as pretty does, I always told her. She modeled all through high school, appearing in *Vogue, Seventeen* and *Glamour*. I was wary of her being alone in New York at some photo shoot, so I usually dropped her off, went about my own business and returned later to pick her up. Nippy was always hungry for more independence—to hang out in New York alone, after a photo shoot or a session. But I always resisted. I finally gave in once and was sorry for it. I let her stay after a shoot with the agreement that she would get the bus at Port Authority and be home in Jersey by eight o'clock. When I called home from the city and she still wasn't home by nine, I got worried. By ten o'clock, I was a basket case. I sent John out looking for her. When she finally arrived home, John had to stop me from giving her a good whipping. "But, Mommy," she pleaded, "I was only window-shopping." Incidents like this confirmed my intuition to set boundaries for Nippy. A few years earlier, when she was fourteen years old, I refused the offer of a recording contract for her. Interestingly, it was Gerry Griffiths, who would later scout Whitney for Arista Records, that came around one of the New York clubs I sometimes sang at with Whitney. Gerry spun a million scenarios on marketing Whitney: beautiful girl, incredible voice, and she's only fourteen. I told him that Whitney was incredible and would be even more incredible when she was eighteen and could sign a contract. But right now, she had a lot of learning and growing to do as a young woman. I wanted Whitney to enjoy her childhood, to be a teenager, a normal teenager. I wanted her to know who she was before she got into the business. Quite naturally, Whitney resisted me.

"I wasn't hurt," recalls Whitney. "I just thought I knew it all. 'Yeah,' my mother said. 'You'll thank me later for saying no.' And God knows, I do. Whooo! I do. So much."

It was hard to rein in Whitney when A&R guys from record companies were throwing contracts at her feet and her face was plastered on the cover of a fashion magazine. Harder still when John and I continued to fight in front of the kids. We fought over silly, stupid stuff. Someone hadn't walked the dog, he'd jumped the fence and I had to go chase him through the neighborhood ten minutes before I was supposed to leave for a session in New York. The wash wasn't dry. Someone had forgotten to pay a bill and we were getting a turn-off notice. It didn't matter what the reason was, we were always at each other's throat. John had very few close friends to pal out with, blow off steam. At least I had acquaintances from my choir, from church. John had no one. After staying home for years raising the kids, the children were his intimates. Now, with Gary off at De Paul and Michael on his way to Hutchinson in Kansas, he was losing his inner circle. The house was no longer filled with neighborhood kids and cousins clamoring around John's backyard grill. John was experiencing the empty-nest syndrome before he even knew what had hit him. We couldn't even agree on a movie to watch. John was a war movie freak—*Patton, The Dirty Dozen*. I hated violence. When he got a good shoot-'em-up on the television, he'd start reminiscing about his army years. I tried to stay interested, but a yawn would eventually slip out. He'd accuse me of not paying enough attention to him. He'd accuse me of never paying him enough attention. If it wasn't the kids that took my attention from him, then it was church, he'd argue. He'd drag up incidents from ten years ago, when he'd taken me out to a nice restaurant and I'd broken the mood by twice getting up and dialing the babysitter. I was always so worried about the kids, I had no time for him, he yelled. He'd asked me lots of times to take a little weekend off in the Poconos—in all my years on Dodd Street, I'd never obliged him once.

I could defend my decisions, but it was no use once John got started. He'd served some time in army intelligence during the war and he knew exactly what he was doing. He'd pound away at you until your brain was putty and you offered no resistance to his plans. One of his ideas was to put the house on the market; something I just wasn't ready to do. He'd marshal his facts, work in the "testimony of experts in the field" (a local real estate salesman he'd shared a cup of coffee with that morning) and then start brainwashing you. Brains—that was one of John's biggest problems; he was too smart for his own good. He was too analytical. What I had once liked about John, the interest he took in me, his curiosity about the way I thought and felt, now annoyed me. I felt like John wasn't happy until he had completely dominated your mind, and I was never one to be dominated by anyone or anything. Once or twice, John threatened to leave. It seemed like a contradiction, but if that's what it would take—a little distance—to get us back together again, I encouraged him to do so.

Whitney experienced the worst of our fighting. Gary was long gone at De Paul, Michael left for Kansas in 1979. That left Whitney, a sophomore in high school.

"I was there. My brothers were away at school," remembers Whitney. "So I was there during the time it began and when they finally separated. Ultimately, my grades dropped; I failed four classes. I became very distant."

Our kids were very upset. They had been raised in a very loving home and this thing just came out of left field. Michael, particularly, was devastated—he was always the family's biggest cheerleader. He still cherishes the days he was a teenager on Dodd Street—those were the happiest days of his life: basketball, John grilling burgers in the backyard and he and Nippy playing in the pool all day. I think they all cherished those days, but there was nothing I could do to bring those days back. If there was something I could have done, I would have. But John and I had some work to do on our marriage. We had been together almost twenty-five years; we had probably changed as individuals during those years. Now we needed to make changes in our relationship to accommodate the people we had become. It was going to take some time. The kids knew that despite what we were going through as man and wife, we loved them. But they made themselves very unhappy with some poor choices. They were old enough to know better; they knew they were loved. But they got into trouble anyway.

"I started hangin' out," recalls Whitney. "In the streets, walkin', hangin', gettin' to know another 'family,' I suppose: the world, the music. I was hangin' around a lotta musicians. Singers, background singers, hangin' out in New York. I didn't wanna be at home. My mother and father were arguing, there was just panic in my household, just unbearable at times. I just wanted peace. As a young girl, I partied. I did my thing. I failed four classes because I didn't want to be there. I was just being rebellious, I suppose. But I was hurting, as my brothers were."

We were all hurting. My sisters knew I was hurting, going through changes. They didn't ask for details but they kept me in prayer. I wasn't much, never have been much, for talking about my problems. People take what they need from you and then put your business all over the street. My friend Bae was the only one I spoke with. But even Bae was not always available; she had just remarried and was cultivating her new marriage. I cried by myself and talked to the Lord.

> *Are you burdened, worn and weary,*
> *Heeding still the tempter's call?*
> *And is your life each day more dreary?*
> *Just tell Jesus, you can tell Him all.*

Don't you need someone to guide you,
To shelter you from the storm and rain?
Let me introduce you to my friend called Jesus.
You can tell Him, you can tell Him all.

Just tell Him, just tell Him
Just tell Him, just tell Him
Trials great, or trials small
He will share them, freely bear them,
So just tell Jesus, tell Him all.
—*"Just Tell Him"*

I didn't always have the answer when I got up off my knees. But I always feel better after I've told the Lord all about it. There's an old saying that goes something to the effect that the man who's had his prayers answered is the man who rises from his prayers refreshed. I have always been refreshed after my prayer. We just weren't made, as human beings, to shoulder some of the burdens we carry. That's when I tell Him all about it.

The kids, in their own way, tried to get John and me together.

"We tried to find answers . . . we tried to put them back together," recalls Whitney. "We tried to mend it and make it right but they had to do it; we couldn't. It was something that they had to deal with, as a man and woman. We didn't know that man and woman; we knew Mommy and Daddy. We didn't know that man and woman that had met many years ago, long before us."

John and I knew that man and woman from long ago. We both still loved each other. Our marriage was weak, but only because we hadn't nurtured it. Right now, we were both convinced that a little bit of space was needful before we could come together again. John took an apartment in one of the old neighborhoods in Newark that he was familiar with. He still picked me up evenings in the city, where I had a regular gig at Sweetwater's and later Mikell's. I made Whitney a permanent member of my background group and called her forward for duets. She was doing so well, watching and learning, that one night I decided she was ready for a bigger challenge. One Friday night, a few hours before the gig at Mikell's, I pretended I was sick. I told her I had laryngitis and couldn't make the gig. She'd have to take my place.

"No, Mommy," she pleaded. "I can't do it."

I convinced her that she could. She knew all the songs, most of the patter, and she had a good pianist, Bette Sussman, behind her.

John picked her up and drove her over to New York. After a shaky start, she fell right in the groove. The audience loved her! Her singing was wonderful, she just needed a little help between the songs. She tended not to talk a lot. I encouraged her just to share things from her own life, what had happened to her that day, little things the audience could relate to. In the studio, I had very little left to teach her. She had watched me record for years, absorbing mike technique and pacing until she was competent enough to make her own sessions.

When she graduated Mount St. Dominic's Academy in 1981, Whitney decided she wanted to go right to work, in the music business. She didn't want to attend college, she wanted to sing. I didn't feel badly about this. Mount St. Dominic's curriculum was so advanced, Whitney's last two years there were equivalent to at least a year of junior college.

If Whitney was going to have a career in the music business, John and I decided that she would be correctly represented. Instead of going the usual route of recording a three- or four-song demo and then taking it around to record companies hoping they'd give you a deal, we signed Whitney with a management agency. Nippy had the whole package— she was beautiful, she could sing and she already had performing and recording experience. The management agency's plan was to create so much interest in Whitney that instead of Whitney begging a record company for a deal, the record company would be begging Whitney for a deal. The agency further enhanced Whitney's résumé by publicizing her participation in important sessions for records and advertising jingles.

Nippy moved out of Dodd Street and got her own apartment in Woodbridge. My little girl was growing up. As her career was getting underway, the whirlwind of sessions, appearances and meetings that the agency scheduled for her sometimes unnerved her. "Mommy, I was so lonely without you," she told me much later. "I used to pick up the phone, dial your number and then hang up and cry. I didn't want to bother you." You should have, I scolded her.

After a year of promoting Nippy to the industry, the agency arranged some showcases open only to record-label executives. Here, record companies bid for the chance to sign Whitney. We chose Paul Marshall, a seasoned music business attorney to negotiate with the most promising bidder. Clive Davis of Arista Records did not offer the largest advance, nor was Arista the company with the biggest muscle. But Clive did impress us with the amount of money he had allocated to spend on promoting and recording Whitney's first album. Whitney signed with Arista.

Now Whitney's career moved into high gear. Clive spent an unprecedented amount of time and money preparing to record Whitney's debut album. He took at least two years gathering the right songs, arrangers, producers and musicians for the project. Whitney's managers were also busy molding her image, working with a designer to create a performing wardrobe for her. I didn't particularly appreciate what they had in mind for my daughter to wear. These dresses were so revealing, cut way up to here and way down to there. I sat there silent with my legs crossed. Whitney is the kind that won't say anything; she just looked real sad.

"My managers thought this was gonna be my image. Ha!" recalled Whitney. "Well, they were wrong. They walked through the dressing room with these clothes that this guy had designed for me. My mother sat through the third outfit, and then she said, 'You can put all that crap right back. I don't know who you got that for, but Whitney's not wearing any of that. She is not shakin' no butt, showin' no skin, nothin' like that. She doesn't have to—she can sing! Anybody can be a strumpet. I'll take care of the clothes; you manage.' And from then on, my mother took care of my clothes."

While Clive Davis readied Whitney's first album for release, Aretha called me to sing on her next two albums. *Jump to It* and *Get It Right* were produced by my friend the hooky player, Luther Vandross. I was very proud of him; both albums took Aretha in a new direction, winning her a whole new group of fans.

I spent many weekends with John at an out-of-state getaway he had bought. In 1983, I had just turned fifty, John was sixty-three. If John's heart attack had set off a midlife crisis a little later than usual in his life, I certainly was more than ripe for one at fifty. I suppose we both found refuge out of town and in each other—Dodd Street was becoming the classic empty nest. Whitney had moved out, Gary had been drafted by the Denver Nuggets and was never home and Michael had married Donna. Only John's mother and I remained in the house.

I became Donna's Lamaze coach as she carried our first grandchild. I went through all the classes with her. But when Donna started getting labor pains, I was nowhere to be found. Donna drove to the hospital and ended up having a C-section. She likes to tell people that when she most desperately needed me as her birth coach I went shopping. I *was* shopping! I was out buying sheets for her new baby's crib. I named our first grandchild, starting a tradition in our family. I get to name or at least partially name all my grandchildren. This tradition is more about practicality than heritage. I don't want any of my grandchildren winding up with some flukey name they have to be shy about their whole lives. I named Donna and Michael's child Gary, for Michael's older brother; the same way my sister Lee named her first child Marie Dionne after her own sister, Marie.

The year or so that Clive Davis took to record Whitney's first album was well worth it. The album produced a string of hits, including "You Give Good Love," "Saving All My Love for You," "How Will I Know?" and "The Greatest Love." It sold over thirteen million copies in the United States and several million more overseas. The album still holds the record as the biggest-selling debut album by a solo artist. Whitney's first album had so many hits on it, the record company had to delay the release of her second album, *Whitney*. Once it was released, it too had several hit singles, including "I Wanna Dance with Somebody (Who Loves Me)," which I sang background on, "So Emotional," "Love Will Save the Day" and "Where Do Broken Hearts Go?" With seven consecutive number one hits, Whitney surpassed even the Beatles' record. I found it annoying that Whitney was criticized by black critics who said her music wasn't black enough. They completely missed the point. The triumph of a Whitney Houston is that as a black performer she was allowed to record a great variety of material—not just R&B.

Suddenly Whitney was an important new artist and a household name. After the music videos, TV appearances and album covers, she couldn't appear in public without causing a mob scene. She couldn't window-shop at any of the New Jersey malls she liked. It took some getting used to. When Nippy's first album was nominated for a Grammy, we flew out to Los Angeles. For the Grammy broadcast, I had picked out a very nice red taffeta dress for her which she hated, but wore. When she won, we were all thrilled. The next night, Clive Davis was throwing a big after-Grammys party at the Beverly Hills Hilton. But Whitney had had enough parties, awards and meetings—she just wanted to be normal. She even tried to get out of going to the party.

"It was this whole 'princess of the industry' kind of thing, and I was feelin' kind of weird about all this admiration," Whitney recalls. "I guess it was also this transformation you go through from being totally unknown to being really known. And all these accolades, and all these new people admiring you, calling your name, and you don't even know 'em. It was just a little much for me.

"I didn't want to go to this party. I was rebellious and I was saying, 'I'm not going, I'm not going. I just wanna be myself; I just wanna be left alone.' And my mother came in that room and she said, 'You are going . . . you're gonna get yourself together . . . you're gonna do your hair . . . you're gonna put your makeup and your dress on and you are going. You're gonna stay for a couple of hours and THEN you can come back and you don't have to be bothered. But you are going to this party. You're going to thank these people.' I wasn't trying to avoid being humble—I was scared. I was frightened. And my mother said, 'Whitney, you must go. They don't know you're scared. If you don't go, they'll take it for something else.' I got to the party and I started hyperventilating. I went to the bathroom and my mother went with me. And I couldn't believe she was so calm. I couldn't breathe. I was goin' like . . . ulp . . . ulp . . . I can't breathe, I can't breathe,

Ma. She's like 'Okay' and she got a washcloth and she put it in cold water, put the washcloth on my head and said, 'Relaxxx, everything's all right, c'mon, get it together, it's all right. Breathe. In your nose. Out your mouth. All right, here we go, you okay? All right, let's go outside.' I don't know why it was so normal for her, but I was freaking!"

In 1987, John finally convinced me to sell our house on Dodd Street. I got a small, sunny condo in Verona, New Jersey, for myself. John continued to keep his place in Newark. Gary had gotten married; a daughter and a son, Aja (I didn't name her) and Jonathan (my choice), followed in 1987 and 1989. That same year, Michael and Donna also had another child. Whitney provided me with no natural grandchild that year, but gave me hundreds to look after when she made me the CEO of the Whitney Houston Foundation for Children. The Foundation cares for children with AIDS and combats illiteracy. As Whitney outgrew her original management, I suggested that she appoint her father CEO of Nippy, Inc., her own management company in Fort Lee, New Jersey. She took my advice. John was finally where he always wanted to be: putting together big deals and guiding the career of a great singer from the Drinkard family. In 1990, John helped Nippy land a deal to become the star in her first motion picture, *The Bodyguard*.

I stayed with Nippy on the set. She was pregnant and wanted me with her. When she went to record a song for the film's sound track, I also accompanied her. From the control room, I watched her sing "I Will Always Love You" and wept. The song summed up everything I felt for my daughter, my sons and John. When she emerged from the studio to listen to a playback, I told her the song was going to be a huge hit. "You think so, Ma?" she asked.

Of course, I was right. The sound track of *The Bodyguard* broke all kinds of sales records because of that song. The film also did great at the box office. There were awards dinners and parties to celebrate the box office and sales records broken by the film and sound track. I prayed that soon John and I would be celebrating together at one of these dinners with our daughter as she gained higher ground in her career. I knew that day would not be far off, just judging by the way John looked lately working at Nippy, Inc., so happy and self-assured. John looked satisfied with himself. He'd put a little management team together, industry people he knew from the old days in New York and a few new faces. He looked like he'd finally escaped the dark cloud he'd been living under since his heart attack. John was dressing better and he even looked like he might have dropped a few pounds.

How many years had I prayed for this to happen—for John to be truly fulfilled in his work. How many years had my sisters prayed for our marriage to be healed. God was so magnificent! He never blesses just one person at a time. In order to bless John, he started with a young girl. He gave Whitney the desires of her heart—a wonderful career doing exactly what she always wanted to do: sing! And through that career, He blessed her father.

I just felt like praising Him, telling Him how much I relied on Him, how impossible my life would be without Him. I went to my kitchen table, sat down with a pen and paper and began to write:

> Without God, I could do nothing
> Without Him, I know I would fail
> Without Him, my life would be rugged
> Just like a ship without a sail.
>
> You see, with God, my life is sublime,
> Without Him, there's no peace of mind,
> And when my enemies beset me
> Who's right there to protect me?
> Without God, I know I would fail.
> —"Without God"

Through all of this He wasn't finished blessing—He had even given me another song. I opened the blinds and let the morning sun fill the living room with light. Just then the doorbell rang. I looked through the window; it was a man from the courthouse, waving a summons in his hand. Great, I thought to myself, a process server. I had to laugh; I had just come off a mountaintop experience, praising the Lord. Now I was back down in the valley. Someone was probably suing Nippy, Inc. As officers of the corporation, they usually went after us too. I opened the door, smiled and signed where he wanted me to. I nodded goodbye and closed the door. I tossed the envelope unopened on an end table. Whatever it was, it wasn't going to ruin my breakfast. I fixed myself some eggs, a biscuit and some bacon. When I finished, I put my dishes in the sink and poured myself another cup of coffee. I picked up the envelope and settled myself on the sofa, ready to read the bad news.

I wasn't being sued as an officer of any corporation. I was being sued by a member of my own family. In fifty years, I had rarely been angry enough to physically hurt anyone. Now, for a moment, I felt capable of murder.

TWELVE

In these days and times we need to know
There's still someplace we can go
In the hour of disappointment and need.
When things get tough and seem a little rough
We often wonder if we will succeed.
Too many times we forget, praise never hurt nobody yet.
Get down on your knees, prayer will change it.
  — "Prayer Will Change It"

I have had three horrible times in my life—three times that broke my spirit. When I was eight years old, the death of my mother made me feel like I was drowning. I felt everything and understood nothing. Ten years later, I was a young woman, watching my father, whom I adored, die in a hospital bed. I nearly lost the will to go on living. Now, the person I loved the most had totally betrayed me.

John was suing me for divorce. After thirty-five years of marriage, he wanted out. Yes, of course, we had been separated for years. But it was a separation we both thought was temporary: the solution for two stressed-out people going through their midlife crises; a therapeutic solution that would eventually get us back together. Some people never even knew we were separated. We saw each other lots of weekends. I stayed at John's place and he stayed at mine. When Whitney toured, we both shared the same hotel room. On particularly good weekends we spent together, it felt like we were dating again; getting to know each other without the stress and worry of children who had all flown from the nest. I knew him better than anyone on earth and he, likewise, was my closest intimate. We had an unspoken understanding: even if we never lived under the same roof again, we would always be husband and wife. We had a public image to maintain. Whitney's fame had put both of us as her parents also in the spotlight. Our lives were no longer private. How could John disgrace me publicly and in front of our children, by asking for a divorce?

I called him up and cursed him out with every low-down curse he had ever taught me. In the middle of his lame explanation, I slammed the phone down. I tore up every photo of John I had in my house. I screamed, I raged, I threw things. And I cried. I felt like a fool who had just been putting a happy face on the last ten years, stupidly hoping that everything was going to work out fine: John and I would get a nice condo and enjoy playing out the role of doting grandparents—together again for the kids and the grandchildren. Now, here I was, approaching retirement age. Where was I going? What kind of new phase of my life was I expected to begin now, at fifty-nine years old?

Unlike me, John had been busy working for months on the next phase of his life. I don't know how I missed it; the hip new clothes, the new, slightly slimmer physique; the air of self-confidence, I should have seen it coming a mile away. John had fallen for a much younger woman.

I was dumbfounded when I heard about John and his new love from someone in the office. I walked around for a few weeks in a stupor, wondering how I could have been so blind. Wondering what kind of huge case of denial I had contracted. Then, once the shock wore off, I went into a rage. I hated him for all the years I'd given him, all the years I'd put in as the main breadwinner. I hated him for all the years I worked while he got to raise the kids: making them breakfast in the morning, kissing them goodbye as they went out the door for school, getting Nippy ready for class pictures, going to the boys' basketball games, being home for them when they came home from school. I thought of all the precious moments he'd had watching them grow up—moments I'd missed because I was breaking my butt, singing on three or four sessions a day or touring with Aretha or the Sweets to pay the bills and put food on the table. It was okay; John and I were a partnership; I didn't mind doing what I had to do. I sang on my sessions and he took care of the kids. We had an understanding; we were different. Sure, I thought to myself, we were different. And now John was going to prove to me how different he was—he was going to get a brand-new, different wife.

The kids wouldn't take my side, which hurt. John had had a forum with them for twenty years, why would they suddenly turn on him now? I had no one to talk to except Bae.

"She felt totally betrayed," says Bae. "She was one mean witch. For about a year, she kicked everybody's backside."

Bae thought my big mistake was not begging John to come home sooner during our separation. But I know how that scenario would have played itself out. John would have always had the upper hand. And he never would have let me forget it. The first fight we would have had, John would have been right up in my face with "Hey, you're the one who asked me to come back." I would have paid the rest of my life.

I wanted to hurt John, hurt him bad, give him back double what I was feeling. But there was no way to do that. He had the love of his children, he had a great job as CEO of his daughter's company and the adoration of a younger woman. I wanted revenge. The Bible says, "Vengeance is mine, saith the Lord." But I was going to get a piece of John for putting me out to pasture. I called my lawyer. If John wanted out, it was going to cost him.

The divorce turned nasty and dragged on for over a year—each of our lawyers firing and returning fire. Month by month, I nursed my bitterness. At night, I raved like a madwoman. I hated everyone: people at our office, people from church, even my grandchildren, who should have been a joy at this stage of my life, got on my nerves. And I still had to suffer the indignity of appearing with John at industry functions, receptions and awards for my daughter. I had to smile and act like nothing was wrong when I knew just what they were thinking: he's thrown her over for a younger woman. I couldn't sleep. I felt a heaviness in my spirit that was blocking my relationship with God. The devil stole my joy and I went right ahead and let him.

Stress will make you sick. In the aftermath of John's big surprise, I found out firsthand, eating myself up alive with bitterness and worry. I had enough stress for six people. In addition to the pain of the divorce, I worried about my kids, who were devastated by the divorce. I worried about their children too. I worried about Nippy. I'd been thrilled for her success, but I was afraid for her too. She had become too big, too soon. This business had a way of building you up only to tear you back down.

I was still living alone in Verona, going out, shopping, driving my car. But I had no energy. The smallest household task, the simplest errand took all of my strength. I complained to Bae, who was spending a few days with me. "You really ought to see a doctor if you're that tired," she said. I kept putting it off, thinking I'd bounce back. But Bae was concerned about me and demanded I call the doctor. When I finally called him and described my exhaustion, he told me to meet him at the hospital immediately. At Orange Memorial Hospital in East Orange, my doctor took my blood pressure and examined me. I was suffering from bleeding ulcers and had already lost nearly half of my body's blood. I was admitted to the hospital without even having an overnight bag. They needed to operate right away. I had been in good health my whole life, visiting the hospital only to deliver my children. I was pretty shook up. Bleeding ulcers had also put my father in the hospital, and along with cancer, had also killed him. In the back of my mind, I didn't expect to survive the surgery.

I barely slept that night. The next morning, just before an attendant wheeled me down to the operating room, I prayed the Lord would spare my life. "I can't leave yet, Lord," I prayed. "I'm not finished with my kids yet." The surgery went well. But they wouldn't release me for ten days, when my blood volume and blood count had returned to normal. I'd probably be dead now if it wasn't for my good friend Bae, who bugged me until I called the doctor.

In the middle of this terrible year, Nippy got married. I should have been thrilled, but I wasn't. Once again, I would have to see John in public and pretend everything was all right. More important, I wasn't happy about Nippy's wedding. I wasn't concerned so much with who Whitney was marrying as that Whitney was marrying at all. She was twenty-nine years old, certainly old enough to take a husband. But I knew once she was married, I would see her less and less. That's just the way it goes. Even the Bible says that the wife shall leave her mother and father and cleave to her husband. But did it have to happen so soon? I had waited almost seven years to have a little girl; now, suddenly, she was all grown up. Where had all the years gone? While I was busy working to put food on the table, pay the mortgage and keep the family car running, almost thirty years had passed. Nippy was a woman. But I wanted to hold on to my little girl just a while longer.

The wedding was the most beautiful I had ever seen. It was held in July 1992, on the grounds of Whitney's estate in New Jersey. I barely recognized the house, it was some kind of beautiful. White tents were set up everywhere, with lavender and white balloons and decorations. The tennis courts were covered with flooring for dancing. No press were allowed. Marvin Winans, pastor and singer, a good friend of Whitney's, officiated. Whitney and Bobby wrote their own vows and were married out by the gazebo. After the ceremony, Whitney had me welcome the guests with a little speech and a toast, then I introduced Bobby's parents, Mr. and Mrs. Brown. John and I were supposed to open the dance floor with the first dance. Of course, we didn't. But Whitney was still happy with me.

"My mother was beautiful," recalls Whitney. "She was a swan."

I was glad to get home that night. I was tired of grinnin' and skinnin' and all the rest of it. I wasn't happy to give my baby away. And the day was made even more tense because of the divorce that John and I were in the middle of.

I continued to dwell in my bitterness. Now I regretted the time I could never recapture with my daughter—when she was still a little girl. Life had flown by, and instead of a comfortable married life, I was now facing the prospect of starting all over again as a single woman. I was tired; so much of my life was about struggle. I felt used up and thrown away.

One day, I woke up and wondered where God was in my life. Had He left me? Had I left Him? Did I know Him? Had I ever known Him? I got down on my knees and poured out my heart to Him. I cried out my troubles and my pain, my bitterness, the anger I had for John. I placed my children and my grandchildren in His hands. I cried and prayed on my knees for an hour. But when I rose up, I didn't leave my burdens with the Lord. I picked them right back up. There I was, just like before, worrying, nursing my hurts just like before.

During this time, a producer over in New York became interested in working with me on a gospel record. I chose to do an entire album of songs by the "father" of gospel music, Thomas Dorsey. He had always been a fascinating person: someone who started as a blues singer, found the Lord, then dedicated his life to gospel. Yet he did not deny the blues he had made early in his career. In fact, his greatest gospel songs were written on blues changes. He was one of my favorite writers; you could tell he felt everything he wrote. Dorsey's most famous song, "Precious Lord," was sung by Mahalia Jackson at Martin Luther King's funeral and by Aretha Franklin at Sam Cooke's grave. But few know that Dorsey himself wrote it in the depth of his own despair—the week following the death of his wife and newborn baby. At a friend's house in Chicago, he poured out his grief in song.

"Right there and then I began to sing," Dorsey remembered, " 'Precious Lord . . . take my hand . . . lead me on . . . let me stand! . . .' and I cast my burden on the Lord."

I cut one of the songs, "When I've Sung My Last Song," as a trio, utilizing my son Gary and Whitney, who met me at the studio on Forty-eighth Street. Gary was going through his own trials and he wondered how I was making a record, staying so focused, despite the pain I was going through in my personal life.

"Ma, I know how you're feeling," Gary said. "I know all the things that you're going through. Yet you come in here and you're focused; you stay focused and you sing like you sing. How do you do it?"

"Gary, that's faith," I explained. "I can't change what has hurt me. I have to pray and I have to let somebody bigger than me take my burden. I have faith that God has taken my burden and will work everything out for my good."

I meant what I said to Gary. But the words sounded hollow as they came out of my mouth. If I really believed what I'd just said, I should have been feeling a whole lot better. The truth was I hadn't left my burden with the Lord. I was still hating John, worrying about my kids and snapping at people; such was the unrest in my soul.

I could only sleep a few hours a night. One particular evening, I was especially distracted: Whitney had miscarried and lost what would have been her first child. I had already been with her in Florida, and done all I could do. But she was still very much on my mind. In the middle of the night, I woke up and was unable to get back to sleep. I went downstairs and turned on the television. There was nothing on. I tried reading, but my attention just kept wandering. I went back upstairs and crawled into bed. I tossed and turned for an hour, trying to get back to sleep. But I just couldn't turn off my brain. I worried about Nippy. I agonized about my failed marriage. Was there something I could have done to save it? Should I have begged John to come home years ago when there was still time? Should I have been more accommodating, taken a vacation with him once in a while like he wanted? Could I have been more attentive? My mind was racing now; I worried about Gary, whose marriage was breaking up, and Michael, who was still devastated by our divorce. What effect would all this have on their children, my grandchildren? Every day the newspapers were full of some horrible thing happening to young children: evil men who preyed on these innocent ones—kidnappings, sexual molestation, murder. I feared for them. I was out of control; frantic something would happen to them that was completely beyond my power to stop. I was scared. I had nowhere to go, no one to call. I was all alone. For the first time in my life, I was scared of my own mind. I felt like I was slipping, becoming unhinged.

I dropped to my knees, beside my bed.

"I know there's a solution, Lord," I confessed. "But I haven't found it yet. I've tried, and I've gone as far as I can go. I need to leave this all in Your hands. I know You'll take care of it. Amen."

My prayer was that simple. But this time I meant it. This time I let go. I left all my worries, my troubles, my fears and regrets with Him. I was crying—but they weren't the lonely, sorrowful tears I had shed for months. These were healing, cleansing tears. I slept like a baby the rest of the night—the first peaceful, dreamless sleep I had in months. When

I got up the next morning, I felt good about myself again—another sensation I hadn't experienced for months.

I hadn't lost my faith; I just hadn't allowed God to help me. God said He would send a "comforter," the Holy Spirit. I can't explain how He, the Spirit, did His work, but He brought a calm to me that night that this world could never give. If you're trusting God, you can experience that calm no matter what this life throws at you. No, I don't mean trusting with just your intellect. I trust with my soul, my heart, and my mind—my whole being is in it. You have to believe God. Take Him at His word. Believe Him when He says He will give you perfect peace if your mind is stayed on Him. Just think about Him; think about all the goodness that He's done for you. Do you think you get up in the morning breathing on your own? No, you can't take anything for granted; it's not yours to take. We only have health, prosperity, any blessing in this life, because we have received it from His hand.

The most important thing is to stay in contact with our heavenly Father—no matter what you feel like, just tell Him. You don't have to wait until you feel "spiritual" to ask Him to help you. Our prayers do not need to be filled with a bunch of thees and thous. Like any earthly father, He enjoys the fellowship of His children. When our fellowship is broken with Him, we lose the opportunity to receive the blessings He has for us, the blessings He delights to bestow upon us.

I knew I had to get motivated about work again. I had no trouble with throwing on some clothes and picking up a session in New York. The studio was a second home to me. I knew exactly what was expected of me; I had been through the drill hundreds of times. But it took a lot to get excited about going into a club and working my show. It wasn't for lack of an audience—I had developed a nice little following at Manhattan clubs like Reno Sweeney's, Mikell's and Sweetwater's. Sweeney's had even bought the club a new piano (Diana Ross's) when I complained in a good-natured way about it once. A club date just took a little doing to call around, get the musicians and singers I wanted, rehearse and make sure everybody knew when and where to show up. It felt like more work than I was used to in a while since my self-imposed exile. I didn't really feel up to it, but I stepped out on faith and called a few clubs.

Sweetwater's was happy to have me back again. My pianist, Bette Sussman, rehearsed the band and made it easy for me just to show up and sing. The audience was wonderful; so appreciative that after a few songs, I felt like singing all night. I practically did—returning twice for an encore. My last song was "Tomorrow" from the show *Annie*. The attention, the applause felt good. I walked off to a standing ovation, shaking hands with some of the audience as I made my way offstage. In the dressing room, I fell in a heap on a sofa, exhausted, but a good kind of tired. After I changed, someone from the club let a few well-wishers in. I don't normally hang around after a show too long—a habit from the days when the kids were small and I wanted to get home to see them. I'm also funny about accepting compliments. I'm my own worst critic; I have my own standard to live up to. If I've sung lousy and I get a compliment, I have to smile and accept it just to be polite. But inside, I feel like a cheat. If I've sung well, I'm happy within myself; I don't need anyone to compliment me. This particular evening, I was enjoying myself and the company of those who came backstage to thank and congratulate me. I knew I'd sung well, sung my heart out, and I ended up staying a little longer. I'm glad I did, or I never would have met "him."

If he gave me his name, I don't remember it. I am bad with names. But I will never forget his face as long as I live. He must have been standing at the end of a small line of people waiting to talk to me; I didn't really notice him until the room had cleared. In fact, I thought everyone had left and I was alone. I started to get up from the sofa, pack up my things and go. He was so quiet and meek that he startled me and I sat back down.

"Hi," I smiled, "did you enjoy the show?"

As soon as I saw him, I knew he wasn't there for an autograph. He was tall, white and good-looking, but he made no effort to conceal his tearstained face. I felt foolish for a second, caught up in my world of well-wishers and fans while this young man was obviously dealing with some heavy trials. I was caught off guard; I didn't know what to say. I just stupidly repeated my question.

"Did you like the show?" I stammered.

He knelt down to address me face to face. His manner and his speech convinced me that he was gay. He took my hand in his and bowed his head for a moment. When he regained his composure, he looked up and began to speak.

"Ms. Houston," he said softly, "I just wanted to let you know that when I came here tonight, I had already decided to kill myself."

At this confession, a sob wracked his body. He dropped his head to avoid my gaze. I was stunned; I didn't know what to say. Here was a stranger sharing his deepest pain with me and except for the quick prayer I could utter for him within, I had nothing to give him.

"Well, you do feel better now, though, don't you?" I managed.

"Yes," he said through tears. "That last song you sáng, 'Tomorrow.' When you sang that song, I changed my mind."

I reached out and hugged him, just from instinct. He never told me what tragic circumstances—the breakup of a relationship, the death of someone close, a grave medical report—had laid him so low. And I'm sure he left the club feeling worlds better than when he first arrived. But if he expected me to let down my hair and relate some tragedy from my life that had also driven me to consider taking my own life, he would have been disappointed. I have no such story. As low as I got separating and then being divorced from John, as hopeless as I felt when my father died, suicide was never an option. I don't understand it, the way I don't understand how people destroy themselves with drugs. As much as I loved John—and I loved him, adored him, had never experienced love until I met John—I never put John before God. There's something wrong, desperately wrong if you're putting man before God. The young man who visited me backstage wasn't even thirty years old and yet he was ready to end his life.

Where was God in his life? I had to pause and think about the heritage I sometimes took for granted. I saw my father pray every day! Not just before a meal but throughout the day and of course in church. He demonstrated, by his life, by the way he carried himself, that he could do nothing without God's direction. He knelt down in prayer and prayed for us, his children, he prayed for our most basic needs. He was not an emotional man, but when he rose up from his knees, he was crying. He knew God had met him; he knew God was real. That's why my religion—I hate to say my "religion"—that's why my faith goes deep. I know He's real! This has been such a fact of life for so many years that sometimes I naively think that everyone is like me. The poor soul who wandered into my dressing room that night came by divine appointment. God could have sent him to any number of more "appropriate" places besides a nightclub. He could have spoken to that young man through something more "spiritual" than a pop song from a Broadway show. And God could have picked a singer to deliver His message who understood suicide, someone a little more sympathetic. But I needed that "wake-up call" just as much as my visitor needed to hear the message of hope in that song. There was a world of people out there without God. And I had grown a little complacent. As my children left the nest and began to make their way in the world, as my role as mother and wife decreased or disappeared entirely, God was letting me know that He wasn't through using me. A new sense of mission was being born in me. In the next few years, He would use me to reach out into the world in unexpected ways. But first, I had important ministry on the home front.

I was concerned for my daughter. The fears I originally had for Whitney when she first decided she wanted to sing seemed to be turning into reality. Everywhere she went there was a mob scene. But after her wedding, and the release of the movie *The Bodyguard,* she began to invite an unhealthy, obsessive attention. Eventually, she would be haunted by stalkers. One individual was even convinced he was related to my daughter.

From the beginning, it would have seemed like we'd done everything we could to insulate Nippy from this freakish behavior. Nippy, Inc., was structured as a family-run organization. Not only was John the CEO but friends and family also had key positions. Both her brothers, Michael and Gary, went on the road with her. Gary sang with Whitney; Michael road-managed and also wrote songs for his sister. Michael's wife, Donna, my daughter-in-law, proved herself to be an extremely capable, even shrewd executive at Nippy. Eventually, she would head the nerve center that coordinated not only Whitney's affairs but also my own activities. On the road, I put my daughter in the best hands I could: those of my longtime friend Bae. Though her official title was "Director of Wardrobe," Bae kept Nippy in the comfort zone, cooking all of Nip's favorite things. I felt good knowing that whether my daughter was performing in Tokyo, London or Johannesburg, when she came back to the hotel that night, she was eating Bae's chicken, biscuits and banana cream pie.

But all the family and friends in the world couldn't protect my daughter from some people who thought she owed them more than a good performance. The tabloids dogged her steps, holding her to a standard that they themselves wouldn't uphold and invading her privacy at every turn. They criticized her marriage, looking for cracks wherever they could. Photographers ambushed her on vacation. Even in the days just following a miscarriage she suffered, the rags continued to beat their drums, printing hurtful lies and rumors about her marriage, her husband and even my sons. After a while, it seemed like it was open season on my daughter's life.

In Kentucky one night, after one of Nippy's concerts, in 1992, all three of my children were put in harm's way. The incident started in the lounge of the hotel where Nippy, Michael and Gary were staying. Michael and Nippy were talking quietly at a table when a few drunks at the bar recognized my daughter. They sidled up and in loud voices demanded an autograph. Nippy refused. The incident should have ended there, but it didn't. A half hour later, these drunks ended up on the same floor as Michael and Whitney. But this time, they didn't want an autograph. They just wanted to verbally abuse Nippy for not obliging them in the lounge. I would prefer that my kids just walk away from a couple of drunks with an ax to grind, not only because I fear for my children but because I hate violence. Throughout their lives, my children have also avoided violence. But once these drunken strangers started spewing obscenities at his sister, Michael, as he had done all through childhood, took up for his little sister. I'm thankful for two things: the police came quickly, before anyone got hurt. But most of all, I'm grateful that Gary was already asleep in his room. Had Gary witnessed either the first scene in the lounge or the name-calling later, the aftermath would have been far worse. Gary is very quiet, peaceful, but if he is wronged, he can go out of control. And I'm usually the only one that can stop him.

A few years earlier, my sisters threw a testimonial dinner for me. I was touched when several childhood friends showed up. But I wasn't moved to tears until my son Michael got up to speak.

"My mother taught us about love," he said. "But out here in the world, there is no love."

I bawled like a baby because I knew he was right.

"Ma, it's gone too far," Whitney says every time the tabloids take a swipe at her or a scene like the one in Kentucky goes down. "All I ever wanted to do was just sing."

When she says that, I flash back on her as a little girl. She is alone in her room holding one of my microphones, pretending it's plugged in and singing her heart out (and out of key) to one of my records, or Dionne's or Aretha's. Except for the years that have passed, she is still the same girl. She hasn't changed. She is warm, friendly, funny and trusting—too trusting. "Aw, Ma," she says, "you don't trust anyone."

"Yes, I do," I fire back. "I trust the Lord."

I could tell her why the tabloids take their cheap shots, but I don't think it would make things any better. This is a business that builds you up just to tear you down. But Whitney incites resentment beyond this. She is rich, young, beautiful, and "worst" of all, she's black. Because she's black, the rags continue to assume that she is physically abused. And because she's black, she continues to "accept" this abuse. In their minds, taking physical abuse is somehow the birthright of every black woman. I have news for these people: Do they think that Whitney's mother and father would stand by while their daughter was abused? Do they think Whitney would? Yet they splash their lies across the pages of their newspapers without even a thought for how John and I feel as parents. I suppose these celebrity hunters also think that because John and I are black, we somehow care less for the welfare of our children.

"Oh, let it go, Ma," Whitney tells me.

I do let it go. Because holding on to that kind of unforgiveness can make you an evil person. Your whole life is caught up in seeking revenge or feeling sorry for yourself. The progress you would have made in life is arrested; so are the growth you would have accomplished in your person and the people you would have been a blessing to.

In the face of persecution, all I can do for my daughter is make sure her life is well grounded, that her faith is strong. This is the only way to survive when your reputation or your integrity is attacked. When someone attempts to assassinate your character, by the time you find out it is usually too late to defend yourself. It's a strange thing; there are few more painful things in life than to be misunderstood. To have your motives for good completely misconstrued, to be portrayed as evil when there was only good in your heart, can make you feel like you are speaking a language no one can understand. Truly, you are a voice crying in the wilderness. Ultimately, it can drive you mad. I've seen lots of "artists" get slighted, cheated, their careers put on the shelf for years—and they became unraveled because that's all they had going in their lives. Their lives were built on this "career" that in the end proved to be nothing more than some empty promises. Don't kid yourself. When you go through trials like this you really have to be walking close to God.

I'm happy that Nippy is. I've been on the road with her, in the same hotel room, and awakened to the sound of her praying out on the balcony. She knows Him for herself. When her daughter, Bobbi Kristina, was born in March 1993 (yes, I gave her the "Kristina") I told Whitney what I've told all my children: Unless you love God and yourself, you can't love anyone. I'm sorry that sounds so strong but it's true. You can lavish material things on your children, you can prepare them for life with the finest education and you can spend all the "quality time" in the world with them, but if you can't love yourself and you don't have the love of God in your life, you'll never be able to love your children with the kind of love that will carry them through life even after you're gone. Don't get me wrong. There are some sweet people who don't know God but are filled with love. They are exceptions to the rule. All my children may still be working at mastering self-love. That's a tough one. But I am thankful they all love God. Now, even if they won't let me fight their battles anymore, even if, like Whitney in grade school, they won't tell me about their little scrapes, because they're afraid of what their crazy mother might do, I'm content. I've left them in good hands. Horatio Spafford wrote the words to the following hymn after his four daughters drowned in an accident at sea in 1873. If Spafford could trust his daughters in death with the Lord, I can trust my children with Him in life.

> *When peace like a river attendeth my way,*
> *When sorrows like sea billows roll,*
> *Whatever my lot, thou hast taught me to say,*
> *It is well, it is well, with my soul.*
> —*"It Is Well with My Soul"*

My father's old expression came to mind: "If you make your bed hard, lie in it until it gets soft." Though I had a lot to be thankful for—a career, my healthy children and grandchildren and my daughter's success—my own bed was "hard." Unlike my sisters, who had the comfort and security of their husbands well beyond middle age, I was alone. My kids were all out of the house. Even the house was gone! John had convinced me to sell it. I still ruminated over the divorce . . . whose fault was it . . . could I have done something more?

I think that house was a symbol for where we started to go wrong. I never wanted to sell it. I had so many happy times with the kids in that house; there was the pool, the barbecue, in the basement a rec room with a pool table and always a crowd of neighborhood kids. When the kids started to leave the house, first Gary in 1975 for college in Chicago, Michael four years later to Kansas, then Nippy, who moved out when she was eighteen, I couldn't bring myself to sell the house. Sadly, with our separation and the kids moving on, it was the only place that still seemed to say we were a family. Maybe John felt the same way but reacted differently. In his mind, the kids were moving on, and rather than let himself slip into getting sad over an empty nest, he thought we should move on too. Dump the house. Come to think of it, John had reason to be just as attached, even more attached to that house than me. For years, his primary job was in that house cooking, cleaning and minding the kids.

But John was really too bright to have turned around at fifty-six years old (the year he had his heart attack), taken inventory and been satisfied as just "Mr. Mom." He was probably caught in between two worlds. His "soft" side said it was okay to enjoy staying home, raising those kids and in the spirit of his own mother—an educator in the New York school system—teaching them, talking to them, giving them a love of words and books and history. But the more "macho" side of his personality condemned him for not "accomplishing" enough in his life. Of course, like lots of brilliant people, John was also too hard on himself. He had a blind spot to his great accomplishment in launching Whitney's career, mine and Dionne's. Had he forgotten how at the height of Dionne's fame, Burt Bacharach, lying on Dionne's floor, looked up at John and mused, "Without you, none of this would have happened."

John was smart, but he outsmarted himself when he left me. That was his big mistake. Because when you have a mind like John's, you need somebody to talk to; somebody to understand you. As John himself has said, there are plenty of "handkerchief heads" out there—submissive women who don't talk, don't question, don't think. Now, I'm not the most brilliant person in the world, but I'll ask questions . . . I'll try to understand you . . . and I'll love you. I'm there. I'll try to help you get yourself together if something's wrong. And above all, I'll tell you the truth. I'm a stickler for the truth, like my dad. "If you lie, you'll steal," he used to stay. My father taught me that without truth between people, there can be no trust. I've carried his passion for the truth one step further: I never lie to myself. "To thine own self be true." To live my life by that standard, I have to admit to myself that the divorce wasn't entirely John's fault. I guess I could have given in and said, "John, don't go," way before he first walked out. Had I done that we might still be together. I don't know; maybe that's what I should have done. But I don't think about it often like that. I'm just not the kind of person to beg for anything. After I've done everything I can do and you know I love you and you know what the situation is—I'm not dealing with it anymore.

But I was lonely. I missed the kind of life John and I had, the places we used to go, the companionship. I had a friend who filled that need, someone I went to the movies with, took little vacations with, but it wasn't the same. I guess I had to lie in that hard bed until my change came along. Waiting's never been my forte. I'll pray for things, I'll wait on the Lord, but I'll also act.

I felt the passage of years most acutely in 1993. In March, my daughter had her first child, Bobbi Kristina, a cause for celebration. But the month before, I said goodbye to my brother Nicky. After a long illness, he died three months short of his sixty-fourth birthday. Nicky was always with me, my accompanist at church, mostly playing organ. I'd work songs out with him, sing him the melody, which he'd transfer to the keyboard. He hadn't started playing organ until much later in his life when we were already at New Hope for many years and he took some lessons from a friend, Professor Banks. Nicky had a wife and family, but after he schooled himself on organ, it became his passion. For the last ten or fifteen years of his life, all he wanted to do was play for me in church. He was there every Sunday for me and at every midweek rehearsal. So quiet and mild, looking over his eyeglasses that were halfway down his nose, like the absentminded professor. I kind of took him for granted. I figured Nicky would always be there for me. When I lost him, it devastated me for many months and still does. Nicky played such a unique role in the Drinkard Singers. It wasn't until Nicky, as a boy, picked up piano that we were really able to start singing gospel. Now, with him gone, the Drinkard Singers would never be the same again. Without Nicky, we were back where we had started; singing a cappella, that is, if anyone even wanted to. In the last few years, we stopped getting together at Lee's to sing on holidays. We were all getting older, and cooking and preparing for a houseful of company was too great a strain on all of us. I'm not one for looking back. Old snapshots bring the pain of lost family members too close—my mother, my father, Nicky, and Hank, who went peacefully in his sleep while living out his last years in an upstairs bedroom at Annie's house. But I do have a few precious moments of Nicky and me preserved on film, rehearsing in church, in a documentary that was made in the late 1980s by director Dave Davidson and Harriet Parker.

My hard bed began to get soft, my change began to come, in 1994. That was the year Denzel Washington asked Whitney to consider taking the female lead in *The Preacher's Wife,* a remake of the old film *The Bishop's Wife,* directed by Penny Marshall.

"When I read the script," says Whitney, "I said, 'My mother is Mrs. Havergal. She's gotta be Mrs. Havergal.'"

I'd acted before: first with James Earl Jones in *The Vernon Grounds Story,* a made-for-television film about the civil rights leader's life, and before that, off-Broadway in *Taking My Turn.* I had no aspirations to be an actor, but this would be the first time I would actually get to play in a few scenes with Nippy. The film portrayed Whitney as the pastor's wife and choir director, and my bit part was Mrs. Havergal, a member of her choir.

"It was fun for me to play her, the choir director," says Whitney, "and for her to kinda be me. She and I had a big laugh over that!"

After a month, my filming was done. I enjoyed being on the set with Nippy and giving input and singing on the several gospel selections in the film. A few months later we were still a twosome, but this time it was my turn to be the headliner. The Rhythm and Blues Foundation had named me and ten others to receive their Pioneer Award at their sixth annual presentation in Los Angeles on March 2, 1995. Whitney would be inducting me.

I had a lot of respect for the Rhythm and Blues Foundation. It was an organization that seemed to have a heart. It was founded by the songwriter Doc Pomus, among others. Doc, along with Mort Schuman, wrote a ton of classic songs for Big Joe Turner, Ray Charles, Elvis and the Drifters. Songs like "Save the Last Dance for Me" and "I Count the Tears" for the Drifters; Elvis' "Viva Las Vegas" and "His Latest Flame"; and Ray Charles's "Lonely Avenue." We sang on lots of Pomus/Schuman songs, mostly Drifters songs like "Sweets for My Sweet." Ailing himself and wheelchair-bound for much of his life, Doc and some other friends had become frustrated begging for money to defray the high cost of medical care for some legendary but broke and forgotten artists. They set up the Foundation to fund needs like this on an ongoing basis. Housed in the Smithsonian Institution in Washington, D.C., the Foundation awards grants of financial assistance to needy artists, and preserves and promotes rhythm and blues music and artists of the 1940s, 1950s and 1960s. Each year, the Pioneer Awards Program recognizes "legendary artists whose lifelong contributions have been instrumental in the development of rhythm and blues music." Doc, the Foundation's most colorful founder, died a few years ago. But not before this big, burly, cigar-chomping Attila the Songwriter put fire to the feet of fat cat record companies who needed to do the right thing by some down-and-out artists. I was proud to be associated with the Foundation; humbled to be one of eleven recipients of the Pioneer Award. But the awards also stirred up a whirlpool of conflicting emotions that even I did not fully understand.

Typically, I ran from music business awards dinners, especially if they involved my getting any kind of honor. They made me uncomfortable. I usually went about covering my uneasiness with my usual tough-chick pose: Hey, it's only a business . . . I was only doing my job . . . what do I need somebody else blowing smoke up my . . . You get the picture. I told myself that half the people that gave you these awards didn't understand what you really did in the studio anyway—so the award was meaningless. This time, however, none of my excuses worked. The Rhythm and Blues Foundation was made up of people just like me—my peers. The musicians, producers and songwriters on the board that selected me as an honoree knew very well what I did in the studio. This award meant something; it meant a lot, actually. Underneath my hard, I-don't-care-exterior, I was really afraid. What did I have to be afraid of? I was certainly secure in my own talent and abilities. I had directed choirs at church since I was sixteen. I had sung on hundreds of sessions, recorded several albums with the Sweet Inspirations and several more as a solo artist. When anyone needed a session singer to back up a vocalist or a nice pop voice for a jingle, I was usually their first call. So what was I afraid of? I was afraid of being praised. It seemed to be a totally irrational phobia. I'd received awards before, had testimonial dinners in my honor; I should have been used to it. But there was still something about receiving credit and praise that scared me. And if I didn't get to the bottom of my crazy fears at this banquet, I never would.

I flew out to the awards ceremony with my daughter-in-law, Donna. Just before heading to the banquet, Whitney shared a little of what she planned to say while inducting me. When we arrived, my daughter-in-law Donna, Bae and I were escorted to our own special table along with Whitney, her husband, Bobby Brown, their daughter, Bobbi Kristina, Whitney's personal assistant, Laurie Badami, and one of Whitney's close friends, the singer Pebbles. One look around the banquet room of the historic Hollywood Palladium made me feel like I was in some kind of music business hall of fame. We were seated at one table, and next to us were the other current honorees: Charlie and Inez Foxx, the saxophonist Illinois Jacquet, the Marvelettes, the Moonglows, Lloyd Price, Arthur Prysock, Mabel Scott, Booker T. & the MGs, Junior Walker, Justine "Baby" Washington and Antoine "Fats" Domino, who would be receiving the Ray Charles Lifetime Achievement Award. Was it just my imagination, or did everyone look a whole lot more relaxed than me?

The faces around the table, and board members and musicians throughout the room, took me through several decades of professional life. At our table I was happy to see another current honoree whom I had known for years—Darlene Love, lead singer of the Blossoms. Chatting with Darlene helped to soothe my nerves. She and her group had been the Sweet Inspirations' only serious competitors. They sang background on lots of records produced by Phil Spector on the West Coast. She made me think of happy times I had on the road with her, backing up Dionne in the 1970s. Early in her career, she sang background on records by Sam Cooke, then moved on to sweeten records by the Ronettes, the Righteous Brothers and the Crystals. Darlene was a lot like me—a background singer who was usually called in to sweeten a track, come up with a background part that fit the groove. Many times we just clamped on a set of headphones and sang our part to an instrumental track, no lead vocal—we didn't even know who the artist was!

Maybe, I thought, that was one of the reasons I shied away from taking any kind of credit: We were just workmen, day laborers on an assembly line that made records. Of course, there were some great records we sang on. But you learned not to get too attached to the records themselves. Your name, after all, wasn't on the record. That didn't mean you did any less of a good job. On the contrary, you sang your butt off! A producer, an arranger, other musicians and an artist were all depending on you to do just that. Punch your part in right and in as few takes as possible.

Still, even if you had created a hip, rhythmic melodic background part that fit right in the record's pocket, a part so appealing that the arranger on the date picked up your lick in the strings or the horns, or was so important it became the reason people eventually bought the record—the hook—still, your name never went on the record. You never got an extra dime for your contribution. We didn't expect any further compensation. There was only the satisfaction that you had taken care of business that day. Your part was good, it added something to the song and you nailed it on the first take. That was enough, or at least it was supposed to be enough. Even my father taught us, you did the best job you could do without the expectation of praise. You had your own high standard to maintain; you didn't compare yourself to others. I didn't need the praise of men, or so I thought.

Darlene looked a lot more comfortable in her own skin. She bloomed when any attention was directed her way, welcoming those who came by to congratulate her with open arms and kisses. I froze if I saw someone approaching me from across the room, dreading the uncomfortable hugs and show biz kisses I'd have to endure. Darlene had moved easily into supporting roles in movies, while continuing to star on Broadway and do her one-woman shows. She seemed to have a love affair going on with the public; Darlene seemed to thrive on praise and acclaim, whereas I shrank from it, though I had some of the same opportunities. Unlike me, however, when the right people pitched a solo career at her, Darlene stepped up to the plate and took a full swing. I didn't.

Perhaps that was another reason for the mixed-up feelings I had about this evening and the honor I was to receive. I could've had a shot at a solo turn, but I never took it. Yes, I had to admit to a few passing regrets on that account. I went through all the motions for a career, but my heart wasn't really in it. I had already paid the dues I was supposed to pay, singing background for almost seven years, from 1961 to 1968. The release of the Sweet Inspirations' first record in 1967 should have been my launching pad for a solo career. In a way, it was. But the constant touring with Aretha, Elvis and now the Sweets put too much of a burden on my family. My leaving the Sweets and the subsequent deal with Charles Koppelman for a solo album in 1970 was another chance to shine. But my kids needed me, especially Whitney. I had longed for a little girl my whole life and finally I'd gotten one. She was seven years old then, and I had to choose: solo career or children. I never hesitated: I chose my kids and I've never had any regrets about that. I looked up at Whitney now, chattering away with Donna. Nippy was so self-assured, well adjusted, and already a good mother herself; I knew I had made the right choice. But every now and then—like tonight, surrounded by my contemporaries—I thought about how things might have been different had I taken another road.

From my table I also spotted my old friend Billy Vera. Billy was on the Foundation's Board of Trustees but tonight was the all-star band's musical director. Billy, the shrimp, finally looked all grown up with a receding hairline, dressed to the nines in a nice tux. It had been so many years since I'd last seen him. It was 1968, and I was watching him and Judy from the wings of the Apollo sing "Storybook Children." I reflected for a moment what Judy and Billy, the white guy and the black girl, meant to us back then—the dream we all had that people were coming together, a dream that, sadly, never came true.

Another Billy I spotted playing on the bandstand took me back to my singing days with the Drinkards. Organist Billy Preston and I were on the same bill at lots of big gospel extravaganzas, where Joe Bostic hyped him (in 1961) as a "sixteen-year-old sensation." Of course, Billy has had plenty of ups and downs in his career since then. He played with the Beatles and had solo hits under his own name. Those were some of the high points. Since then, I'd heard he'd had darker times and trouble: drugs and jail. Billy never had a normal childhood. He was out touring on the gospel circuit even earlier than sixteen. He was a preteen on the road playing for people like Mahalia, and a child playing a young W. C. Handy in *St. Louis Blues*. I could have easily been on the same road—"a seven-year-old sensation"—if the Coleman Brothers of Newark could have had their way with me. This black family of entertainers and entrepreneurs offered my father the chance to develop my career singing whatever I wanted—gospel or pop. But my father categorically rejected their offers. No child of his would go into show business. When I was almost nineteen years old, he gathered us around his death-bed and restated his plan for our lives: that we would never stop singing as the Drinkards. Each of us knew implicitly that he also meant that we would never sing secular music. Nine years after he died, I disobeyed him. I sang on my first pop session. Had he been alive, chances are I never would have done it. Had he found out about it, he was the kind of man, the kind of father that never would have stopped loving me. I was his baby. But he still never would have agreed with the road I took.

I missed my father terribly back then—still do—but I had choices to make for the welfare of my children and our survival as a family. Early on, I was convinced in my heart that I could sing almost any kind of song and not compromise my faith. The boundary lines between sacred and secular were drawn by men. I knew Who had taken up residence in my heart when I was fourteen years old and no lyric or drumbeat could ever change His address. My father's world was a much different world. Show business in Newark's Third Ward had a whole different connotation then: a world of racy burlesque at Miner's, cheap hustlers hanging out backstage at the Kinney Club and blues-singing women strung out on dope.

But even as I took a road my father never would have agreed with, I honored him. Subconsciously, I found a way to keep his spirit alive in my life: I fathered myself, if you will. I took care of Cissy, made sure that though she had to be in the world to make a living, she would not, in the process, become part of the world. Ironically, *I* now drew the boundary lines dividing the sacred from the profane. I never socialized after a recording session; certainly, I never went drinking with the boys, the other musicians, at their favorite hangout, Jim & Andy's bar. *Sing and split*—that was my motto. I liked these people I worked with week to week, cared about them and even loved some of them. But there was a fixed distance between us. I maintained that distance so that I would never become something other than what I was: mother of three children, wife of John, choir director at New Hope Baptist Church, Christian woman and Nitch Drinkard's daughter. If I became too comfortable in that studio, if I took too much ownership in what we created there, my perception, my lifestyle would slowly change and I would upset the delicate balance of who I really was. There was always the danger that in becoming too closely associated with the work I did, I would one day find myself not only in the world, but of it. As Nitch Drinkard's daughter, and even as my own person, I don't know how comfortably I could have crossed that line, let alone lived in that world.

My father was a good daddy. He took me as far as he could, protected me, as a child, from a world he feared might steal my soul. He was right to do that, and I will be eternally grateful to him for that. But what Daddy didn't know, couldn't have known, was that one day, when I came of age, the gospel would need to be taken into the highways and byways, the nightclubs and concert halls of the world. How could Daddy have foreseen the love of God reaching out through a darkened nightclub to a young man about to commit suicide? How could my father have envisioned his daughter changing that young man's mind while singing a song from the music halls of our day? How could my father know that I would inherit his strength to fend for myself in that world and come to rely on the same God he did.

So there was my answer. It was no longer such a mystery to me why receiving praise for my work made me so uncomfortable. I kept what I did in the studio at a safe distance by treating it, all these years, as just a job. Something to put food on the table and clothes on our backs. But not something to build any kind of identity on, not something to get grand about. It was my way, the only way I knew, both to survive in the new world of recording studios and to preserve the old world of my father.

As I sipped my after-dinner coffee, reflected on these things, and looked into the grateful faces of the other honorees, I learned something else: how much we all do need praise and encouragement for our efforts. For years, I'd fooled myself into believing I didn't need it. But I did. For years, I believed that it was somehow "unspiritual" to receive the praise of others. Scriptures like "Only God is good . . . Beware of the scribes who wear long robes and love the praise of men" preyed on my mind. While I ignored passages that preached the value of encouraging each other, like "Pleasant words are as an honeycomb, sweet to the soul, and health to the bones," or "A word fitly spoken is like apples of gold in pictures of silver." Even Nitch Drinkard was blessed by the praise of men; what else was he receiving as he sang his heart out, down in the Singer foundry locker room? Of course, we only learned about his lunchtime concerts on the job many years after he was gone. In my mind, I had confused seeking the praise of men as the be-all and end-all of my efforts—being a glory hound—with receiving a well-deserved pat on the back. I told myself I didn't need compliments, accolades and kudos. In a way, I put myself above needing encouragement. From my lofty perch, I missed out on a whole lot of blessings, sincere compliments and "pleasant words" that could have been "healing to the bones . . . sweet to the soul."

So much of my self-worth was also tied up in losing my mother so young. At eight years old, your mommy is like some kind of superwoman, a caregiver you are so dependent on, she seems to be larger than life. You are too young to see her flaws, her weaknesses. In later years, it was this all-powerful mommy that became my standard of motherhood and womanhood—a standard against which I judged myself harshly, one I was unable to reach.

As I listened to the acceptance speeches of other honorees, looking so comfortable acknowledging their past triumphs, I realized I hadn't given myself half as much credit for what I'd achieved, or nearly enough love.

Something began to melt inside me, and I suspect a lot of others, judging by how many were dabbing their eyes with handkerchiefs, when current honoree Arthur Prysock got up. Arthur brought me all the way back home to Newark and my childhood in the 1940s. When I was still a kid, Arthur, a velvety balladeer with matinee idol looks, was a regular in the Third Ward's notorious Kinney Club. He sang for several years with Buddy Johnson, whose records Jolly Dean, Evelyn "Black Beauty" Nelson and I used to dance to at the Green Lantern. Tonight, I really was in the company of giants. My normal skeptical self had left town hours ago. Tonight really meant something. I was surrounded by my peers: musicians, arrangers, unsung creatives who kept giving one hundred percent even when the spotlight wasn't shining—even if it never shined—on them. I felt a great sense of fellowship and solidarity with the men and women in that room. This was finally our night.

As Arthur Prysock reached the stage and stepped into the spotlight, the room almost gasped as one. People who had not seen him in forty years strained to reconcile the man who ambled onstage with the image of a forty-year-old album cover etched in their memory. The once vibrant, handsome, matinee idol looks of fifty years ago were gone. Arthur was old and thin, unsteady and perhaps ailing, as he approached the microphone. His voice was thinner, yet traces of his signature velvet tones were still there, reassuring us. He expressed his gratitude for finally being recognized publicly by his peers, after a lifetime of making records, and taking all the hard knocks the business had to offer him. He spoke and sang with such eloquence, it brought tears to the faces of scores of guests. I too was crying.

Just then, someone from the Foundation was tapping me on the shoulder. It was my turn to be inducted. As I got up from our table and followed him backstage, I prayed that I could maintain my composure and not lose it onstage. It had already been an emotional evening for me; I figured it could only get more so. A presenter would first introduce Whitney. I was instructed to wait in the wings until Whitney introduced me and called me onstage. I stood in the wings and got butterflies when they announced my name. I worried about the little speech I had prepared; was it too short, too long? How did I look? My heart was racing; blood pounding in my ears, I could barely hear the presenter reading a list of artists I'd worked with and records I'd sung on. Then they introduced Whitney. The sound of her voice restored some of my calm. She spoke about me for a moment, words that were familiar to me, words she had previewed with me. Even coming through the house sound system, the sound of her voice was familiar and relaxed me. She spoke about what I'd taught her as a singer, how I told her to always feel what she sang. That you didn't have to be the greatest singer in the world, but if you sang from your heart, then people were bound to give you back a hundred percent. She spoke a few additional moments, more familiar words I remembered her sharing with me earlier, then got a laugh for something she said. What she said I didn't hear; I was busy fussing with my dress, nervous, because I knew that in a few seconds she'd be calling me onstage.

Then, suddenly, without any kind of warning, Whitney veered from the "script" and started to ad-lib. I was in shock! I wanted to kill her! That delightful, talkative, fresh-faced, hammy kid of mine that everyone liked was taking liberties on my evening! Now she was starting to sing something she'd learned in my choir at least a hundred years ago. When I realized what she had started singing, I thought I might really need help to get out onstage.

". . . and something else my mother taught me, most importantly," Whitney ad-libbed, and broke into song:

> *I sing because I'm happy,*
> *I sing because Jesus set me free,*
> *Ohhh . . . Ohhhh . . . Ohhh*
> *His eye is on the sparrow,*
> *And I know He watches over me.*

She was singing "His Eye Is on the Sparrow." Somehow, in all the years we'd sung that hymn in church, I had never gotten around to telling Whitney that this was one of my mother's favorite songs. Nippy just liked it. The shock of hearing it now, so unexpected, unnerved me. I always associated it with my mother. But now that song spoke to me.

Are not two sparrows sold for a farthing? and one of them shall not fall on the ground without your Father. But the very hairs of your head are all numbered. Fear ye not therefore, ye are of more value than many sparrows.

—Matthew 10:29–31

In this passage of scripture that inspired the hymn writer, the Lord is sending out His disciples. In describing the hard road that lies before them, He tells them that they will encounter persecution because they represent Him. But He tells them not to worry, not to be anxious. He has them in His care. To illustrate their value to Him, He directs the disciples' attention to the sparrows. Though the sparrows seem to be of little value to man—two of them are sold for a penny—not one of them will die unless God has decreed it. Cheap but precious.

It made me think of us Drinkards. What were we, after all, but a handful of sparrows, flying up from Georgia in 1923? Poor, like thousands of others of us, then; running North for higher ground. Higher ground that turned out to be a hill in Newark's Third Ward. And there was tribulation just like He said there would be. Poverty and sickness and death. But He said, Don't be anxious. Trust me . . . don't go by appearances. I'll take care of you. And He did.

I heard Nippy's voice call me, shaking me out of my reverie in the wings. I was no longer anxious about my speech. As a matter of fact, I purposely left it backstage. I'm a singer, and I'll sing all night if I'm in the mood or the Spirit falls. But I am a woman of few words. I knew exactly what I had to say—no more, no less.

". . . and I am so proud," Whitney said, "to present her with the Rhythm and Blues Foundation Pioneer Award. It's about time!"

I felt myself step out of the wings and walk toward Nippy. Billy Vera caught my eye, gave me a big smile and struck up the band. Whitney and I fell into each other's arms and began to cry. I held her for a long moment, getting myself together. Then I stepped up to the microphone.

"To the Rhythm and Blues Foundation," I said, "and to the Board of Trustees . . . and to the Almighty God Who is the head of my life

. . . and has been the head of my life for a long, long time, thank you. Thank you so much.

As I looked past Whitney and saw my granddaughter sitting proudly with her daddy, I thought of what she and her generation might experience in their lives. She was seeing me at the height of my career—receiving the Pioneer Award—but there were many things in my life that she knew nothing about. Neither of us would have been here if it hadn't been for my pioneering ancestors: Nitch and Delia Drinkard, John and Susie Bell Drinkard, John Sr. and Victoria Hansom Drinkard. These days, people could care less about the values that my parents, my grandparents and my great-grandparents lived by. I wondered whether Drinkard values would be passed on to Bobbi Kristina and the rest of my grandchildren.

CODA

Receiving a prestigious award, having my daughter at my side, and accepting the applause and admiration of my peers makes for a nice ending. But if you have read this far, you probably have learned that these things have not been the sum total of my life. Yet there was still within my heart a desire left unfulfilled, a wish I thought so far-fetched, I could barely bring myself even to pray about it.

It had been twenty-five years since I had released a solo album. I stayed away from such a project for several reasons. First, as I already mentioned, my last solo album had left a bad taste in my mouth. There were so many good songs on that album that deserved to see the light of day and never did. The dissolving of the Commonwealth United label, then the album's adoption by another company that could have cared less for my efforts killed the record. I had no wish to relive this experience with another label that was not behind me 100 percent. Second, the record of Thomas Dorsey gospel tunes I made in the 1980s had also broken my heart. It was still lying unreleased on the shelf of some record company somewhere. Finally, I was certain that no record company in the 1990s would give me the artistic freedom I desired: I didn't want to make another pop album—I wanted to record a gospel album.

A gospel album. Where did I get the nerve to think some label would give me the freedom to cut a gospel album? Gospel had changed so drastically in the last twenty years. New artists like Kirk Franklin were pulling in the young people, rockin' the house with that heavy bass. I had nothing against it, but it wasn't my kind of gospel. I was trying to get those young mothers and adults to listen up to the message of a good old Thomas Dorsey or Alex Bradford tune. I couldn't see changing my stripes, recording some kind of "contemporary" gospel to please the record company's idea of what was commercial. Nor could I see a record label giving me carte blanche to record whatever I wanted, whether it sold "units" or not.

That's why I was leery when Joel Moss, a record producer from L.A., telephoned. I wondered what "bag" I would have to fit in to make the record attractive enough for a label to buy it and promote it. When Joel told me I could make the record exactly as I saw fit, I started to listen more closely.

We had never met, but Joel had seen me and my choir at New Hope a few years ago. After hearing us, he vowed one day to cut an album with me. Joel had grown up in Detroit, a Jewish kid who was so crazy about gospel, he'd sneak into black churches to hear it. After a patch-work music career, Joel was now producing records in California. He had been nurturing his little dream to do an album with me for a few years when He found himself pitching the project one day to Isaac Tigrett, the owner of the House of Blues clubs. Tigrett had just launched a House of Blues record label, with mostly rootsy artists. But Isaac wasn't familiar with my work. Joel asked Isaac to think for a second and name five of his favorite records from the 1960s. After pondering for a moment, Isaac ticked off his list of all-time favorites, and I had sung on four out of five of them. (They were songs by Wilson Pickett, Solomon Burke, Dusty Springfield and Aretha.) That clinched it for Isaac—he gave Joel the green light to record a gospel album with me, any style I wanted.

Joel and I discussed musicians and repertoire. We were both on the same page and even wrote a song together. In the closing months of 1995, the two of us met at the Hit Factory on West Fifty-fourth Street to start recording. As you can imagine, our musicians were all "first call"—the best. There was drummer Steve Jordan, a real character, with short dreads and a knockout session résumé. Will Lee (bass) and Jimmy Vivino (guitar) were also both veteran session guys. Will played with Paul Shaffer's David Letterman band and Jimmy was with the Max Weinberg Seven (from *Late Night with Conan O'Brien*). Longtime session organist Leon Pendarvis, a member of the *Saturday Night Live* television band, was a great compliment to the voices as was my pianist, Ouida Harding.

During the sessions, I tried to keep my ears open to suggestions. Some I didn't completely understand, but I went ahead anyway. It was Jimmy Vivino's idea to cut Willie Johnson's "God, Don't Ever Change." I got my son Gary to sing the sparse harmony with me. It was so retro it sounded like we were singing down in the delta in 1910. But in the final mix, I came to like it for its "atmosphere." Joel encouraged me to take Marvin Gaye's "How Sweet It Is," an old Motown tune, and interpret it as gospel. Initially, I couldn't see it, but when I started to rehearse, I wondered why nobody else had ever discovered its gospel possibilities. Once I added the voices, I could feel the anointing. In addition to these songs, I included a Thomas Dorsey favorite "The Lord Will Make a Way Somehow," and several that I wrote, including "I'm Somebody" and "Just Tell Him." I'd always wanted to tackle Alex Bradford's "Too Close to Heaven." I could remember standing in the wings at the Apollo thirty years earlier when we were on the same show, watching Alex sing it. But now the words spoke to me so clear it might as well have been my personal testimony:

> *I'm too close to my journey's end.*
> *I'm too close to turn back into a world of sin.*
> *I wouldn't take nothin' for my journey right now.*
> *Lord, I just got to make it to heaven somehow.*

> *'Cause I'm too close—I'm about to reach my goal.*
> *I'm too close to finally saving my soul.*
> *I'm too close to heaven.*
> *I'm too close. No, I can't turn around.*

I'm too close. I can almost see my God's face.
I'm too close. I'll tell the world how I love this race.
You see, I'm so close, how do I know?
'Cause He's holding my hand,
I know I'm gonna make it to that promised land.
I'm too close.
I want to see my mother and father again.
I'm too close to miss shaking hands with all of my friends.
I'm too close to heaven.
I'm too close to heaven.
I'm too close to heaven.
I'm too close to heaven.
I'm too close and I can't turn around.

It was exhilarating after almost twenty-five years once again to be releasing an album. But not just any album. *Face to Face* was the gospel album I've always wanted to record—an opportunity I never thought I would get. I wouldn't have changed one note—I was so happy with it. The record company released it in March 1996. For a few months after its release, it was even fun playing "meet the press"—sitting down with writers from newspapers and magazines. I made the rounds of radio and television interviews and did some concerts. Then, several months later, early in the new year—and early in the morning—Joel Moss called from California. He woke me up to tell me that *Face to Face* had been nominated for a Grammy Award in the Traditional Soul Gospel category. I was stunned. I had been nominated for a Grammy once before. In 1968, the Sweet Inspirations' first album had been nominated, but we lost to the Temptations.

This time I also found myself up against some heavy competition. Stalwarts like Albertina Walker, Dorothy Norwood, Shirley Caesar and the Edwin Hawkins Singers—people who had released gospel albums their whole lives. But several weeks later at the live telecast from New York's Madison Square Garden, *Face to Face* won a Grammy for Best Album in the Traditional Soul Gospel category. As my daughter-in-law Donna and I left the Garden that night through a talent entrance, fans were screaming my name in the cold, misty rain.

I am still incredibly grateful that I was able even to record *Face to Face*. I don't think enough artists or record companies cater to adults who listen to this type of gospel music—the kind of gospel I cut my teeth on. It gives me hope that a whole group of listeners will not go unreached since the Grammy committee has created a category to represent this traditional gospel.

The Grammy Award was another wonderful milestone for me. But it didn't change my life. I still miss John. We were happy, very happy for many years. I love John to this day and I guess I'll love him until I die—as he will me. It hurts me when I see him alone, and I'm usually alone, too. We live only a few miles apart, both of us on the Jersey side of the Hudson, watching the sun go down everyday on the prettiest skyline in the world: Manhattan. I miss him always teasing me about something, though he still gets to mess with me over the phone. I call him at least three times a week to check up on him—he's not in the greatest health. He always ends our calls the same way, with "I love you," and I'll say, "I love you, too."

The truth is, I'm sorry we ever separated. And I'm sorry how much it upset our kids. I still don't completely understand what happened to us—I guess he went through his midlife crisis and I went through mine. Could we live together again? I don't know. John is a very headstrong, crazy person and I'm about the only one who can do anything with his butt. But I've also gotten used to being alone. I don't mind staying by myself—I like me.

From time to time we see each other at public events, and we banter like old times. "You'll always be my wife," he growls, unable to escape our long history. Of course, this change of heart didn't come overnight. I was very bitter with John for a long time. But I could only carry that bitterness for just so long before it poisoned me, too. There came a reckoning one day when I had to do a little self-examination. If I really believed what I sang about, if I really believed that the God I served was a God of mercy, then what right did I have to walk around with an attitude of unforgiveness? But I didn't forgive John because I'm some kind of "good" person. I was able to forgive because God had first forgiven me. That's what that old hymn "Amazing Grace" is all about.

Coda

Amazing grace, how sweet the sound,
That saved a wretch like me . . .

That's right, I am that wretch. I'm selfish, I'm self-centered, and I want my own way, and to hell with you. When you slight me, when you mention everyone's name but mine, when you drag my child's name through the mud, when you cheat me out of my money—my first instinct is not forgiveness. I want my pound of flesh. I want revenge.

How unlikely we are to turn the other cheek. How foreign a response this seems to us, in a culture of "do unto others before they do unto you." We are a society that sees no need to forgive, nor to be forgiven. Forgiven, for what? It's always somebody else's fault. How self-sufficient we think we are. "I am master of my fate, captain of my ship," we love to claim, brushing aside, ignoring the great care, the great love God has lavished upon us right up to this moment. Until we are convinced of His reality, forgiveness is just an abstract concept. But from the first moment we acknowledge Him and realize how good He has been to us and how we have ignored Him, our only impulse is to seek forgiveness, grace. It's automatic. This was the testimony of the English slave ship captain John Newton, who surviving a terrible storm at sea, realized he wasn't master of his fate, captain of his ship, and wrote "Amazing Grace." It was the experience of the prophet Isaiah, who, seeing God, cried, "Woe is me . . . I am a man of unclean lips." And it was my experience at fourteen in a back pew at St. Luke's AME Church. Sitting there, it dawned on me how easily my life could have gone wrong as a result of my mother's death, my family's lack of street-smarts, or just my own headstrong ways. I realized how close He must have been walking with me, though I knew Him not. Now I wanted only to thank Him for His mercy. That's the only reason I'm able to forgive—John or anyone else.

I'm mystified by people who continue to ignore the reality of God. Do they really think that their life expectancy is governed only by good genes, exercise and a cholesterol-free diet? The problem is these people are not living their faithless lives unobserved. Their children are watching them closely. Because these parents are not leading their children to

God, they are reaping a whirlwind of disobedience, disrespect and even violence from their offspring. These kids are filling the emptiness inside them with everything but God. Materialism, sex and drugs—the only thing that seems to count is feeling good. I'm afraid my father's expression, "If you make your bed hard, lie in it until it gets soft," would be lost on these kids and their parents. It still rings true to me. I don't always feel good. Sometimes a sadness will come over me—I don't know where it comes from. Maybe it's the memory of my kids leaving home that sends a lonely chill through me. Or a long ago flashback of my mother, who I still miss everyday. I cry by myself—I'm still not a big talker to people. Me and the Lord work it out together. But I go through the bad feelings. I don't duck 'em by smoking something or drinking something. Because when you go through the fire, there's a bonus on the other side: You find out who you are.

The burden I have for the young is not simply to tell them to be present in their own lives. They can get that from any motivational speaker. What I want them to learn is that they don't have to walk through the trials and fires of life alone. There is a God who cares, who acts on our behalf in ways that we can't even imagine until we try *Him*.

That's what I want my children to know. They're out of my house, but I'm not done with them yet. We don't have our Saturday morning beef sessions anymore, although we still have a heavy powwow every so often. My biggest complaint, like every grandparent, is I don't get to see my grandchildren half as much as I want to. I have six now and I like being around them. Besides my natural children and my grandchildren, I have a few adopted daughters, two of them I met at New Hope. Towanna Choice is a year or two younger than Whitney; as a matter of fact, they were both in my choir together as teenagers. Fatima Jones is only twenty-three, but already she is showing promise as a choir director at New Hope. I'm more comfortable around young people; they're more positive, they're always starting something new—school, a new job—there's always a dream to catch. I still feel young enough to catch a few dreams myself.

I've just released another gospel album. The Grammy gave me the push I needed to finish up some songs I had on the shelf and also write some new ones. The writing came so easy. Some of the experiences in this book even found their way into the songs. I guess I'm finally getting comfortable in my own skin. I know who I am. I want to let go and start to live my life now. Try some new things, have some adventures. And when I've run the course, and I close my eyes, I want my children to know that I was content with who I was. I want my grandchildren to know that I was proud of who I was created to be and what I became. I don't know what awaits on the other side. All we know is that "eye hath not seen, ear hath not heard, nor hath it entered the heart of man, what God hath prepared for those who love Him." When I open my eyes on the other side, I am certain about only one thing: I will be singing and it will be oh so sweet.

When I've sung my last song,
When I've prayed my last prayer,
When I've borne my last burden,
When I've had my last care,

When I've felt my last sorrow,
When I've breathed the last air,
When I've sung my last song here,
You'll find me singing over there.
—*"When I've Sung My Last Song"*

THE LIFE OF CISSY HOUSTON

1933 —Born, Emily Drinkard, Newark, New Jersey, September 30.

1938 —Attends Overcoming Church of God in Christ, Mercer Street, Newark: first exposure to gospel music.

1938 —As five-year-old, begins singing with brothers and sisters, the Drinkard Singers, at home church, St. Luke's AME Church, Charlton Street.

1951 —Drinkard Singers appear with Mahalia Jackson, the Ward Singers, the Davis Sisters and others at Carnegie Hall.

1952 —Cissy, nineteen, begins directing choirs at Newark's New Hope Baptist Church.

1957 —The Drinkards appear at historic Newport Jazz Festival. Gary Houston is born, Newark, New Jersey.

1958 —As RCA's first gospel signing, the Drinkards record *A Joyful Noise* album.

1959 —The Drinkards appear with Alex Bradford at the Apollo.

1961 —Cissy first sings background on Ronnie Hawkins session. Michael Houston is born, Newark, New Jersey.

1962 —Begins singing background for the Drifters, Dionne Warwicke, Chuck Jackson, Tommy Hunt, Solomon Burke, Wilson Pickett, Gene Pitney, Ben E. King and others.

1963 —Cissy and group become first-call background singers for producers Lieber and Stoller, Burt Bacharach, Luther Dixon,

Clyde Otis, Jerry Ragavoy, Bert Berns, Jerry Wexler, Ahmet Ertegun and Tom Dowd. In one year alone, she sings on the following Top Twenty hit recordings: "Tell Him" (The Exciters, Jan. '63), "On Broadway" (The Drifters, Apr. '63), "If You Need Me" (Solomon Burke, Apr. '63), "Just One Look" (Doris Troy, July '63), "Cry Baby" (Garnett Mimms and the Enchanters, Sept. '63) and "Anyone Who Had a Heart" (Dionne Warwicke, Nov. '63).

Whitney Houston born, August, Newark, New Jersey.

1967 —Forms the Sweet Inspirations with Myrna Smith, Estelle Brown and Sylvia Shemwell. Signs with Atlantic Records.

Creates and sings background parts with the Sweet Inspirations on virtually all Aretha Franklin hit records. Tours with Aretha Franklin.

1968 —Receives Grammy nomination for "Sweet Inspiration" single. Records gospel album with the Sweet Inspirations.

Backs up Elvis Presley with Sweet Inspirations during his historic comeback engagement in Las Vegas.

Receives prestigious Mary Bethune award.

1969 —Leaves the Sweet Inspirations.

1970 —Releases first solo album, *Presenting Cissy Houston.*

1972 —Continues background work for producers Joel Dorn, Tom Dowd, Arif Mardin, with artists Roberta Flack, Herbie Mann, Bette Midler, Judy Collins, Paul Simon, Average White Band and others.

1977 —Begins association with producer Michael Zager and several hit recording projects. Sings on numerous national advertising jingles.

1978 —At United Negro College Fund benefit, Carnegie Hall, she introduces and sings duet with fourteen-year-old Whitney.

1980s —Performs regularly at New York cabarets Reno Sweeney's, Mikell's and Sweetwater's.

Appears in off-Broadway show *Taking My Turn.*

Continues as Director of Music, New Hope Baptist Church, Newark, New Jersey.

1986 —Documentary by Dave Davidson, *Cissy Houston, A Sweet Inspiration*, details her life in pop and gospel music.

1988 —Appointed President, CEO of The Whitney Houston Foundation for Children.

1993 —Makes film debut in *The Vernon Johns Story*, unsung hero of the civil rights movement, with James Earl Jones.

1994 —Receives Honorary Doctor of Humanities degree from Kean College, New Jersey.

1995 —Receives the Pioneer Award from the Rhythm and Blues Foundation, Los Angeles, California.

1996 —Appears as Mrs. Havergal in the film *The Preacher's Wife*.
Receives Honorary Doctor of Humanities degree from Essex County College, New Jersey.

1997 —Receives Grammy award in the Traditional Soul Gospel category for *Face to Face* album, New York.
Appears in gospel musical *This Is My Song*, New York.

1998 —Receives the Women in Music Award along with Ruth Brown, Ellie Greenwich and others, New York.

SELECTED DISCOGRAPHY

The following is a brief sampling of the more than five hundred records Cissy Houston has recorded either as a member of the Drinkard Singers, a session singer or a solo artist.

THE DRINKARD SINGERS

A Joyful Noise (RCA) 1958
Joy Unspeakable Joy (Choice) 1960
Yield Not to Temptation (Choice) 1961

SESSION SINGER

The Best of Ronnie Hawkins (Rhino) 1990
"Mexican Divorce"/The Drifters (Atlantic) 1961
"Some Kind of Wonderful"/The Drifters (Atlantic) 1961
"Sweets for My Sweet"/The Drifters (Atlantic) 1961
"When My Little Girl Is Smiling"/The Drifters (Atlantic) 1962
"Any Day Now"/Chuck Jackson (Scepter) 1962
"Don't Make Me Over"/Dionne Warwicke (Scepter) 1962
"Cry to Me"/Solomon Burke (Atlantic) 1962
"Anyone Who Had a Heart"/Dionne Warwicke (Scepter) 1963

"On Broadway"/The Drifters (Atlantic) 1963

"Tell Him"/The Exciters (UA) 1963

"Cry Baby"/Garnett Mimms (UA) 1963

"Just One Look"/Doris Troy (Atlantic) 1963

"If You Need Me"/Solomon Burke (Atlantic) 1963

"Walk On By"/Dionne Warwicke (Scepter) 1964

"Everybody Needs Somebody to Love"/Solomon Burke (Atlantic) 1964

"Goodbye Baby (Baby Goodbye)"/Solomon Burke (Atlantic) 1964

"You'll Never Get to Heaven (If You Break My Heart)"/Dionne Warwicke (Scepter) 1964

"Reach Out for Me"/Dionne Warwicke (Scepter) 1964

"What the World Needs Now Is Love"/Jackie DeShannon (Imperial) 1965

"Message to Michael"/Dionne Warwicke (Scepter) 1966

"634-5789"/Wilson Pickett (Atlantic) 1966

"Mustang Sally"/Wilson Pickett (Atlantic) 1966

"Trains and Boats and Planes"/Dionne Warwicke (Scepter) 1966

"I Just Don't Know What to Do with Myself"/Dionne Warwicke (Scepter) 1966)

"Do Right Woman—Do Right Man"/Aretha Franklin (Atlantic) 1967

"Why (Am I Treated So Bad)"/The Sweet Inspirations (Atlantic) 1967

"Brown-Eyed Girl"/Van Morrison (Bang) 1967

"(You Make Me Feel Like) A Natural Woman"/Aretha Franklin (Atlantic) 1967

"I Say a Little Prayer"/Dionne Warwicke (Scepter) 1967

"Chain of Fools"/Aretha Franklin (Atlantic) 1967

"Ain't No Way"/Aretha Franklin (Atlantic) 1968

"Sweet Inspiration"/The Sweet Inspirations (Atlantic) 1968

"(Sweet Sweet Baby) Since You've Been Gone"/Aretha Franklin (Atlantic) 1968

"Think"/Aretha Franklin (Atlantic) 1968

"To Love Somebody"/The Sweet Inspirations (Atlantic) 1968

"I Say a Little Prayer"/Aretha Franklin (Atlantic) 1968

"Son of a Preacher Man"/Dusty Springfield (Atlantic) 1968

"Sweets for My Sweet"/The Sweet Inspirations (Atlantic) 1969

"I'll Never Fall in Love Again"/Dionne Warwicke (Scepter) 1969

"Put a Little Love in Your Heart"/Jackie DeShannon (Imperial) 1969

"Suspicious Minds"/Elvis Presley (RCA) 1969

"Mother and Child Reunion"/Paul Simon (Columbia) 1972

"I'm Every Woman"/Chaka Khan (Warner) 1979

"Jump to It"/Aretha Franklin (Arista) 1982

"How Will I Know"/Whitney Houston (Arista) 1986

"I Wanna Dance with Somebody (Who Loves Me)"/Whitney Houston (Arista) 1987

"I Know Him So Well"/duet with Whitney Houston (Arista) 1987

"Never Too Much"/Luther Vandross (Epic) 1989

"Here and Now"/Luther Vandross (Epic) 1990

ALBUMS WITH THE SWEET INSPIRATIONS

The Sweet Inspirations (Atlantic) 1967

What the World Needs Now Is Love (Atlantic) 1968

Songs of Faith and Inspiration (Atlantic) 1968

Sweets for My Sweet (Atlantic) 1969

Sweet Sweet Soul (Atlantic) 1970

A compilation album on CD, *The Best of the Sweet Inspirations* (Ichiban), features a selection from the above releases

ALBUMS AND SINGLES AS A SOLO ARTIST

Presenting Cissy Houston (Commonwealth United) 1970

"Be My Baby" (Janus) 1971

Cissy Houston (Private Stock) 1977

"Tomorrow" (Private Stock) 1977

"Think It Over" (Columbia) 1979

Warning—Danger (Columbia) 1979

Step Aside for a Lady (Columbia) 1980

Mama's Cookin' (Charly) 1987

A compilation album on CD, *Midnight Train to Georgia: The Janus Years* (Ichiban), features a selection from the above releases

Cissy Houston with Chuck Jackson, *I'll Take Good Care of You* (Shanachie) 1992

Cissy Houston, *Face to Face* (HOB) 1996★

Cissy Houston, *He Leadeth Me* (HOB) 1998

Cissy Houston can also be heard on albums by Gene Pitney, Tommy Hunt, Esther Phillips, Connie Francis, Carmen McCrae, Freddie Scott, Billy Vera and Judy Clay, Burt Bacharach, The Rascals, Jimi Hendrix, Nancy Wilson, Nikki Giovanni, Bette Midler, Yusef Lateef, Herbie Mann, the Neville Brothers, Judy Collins, Lorraine Ellison, Average White Band, Chaka Khan, Whitney Houston, David Bowie, Luther Vandross and *The Preacher's Wife* sound track.

Ms. Houston and her choir are also featured on New Hope Baptist Church's weekly radio broadcast, WWRL (1600 on the AM dial), Sundays, 1:30 P.M.

★ Grammy Award Winner, 1997, Traditional Soul Gospel

FOR FURTHER REFERENCE

Broughton, Viv. *Too Close to Heaven: The Illustrated History of Gospel Music.* London: Midnight Books, 1997.

Davidson, Dave. *Cissy Houston—Sweet Inspiration.* New York: Hudson West Films, 1986.

Heilbut, Anthony. *The Gospel Sound.* New York: Limelight Editions, 1985.

PERMISSIONS

TEXTUAL REFERENCES

Bacharach, Burt and Hal David. "What the World Needs Now." Copyright © Hal Leonard. Reprinted by permission.

Berns, Bert. "Heart Be Still." Copyright © Sloopy Two Music. Reprinted by permission.

Berns, Bert. "Tell Him." Copyright © Sloopy Two Music. Reprinted by permission.

Bradford, Alex. "I'm Too Close to Heaven to Turn Around." Copyright © Unichappell/Warner Brothers. Reprinted by permission.

Cleveland, James. "Peace Be Still." Copyright © Screen Gems. Reprinted with permission.

Coates, Dorothy Love. "Come On and Go with Me to My Father's House." Copyright © Embassy Music Corp. Reprinted with permission.

Coates, Dorothy Love. "That's Enough." Copyright © Sony ATV. Reprinted by permission.

Cooke, Sam. "Change Is Gonna Come." Copyright © ABKCO. Reprinted by permission.

Dorsey, Thomas. "The Lord Will Make a Way." Copyright © Hal Leonard. Reprinted by permission.

Dorsey, Thomas. "When I've Sung My Last Song." Copyright © Hal Leonard. Reprinted by permission.

Richards, Jack and Richard Mullen. "He." Copyright © Hal Leonard. Reprinted by permission.

PHOTOS

The following photos are from family collections:

Cissy's mother, Delia Mae McCaskill Drinkard *(1930)*

Cissy's father, Nitcholas Drinkard, with oldest brother, William *(1923)*

The Drinkard Singers *(1943)*

Cissy's sister Marie (Reebie) Epps *(1972)*

Cissy's brother Nicky *(1972)*

Classic 1950s portrait of the Drinkard Singers

Michael, Whitney (Nippy), and the Lincoln *(1968)*

Nippy and Michael *(1973)*

John Houston *(1971)*

John and Nippy outside house on Wainright Street

Cissy and John after church on Sunday in Newark

Cissy singing "Ain't No Way" with the girls

Gary, Whitney, and Michael as adults

Other sources:

Gospel poster featuring the Drinkard Singers *(1963)*, courtesy of Mitch Diamond

The Sweet Inspirations *(1968)*, courtesy of Atlantic Records

Cissy directing her choir as they perform for the *Face to Face* album *(1996)* used with the permission of James Minchin III

Cissy handing Whitney award at World Music Awards (1994), used with the permission of Reuters/Eric Gaillard/Archive Photos

Cissy receiving her 1996 Grammy Award for *Face to Face (1997)*, used with the permission of Sonia Moskowitz/Globe Photos, Inc.